THE POWERFUL THOUGHT OF "A COURSE IN MIRACLES"

Copyright © 2015 Sharon Moriarty

Author Photograph Courtesy of David White Studios

ISBN : 978-0-9971179-1-2
Library of Congress Control Number (**LCCN**) : 2015959746

Published by GatewayToEternity Publications
Join my mailing list to get advance notice of new releases.

mailto:now@GatewayToEternity.com
http://www.GatewayToEternity.com

DEDICATED TO ALL

WHO WILL ACCELERATE

THE GREAT AWAKENING

CONTENTS

Prologue 7

1. Finding the Clown in the Show 11

   The Incompleteness of Various New Age Systems 17

   Choosing Between the Red Pill and the Blue Pill 20

   Truth Alone Brings Bliss... 23

   The Deceptions of the Ego.. 25

   Healing the Dream Through Love 29

   A Zen Master Points us in the Right Direction................................ 32

   Reality as the Home of the Imperishable 34

   Our Perennial Groundhog Day.. 37

   Coming to Terms with our Authority Problem 38

   Our Many False Beliefs Are the Only Barrier 43

   The Atonement, as a Spiritual Filtration System, Which Avows only Truth 45

2. The World as Projection of Your Subjectivity 49

   Our World Experiences Are Not at Random........................... 55

   The Illusion of an Objective Universe 58

   God Becomes our Patsy.. 60

3. Searching For a Place called Home 65

   Developing a Miracle Minded Awareness, as Our Healing Recipe 69

   A Course in Existential Dialectics 71

   The Magic Wand Of Forgiveness 77

4. Ideas leave not their Source................................81

   All Is Idea.. 84

Our Treasuring of Idols made From Dust 86

Our Denial Enables Empty Ideologies to Proliferate........................ 92

This Holographic Universe is Powered by Our Beliefs 94

5. Taking Off the Blindfolds....................................98

The Planets and Cosmos are Living Off Our Psychological Energy 102

More Conspiracy Theories..103

Our Lost Illumination and Misdirected Energies 109

Guilt, The Illuminati and Various Piss-pots in the Boonies 113

Taking Responsibility, For The World we Invented 117

The Hopeless and Despairing Plans of the Ego............................121

The One Alternative 125

6. I Am the Light of the World..................................127

7. Only God IS 132

Enlightenment and Innocent Perception 137

8. This World is not God's Creation...........................141

9. Perception and the Dream Nature of Existence 144

Zen and the Art Of Dream Machine Maintenance 148

The Prisoner's Dilemma 154

Hysteria, Trauma and PTSD 158

Taking Responsibility for Our Dreams, As The Means to Liberation .160

Dr. Gobbler's Knob's Wisdom on Samsara and Nirvana 162

10. The Son 167

The Son's True Identity and Purpose 171

Perfectionists and Perfection 176

11. Finding your Way out of the Fog 184

STOP THE MADNESS! 186

Lucid Dreams, And Our Critical Need Of Awakening 190

Solving the Rubik's Cube of Truth, Through Atonement 195

12. The Only Solution For A Broken Down World 197

Our Anxiety, Angst, Eccentricities and Self-Contraction.................199

Worldly and Behavioral Solutions Cannot Work 205

Forgiveness Undoes all Effects of the Tiny Mad Idea 209

13. The Panacea is Found Within 212

Making the Smart Decision, for a Volte-Face 214

The ego's House of Cards Comes Tumbling Down 217

Teaching The Laws of the Kingdom As the Means to Remember It ..220

14. The Two Thought Systems 223

The Need For Flipping Our Thought System Completely Around 226

This Old, Aching and Worn Out World..228

Embracing The Holy Spirit's Wisdom, to End Our Dream Miseries ...237

15. The Power of Your Decision 256

Deciding to Hear the Holy Spirit Instead 260

16. The Two Emotions..263

Tuning into our Feelings, to Escape Dark Trains of Thought............267

We are Not Victims of Our Emotions. We Choose Them! 272

Curing All Our Fears and Phobias, Through Love............................282

True Living Requires us to Relinquish All ego Control 285

Recognizing the Presence of Fear Behind all Dark Emotional States 290

Escaping the Dark Room, By Amplifying and Avowing Only the Healing Light 295

17. Quantum Forgiveness Is the Key to Happiness......299

Quantum Forgiveness is Love's Face in the Relative Existence........301

Judgment and Love Cannot Coexist.................................303

The Correct Interpretation of Forgiveness.......................311

18. Time V Eternity...323

Discovering our True Reality Through Forgiveness 329

The Correct Use of Time, is to Heal all our beliefs in Guilt 335

A 3D Being Provides Enlightenment 342

The Carpet of Guilt.......................................349

Gaining Perspective, On Our Learning Limitations 351

Our Decision Options are Always Ego or Spirit Based 356

Don't Be Fooled by The Ego's Rosy Picture, of your Future 366

Zeno's Answer to the Objective View of Time.................371

Evolution in Our Consciousness is Desperately Needed..................384

The Present Moment is Our Gateway To the Eternal.......................387

We Are Hypnotized by Orders, Magnitudes and Our Partialities......391

The Power of the Unseen, and Unsymbolized 393

The Important Link Existing Between Awareness, Time Dilation and Consciousness Evolution 398

19. The Journey Home 403

Failure is Inevitable for the ego, But Success is Guaranteed For You405

Your Escape Plan Home..411

Appendix A - Dynamics of The Holy Spirit V The Ego..419

PROLOGUE

In December 2000, I was enjoying some cocktails at the airport bar while awaiting for my flight home to Ireland for Christmas. There a woman engaged me in light conversation. I immediately had the inner intuition that she had never progressed beyond young girlhood. Her voice sounded so fresh, giggly and excited - even excessively alarmist on the most trivial matters. Yes, I could sense that she remained trapped there after sixty plus years of living, possessing the looks of someone in their thirties and the psychology of someone in their preteens. I gained the distinct impression that she had quite the breadth of life experience and intuited also that she saw deeply into things and people. Since we hit it off, we exchanged numbers before leaving for our respective flights. Immediately, I put the encounter completely out of my mind. I was surprised therefore when she called early January, to wish me a happy New Year. Since we continued to connect pretty well, we started having phone conversations every other week or so. In many of the calls, she kept referring to a book called "*A Course In Miracles*". I was not familiar with it, nor remotely interested in learning more. I was tremendously busy leading a hardware team in a Silicon Valley startup, at the time.

What sparked my interest most, was the way she somehow managed to squeeze this topic in, to even our weirdest and most oblique conversation threads. She kept on pressuring me to read it, which deeply irritated me. Eventually, I realized that the only cure for this particular poison was the poison itself. So I promised to give it a read. Then in the early Spring of 2001, I was awoken late in the night by a mysterious vibration and rattling sound in my apartment. The upper story where it was located had begun to shake. My first thought was that we were experiencing an earthquake. So, I put on my dressing gown and took a look out to see if any damage had been done. Yet, all was quiet and serene, apart from some expected chirping sounds and croaks. Everyone in the neighborhood was soundly asleep.

Then I noticed a package close to my door. Inside was this large blue book titled "*A Course in Miracles*". I did not think much of it at the time and tucked the book into one of my cupboards. I was thinking to myself, "*Now that sure is some verbal mausoleum of hocus-pocus nonsense that I am never going to read.*" Why had I given in to her? Even the audaciousness of the title was off-putting. It somehow suggested miracles were something we all could do. Like we just needed to gain some New Age certification first from an accredited source. I expected to see a subscription service on the back cover, along with photos of some retreat center offering training courses that cost thousands of dollars for a weekend seminar.

Yet, one night soon afterwards, I got drunk and needed some quick laughs. So I searched the cupboard for this book and started to read. All I needed was to fetch a few quick lines by which I could ridicule its content to my friend. Then she would leave me alone. Yet, almost immediately, I was hooked by its consistency, depth, precision, lucidity and the lack of contradiction in its content. And as an Engineer, I am trained to spot deficiencies, weaknesses and contradictions quickly and then go in for the kill. Even at that time, I possessed a thorough working knowledge of Philosophy, Metaphysics and Zen. Absorbing and understanding thought provoking literature was a hobby of mine for over a decade. Yet, this book was answering questions for me in simple English, which I didn't even yet know how to properly formulate or verbalize. It swiftly spun out many profound messages, that I had never even heard. They came like bullets of wisdom that were quickly destroying the existential foundations of my world.

As I read on, I immediately grasped that here was a very wise Authority. One possessing a freshness and directness that was positively appealing. A sagacious voice that could immediately penetrate to the heart of a matter and demystify complex themes, while casually brushing aside and obviating all nonsense ideas. All such interferences were easily dispelled like leaves before a leaf blower. It held the essence of all religious systems and yet went beyond even their most core messages to the deeper reality they could never reach. I was simply astounded by a number of bold statements it made. Awed and inspired by its dizzying symphonic capacity for continuously reinforcing its own ideas and themes, from so many lustrous angles. So began my adventure with and love for the Course.

In this writing, I share some of my own insights into the Course material along with certain trinkets of wisdom I have gained over the years. I also share some of my own direct life experiences. Ones that serve to validate its message. It goes without saying that some may disagree with a particular insights and interpretations, I share. This is natural. Confrontational positions are the first and often most progressive step in reaching to clarity and meaningful resolution. Also some egos by projecting their own learning failures may seek to crucify. But those most likely to get bogged down in conflicts, pertaining to different interpretations, are those most likely to miss the Course's key message. The Course teaches that only when we practice and assimilate its message, will its gifts be received. Then healing and transformation can begin. Ultimately the faith, trust and conviction we gain through our experiences and application of its ideas is what enables us to finally transcend the ego and its world.

An unheard and unassimilated message is powerless to change one. So it is without all worth. Most of us reject that which we either do not understand or have not experienced for ourselves. We have a conditioned visceral reaction to the new. Consequently we continue to harness to ourselves numerous fatal flaws, which we wear like badges of honor. These become our Achilles heels and they portent our eventual demise. In the end, I am just sharing from the window of my own insight and personal experience, hoping that it may help some travelers on the path. Even if no travelers are helped, I have been. I have reached a far deeper understanding and gained significant trust in the Voice of inspiration, the Holy Spirit (HS), in writing this. Today, fifteen years later I remain as inspired as ever and continue to receive important new insights on a regular basis. In the end, Truth cannot be attacked, nor does it seek to attack. Ideas will be right or wrong, depending on the content they reflect and encapsulate. True ideas should be welcomed as gifts and fallacious ones can be easily discarded. The Course itself is to remain the one and trusted source of its own message.

1. FINDING THE CLOWN IN THE SHOW

I

You have Never Heard of Me!

Yet, I exist all Around,

And within You!

I am in all Things

and all Things

Are in Me!

I am the Formless One,

Amid the World of Form!

Yet, Form and the Senses

are both Blind to Me!

II

Out of Me,

All Manifold Universes Arise!

and Back into my Bosom

Again Disappear!

Only to Spring Forth Again,

Through the Defilement,

Of ego Desires!

For in Me, lies all Potentiality!

All Worlds Manifest

and Non-manifest,

All Existence and All

The Seeming non-Existent!

III

I Exist before Time Was

and will be Known Again,

When Time is no More!

For Spacetime and Form,

Arise from the Ignorance,

Of Not Knowing Me,

This is the Relative Existence!

The Hell of the everyday Dreamer!

The Dark World of Despair,

That has Never Been!

IV

Yet, the Pure in Heart

Know me Once More!

And so their Minds with

Spiritual Light Glow!

They Follow the Golden Path

of True Forgiveness!

The Joyous Path,

Leading to Love!

Then they Disappear,

Behind the Veil!

And enter my Body,

The Formless One!

[The Formless One]

Be still a moment. Freeze all your current activities and take a gander at the world around you! Glance at the words written here, at your hands and feet and at the faces of the people passing by. Absorb in, all those trinkets and technical gadgets that surround you, which you feel you need to survive. Survey the buildings nearby and the street lights. There may be vehicles coming and going. Examine the spaces between them – this unwritten and unknown magical space, existing between all things. This alive and miraculous space, that you have never really looked at before. Look up at the sky, the clouds, the airplanes flying by and at the moon and stars, if they are out. Review the whole cosmic show and then reflect on this thought. **"None of this exists. This is my personal hallucination."**

Now you finally know the secret, of why your life feels like such a disaster zone, why you are miserable most of the time, why you aimlessly plod about, feeling like your best intentions come back to stab you. You have been duped into playing out a role in your own mind-generated game. A game you cannot win because you are up against the greatest power in the universe - **your own mind**. The enemy is within all at the time, so nothing you do out-there can ever matter. This is why your world seems so unpredictable and chaotic. Why you feel hopelessly trapped in a meaningless, merciless and cruel place, that cares not for you. Ultimately, this is the reason why you cannot succeed and will only find increasing despair. An hallucination has no real rules. It is powered entirely out of the imagination of its thinker. Taking on his thoughts and going with them entirely. To seek for guidance from an hallucination, is to ask for trouble. For it can only ever reflect back to you, your own misguided thinking, your own arbitrary fears and desires. It exists but as a series of pictures on a screen, projected from your mind and made to seem, as if apart. Not recognizing it as your projection, you take it for reality and so become identified with it. So begins the most destructive dream of your Self-forgetfulness.

William Shakespeare once wrote that "*A fool's paradise, is a wise man's hell.*" He could just as easily have written : "*A wise man's paradise, is a fool's hell.*" This world is that fool's paradise and it is also a wise man's hell. Hell could be equated with being the only sane voice left in an insane man's universe. In what follows, you will learn exactly how your hallucination arose, how it is maintained, and how it can be relinquished entirely from your mind. Our only goal is for you to wake up, so that you can be restored to unconditional love, peace, happiness and knowledge. Restored to immortal sovereignty and true Being. Restored to all that you have lost, living in the land of separation. This noble goal, we hope you will share and come to be grateful for.

I do not want you to take my word on anything. My word is worthless in itself. In the final analysis, you stand naked and alone. After all, this is your universe and I am just another lone voice in your personal hallucination. It is only real experience and the transformation that follows, that will bring conviction of the veracity of this to your mind. The sheep mentality believes, the lion mentality roars. It roars out from the conviction of its own direct experience, its own incontestable knowledge. No one can give Enlightenment to you. It is after all, not a marketable commodity that can be bought and sold. Nevertheless many false prophets and slick willy opportunists attempt to sell it everyday, from their altars dedicated to spiritual materialism. Yes they spit out their futile offerings, methods and deceptions, from every vortex and cranny in this cyber-luniverse. In the end, Enlightenment can only be reached through deep discovery and intense desire, through your willingness not to settle for all the valueless mediocrities of this world.

There is a temptation to be hypnotized by words. We like to deceive ourselves, that we are always increasing in our store of knowledge and being. But we have merely substituted symbols for reality. We are still only scratching the surface, resting in a toxic home of gibberish, spouting mental nonsense and the diarrhea of ill formed thoughts. We are merely peeking through a darkened window, back to earth, ground-zero of hell, peering at the same old insanities. Our minds are so full of undigested teachings and esoteric novelties, that we have become a spiritual wasteland. Barren of purity, barren of benevolent instinct, barren of accomplishment. Our only ripened fruit has been a gradual poisoning of our mind system and a mind-numbing intoxication with words. We remain merely wilted flowers, thinking ourselves spiritually enlightened, enduring as the ultimate witless heralds of a spiritual materialism that kills.

Now is the time to set yourself on fire from within. Now is the time to successfully burn all those illusions that conspire against you. Illusions that have perfumed you with nothing more than a severely opinionated grandiosity, since time began. The illuminated reality is self-evident to all those, who find royalty in simplicity and are not corrupted by the wishfulness of their imaginations. You just need to become a light unto yourself. A consciousness that is capable of tracing its inner rays back to its Source. You may still be resistant to the idea, that *"This world is nothing but my hallucination."* I wouldn't be surprised, if you flat out laughed it off. Yet, what part of you is laughing? And beneath your hollow laugh, isn't there a subtle trembling and fear?

THE INCOMPLETENESS OF VARIOUS NEW AGE SYSTEMS

Yes, we all like to extract, only that which we want out of life. We want the steak and onions, but not the broccoli, carrots and cabbage. We think we can leave, all that is unseemly, at the side of our plates, and go on unaffected. I wouldn't be surprised, for example if you subscribed fully to a number of New Age belief systems, that are to your particular liking. Teachings such as *Creative Visualization, 'The Secret', 'The Law of Attraction'* and *'The Power of Positive Intention',* and a number of others come to mind. They have a very strong and compelling attraction, because they are presented to you in a very alluring package. One that promises to give you, all that you wish for. They pander to all your ego desires and needs. They elicit the genie from the lamp and place him before your very eyes. Yet, they are all powered by the exact same underlying mechanisms and understandings. Their fundamental teaching is **'Thought is Tremendously Powerful, it Attracts in its own Likeness, and the Universe is nothing but Thought."** Yes your thought is hardly innocuous. As you think and desire, so will you receive.

Yes, their fundamental message, is that the everyday world of your perceptions is nothing but a projection of your thoughts. This is the essential backdrop that gives all these belief systems, all their fuel and momentum needed to survive. It is the seed idea by which they flourish to bring miracles into your life. Unfortunately they tend to emphasize only one side of affairs - the positive side. They tend to deemphasize or ignore completely the flip side of this coin. Because the universe is not just a projection of your thought, **it is a projection of all your thought.** Your thought is like a jet-stream that can also bring many negative fruits in its wake. The truth is that all your toxic thoughts, negativity, warped understandings, contracted states, feelings of limitation etc. are also showing up in your world. Similarly all that you have denied and buried deep into your subconscious mind, is still very much shaping your perceptions and world experiences, moment-by-moment.

Wanting to sell themselves to you, they ignore all this. They play into your desires and teach how you can attract only those particular aspects you like, into your perceptions. This is accomplished, through nourishing and visualizing these aspects very clearly, within the rich inner soil of your mind. They are not incorrect on this. Yet, if your desires are just for worthless ego toys and "powers", you will remain unhappy. The goal is not to fulfill all your desires, but to remove all your foolish wants. Once you remove all your foolish and unnatural wishes and wants, you will see that you are already complete and in need of nothing. Yes the real goal is for you to learn how to meaningfully evaluate and appraise, what is worthy. Only then, will you come to true peace and bliss.

Apart from the Course, most New Age systems steer away from teaching this higher understanding. The teaching that this world is nothing but your personal hallucination. That the relative existence is merely a product of your own split-mind. Mind that has become so tarnished and defiled by false understandings, that it finds itself inhabiting a world of illusions. The Course recognizes that almost no one is mature enough, to take this step. Almost no one is ready to take full responsibility for their world. Most will run quick for the door, if they feel badgered or coerced into accepting, even partial responsibility for their world experiences. We have become so passive and of the "victimized" mindset, that we do not want to accept any ownership for our thoughts and feelings, and their unavoidable effects. To teach another, their exclusive responsibility, for the often bleak, brutal and chaotic world of their perceptions, is to make an enemy fast. Yes, many function as barflies. They are happy to nurse a very superficial acquaintance with power and truth.

They may be happy to rub shoulders, with their true selves momentarily, but they are not ready to put on the full ceremonial regalia and garb for good. They want to be able to use their escape clause and slink back into their holes. Return to theirs dens of iniquity, temptation, false images and idol worship.

Yet, this one idea is the central idea that leads to your freedom. No one bound to belief in mistruth can be free. All he will ever witness are illusions and distortions. So he becomes enslaved, because a mind continuously tormented by misbeliefs, fumbles and bumbles in the dark. Many contradictions reign in his mind and his only freedom left, is in choosing which illusion he will charm that day and have as his soup-du-jour. Yet, this is just choosing between one form of abject slavery and another and represents no real freedom at all.

> **"There is no world! This is the central thought the course attempts to teach. Not everyone is ready to accept it, and each one must go as far as he can let himself be led along the road to truth. He will return and go still further, or perhaps step back a while and then return again."**
>
> **[W.132.6:2-5]**

It must be obvious to you that a single lie must create a powerhouse of lies. A single lie unleashes a massive web of deception that binds and fastens your mind to darkness. It can become so dark that you forget your original deception. Yet its deceptive power only lasts so long as you believe in it. It must be equally evident, to you, that a thought system claiming to be whole must be without all flaw. All its premises must be correct and all deductions and inductions streaming from it must be utterly consistent. One false statement anywhere and the entire edifice crumbles into the dust. This one statement would displace it to an insecure foundation and render it worthless.

What if a thought system could be presented to you, that is totally without contradiction? One that can prove its validity, value and strength to you, not by your belief but by the conviction of your own direct experience? One that you come to esteem because of all the beneficial changes and healing transformations it brings. One that will transform you from a sickly, confused and fear weakened creature to the very picture of omnipotence, peace and radiance. Then by ignoring it, you are denying yourself its many gifts. Gifts which include vision, unconditional peace, love, bliss, empowerment, awareness of truth and escape from all illusions.

> **"If the center of the thought system is true, only truth extends from it. But if a lie is at its center, only deception proceeds from it."**   **[T-6.B.1:10-11]**

CHOOSING BETWEEN THE RED PILL AND THE BLUE PILL

Do you want such gifts? Or does your reticence indicate that you are content to remain on the cabbage patch? If you are ready, then you should be able to answer this simple question. "Do I want to know the truth, or continue to believe a lie?" It is like the choice Morpheus had to make between the red pill and the blue pill in the movie "The Matrix". Choosing the red pill is the choice to have reality and truth revealed to you. Yet, with this choice you are also accepting whatever powerful changes come in its wake. You will not be able to turn back the clock and reenter your slumber of delusion. It is this that accounts for your reticence and fear. For we do not really want truth. Because truth necessitates change. What we want is lasting comfort and happiness. If you could have these without truth, you would be happy to remain ignorant forever.

Yes, the red pill does bring change, because it is the choice to awaken. With it, all your illusions must go. Profound transformations will occur, until you arrive back at the changeless. Yet, all this change will only be happening ever at the level of illusion, because truth itself remains forever changeless. With the red pill, you are making the choice to have your eternal Inheritance returned to you. Proclaiming that you are no longer happy living, in the deep sleep of your mind generated illusions. The blue pill, in stark contrast is the decision to remain asleep, bound to illusion and ignorance. It is the choice for nothing. It has the comfort of a worn out pair of shoes, that you have known for so long. Soon however these shoes will develop large holes, come apart and need to be thrown away. Soon your situation will become beyond repair. You will have become too closed-minded and rigor mortis in your ways. The forces of evil, inertia, ignorance and darkness will pull you back once again into the bowels of the earth. First you will settle for mediocrity and in the end you will settle for anything. Your unquestioning compliance will make you a candidate for deception by all artful lies, concealed as half-truths. Your thought process will become so circumvented, as to occlude all light. So you will have to be discarded, only to try again in another life.

In the movie, in contrast Morpheus's choice for the red pill leads him to awaken to a painful and fearful reality, while the blue pill would have kept him in a blissful sleep, where he remained fed upon and used by the machines. Yes, the world has always taught us that "Ignorance is Bliss". It teaches us not to question things, not to step out of line, never to rise above our position, class or rank. "Be not restless", it says. Stay where you are. We want to keep you hooked in, so that we can continue to spoon-feed you on platitudes, ideologies and distortions, flown in on electronic beams to your living room. You do not really need, nor want, the intense burden that knowledge brings, that fierce searing jaw-biting pain of naked truth. Yet, the reasoning mind knows this is not so.

Ignorance, is but the choice for increased disempowerment and confusion. In ignorance, nothing can be truly seen, because what is hidden and denied must lead to distortion and blindness. Ignorance opens you to exploitation by those savvy operators in the field of life, those opportunistic of your ignorance and predacious of your fears. No sane mind willingly would choose ignorance over truth and no sane mind does. However ignorance is rarely seen in its raw and naked essence. It always comes masked and garmented in some ideology or form, that is to your liking. It is only because of the attractive and alluring nature of the forms in which it is packaged that you graciously swallow it whole. So you gulp down the chocolate covered poison or the apple laced with cyanide. Only afterwards, when you are feeling pain in your stomach and viscera and vomiting out the poison, do you realize that you have been had.

Dr. Gobbler's Knob walked into a pub holding a bright shiny penny in his hand. He says to the bartender, "This is a magical penny, a penny, so powerful indeed that it could smash two coconuts together." The bartender replies, "No way, I bet you a pint your penny could never be that powerful." At that moment, Dr. Gobbler's Knob drops his penny to the floor. Two Scotsman who were sitting nearby proceed to bang their heads together while furiously scurrying to pick it up. As I promised, said Dr. Gobbler's Knob, "It can easily bang two coconuts together." Then he sat down to enjoy his well earned pint.

TRUTH ALONE BRINGS BLISS

The truth is an open secret for those who care to look. The reality is that "Truth is Bliss." It alone has the certainty that brings power and peace. Truth illuminates with transparency, while ignorance only serves to obfuscate. You have always been taught to associate rest with sleep. But have you ever wondered, 'Rest from what?' At a superficial level, you may think, rest from your job, your wife, your financial problems, your many addictions and nervous anxieties. Rest from all the harassment, injustice and special hatreds you experience in your life. Rest as well as from all the uncontrollable tragedies, chaos and freak encounters. That constant stream of nonsense running through your mind, that you cannot shut out or shut up. Yes, it is foolish to think that the dream of ignorance can ever give you rest. After all, it is what causes all your loss of peace in the first place. Yet nothing in the "outside" world can give you pain, unless you empower it to do so. All rest, is rest from your ego self and its Source is found deep inside yourself, where truth still shines and the ego cannot enter.

One powerful Course idea that is important to fully absorb is that "Rest does not come from sleep, but from waking." [T-5.II.10:4] Reality and truth are not frightening. It is in choosing the red pill alone that you finally enter into a world of bliss. So will all fears and any traumatic chaos, present in your life come to end and completely disappear from the runway of your mind. Because you have made the decision to find unconditional peace and the only Home of true rest. With the blue pill, you remain a hostage to fearful dreams and at mercy to the multiplicity of poisons and demons born out of your continued ignorance. A veritable Pandora box of hell, revealed to you in living daylight. Ignorance always leads to eventual despair, because in its barren and lifeless soil, all illusions easily flourish and proliferate. They will grow into powerful weeds that will completely darken your mind over time. Yet, illusions are powerless to give you anything real. They cannot fill your cup, nor satiate. You will grow increasingly weary and disenchanted by them.

Truth cannot be lost, but it can be denied. Yet through denial, it becomes as good as lost, since it is lost to your awareness. So it is powerless to help you. The decision, to welcome truth back into your mind, is therefore the decision to release yourself from the darkness and imprisonment of illusions. With this decision, you will find your mind becoming gently transformed and healed and increasingly attuned to light. Restored to vision, you will find the peace and rest within, that you have always sought for without. You were at Home, all the time and simply wandered away to entertain futile dreams.

Your progress will start in tiny glimpses at first. Tiny glimpses of experiencing something entirely new, fresh and vibrant showing up in your daily life. A sudden subtle reordering of the universe, revealing new meaning in place of the chaos that was there before. There may be light flashes, meaningful patterns developing, synchronicities as well as light rims seen surrounding the periphery of objects. You may begin to feel a new fusion or immersion with all around you, an effortless blending in and healing of all invisible barriers that were present before. Expect moments of discontinuity, in time and space, permeated by definite quantum leaps that increase your awareness and self-understanding. You are being gently restored to vision, through your desire for truth. You are learning to see the world anew. For it reflects now your own illumination - your increasing attunement to Spirit and its Knowledge.

The extent of your progress depends on your sincere willingness to open-mindedly evaluate and displace all your current beliefs and interpretations. Yes, all must be held to ransom. There can be no sacred cows. As you put these new ideas, you are learning into practice, you will tune in and harmonize with the laws of truth. This will have a monumental life-changing impact on your perceptions. You are changing and so your world is changing also as a natural consequence. It is as simple as that. As you witness your world transforming before you, in miraculous proportions, you will realize also that you were the lie, all along that needed to be exposed. You had been too hard-crusted, inflexible and set in your ways – far too defensive.

You were like a clam trapped in its shell, too fearful to open up to the world around it. Your worldly misadventures told many tales of tragedy and of wasted investment. But now you see, they never had any real effects. Because illusions are powerless to affect the real. You were but dreaming with your eyes open. A costly dream indeed and one that kept you from truth. The dream had been going on for far too long. There was nothing really new, potent and fresh ever showing up in it. Just the same old insanities percolating about. Just the same old dregs and slops of the ego world. An ego that continues to dance frantically about while engaging in much flash-dash. One continuously vying for your attention. One you must decide to terminate, so ending its charades of smoke and mirrors. One continuously vying for your attention. One you must decide to terminate, so ending its charades of smoke and mirrors.

THE DECEPTIONS OF THE EGO

The ego always gesticulating in its madness, was but a puff of smoke that allured and hypnotized. So it entrapped you into watching a vain and empty show, a theatrical flop that cost you far too much. Worse still, you had lost the capacity to see it as but a dream. You saw only through the overlay of memory and false thought-forms. These conditioned the viewing lens of your perception distorting everything you saw. Looking out through those peepholes, afforded by your myopic vision, you had become a ragdoll mindlessly tossed about. Space-dust foolishly trying to agglomerate as much pleasure as you could before the salt-shaker ran out. You were fooled into identifying with shadows you projected on your cave wall - that cave wall of the world. All that ever showed up there were the shadows of your own distortionary venom. You were hopelessly obsessed with the 'never-was' and could not see the immaculate reality, that has always remained before your unseeing eyes. Reality became lost to your awareness. The Home of Love no longer known. So you navigated about with this giant gaping hole in your pulp, covering it over with sticky tape.

One day I was meandering my way through the marketplace in the center of the town, trying to remain as incognito as possible. That is not hard for me. I would forget myself, if I did not come already packaged in this meat suit. There in the center of the town was this pathetic exhausted looking figure. He was cast in chains and circling mindlessly about this obelisk. As I came closer, I realized it was none other than Dr. Gobbler's Knob. A friend, that I had known for many years, even decades. He looked so worn out, fatigued and dehydrated. I immediately inquired, "What is happening here?" He said some crafty old man had put him up to this. This man had totally discredited him in public, saying he would never amount to much and remain just a great big fat zero all his life. To which the Dr. had replied, "You just watch, I will walk around this obelisk continuously and just see how much more substantial I become in the eyes of the world."

So he became obsessed with outwitting this gnarly old man and the bet was on. It was a matter of honor and pride now. Yet inwardly, he was feeling very upset by what the old man had said. It had struck a chord which ran too close to the bone. For the Dr. himself knew he was indeed just a false prophet of no real worth. All his credentials were bought through mail order from Mexico. So he was always attempting to compensate. Going about behaving like some prized drama-queen, obsequiously begging his way through life, desperately attempting to procure at least five minutes of fame.

He started off real energized and zealous about his mission. Each time he circled, a great big neon sign delimited his progress. It read out clearly how many times he had successfully circled about the obelisk. At first he had been bolting around, but now he had fallen back to a mere trot. Yet, the number of successful loops boosted his confidence and pride even more. His leg muscles were beginning to bulge and tighten and look very impressive. His mind had started to wander. He was cerebrating now on all the sexual orgies he would be able to milk from this fact alone. He was becoming a "Someone" now in the eyes of all those gathered there at the marketplace. A personality that was no longer a zero. He could see the admiration exuding from all their faces. They were positively bonding with him and seeing him as one to honor and esteem. So, even though he remained chained to his task, he represented for them some invisible freedom. Yes, he was their 'cool hand Luke'.

Yes he was on the pedestal now for once, soaking up all their psychological rays and energies. He had become the living symbol of foul smelling lowlife swamp pulp transfigured into immortal grandeur. So he continued at this for days, becoming ever more tired and thirsty. Yet the numbers were increasing all the time and so his ego pride was exploding into the stratosphere. He could not give up and disappoint everyone - he could not afford to fail. He would just become another mangy stray, to be kicked about and pissed upon, starved, forgotten and thrown into the gutter. No, he recoiled from all this and had to go on. He could not go back to those stale old days of such vapid mediocrity.

And now he was beginning to sport this stupid fatuous grimace on his face - 'the gimp look', like he had just had sex with a leper and didn't care anymore. Yet, the deeper truth, bubbling in the inner cauldrons, was that he no longer relished his interminable task. He could no longer find any pleasure or meaningful purpose in it. He felt like an Atlas duped into holding the world on his shoulders or like a Forest Gump running aimlessly across America. The chains to his freedom were beginning to represent the chains to a hopeless despair. It was all some sick joke, but he could not stop and take a rest. He no longer wanted to be a God, but he did not want to plummet back to mediocrity either. He would just be that zero once again.

So, he continued for a few days more. Then finally malnourished and exhausted, he dropped down dead from a heart attack. Once again his life had reaped itself as a dismal failure. Yet, we should not be tempted to laugh too much at his failings. Because this is our story too. The ego has had us circling the world for hundreds of thousands of years, trying to build us up into something more substantial - something far greater than the zero, it tells us that we are. Each dream we start out again very energized and idealistic, all puffed up with pride and conceit, until finally extremely disenchanted, exhausted and fatigued we drop down dead, once again. Another life wasted. It always ends the same way.

Every ego likes to hold this grand portrait of themselves as loving, kind and considerate. We love to deceive ourselves on this. Yet, it must be obvious to all, that we do not really experience ourselves as loving most of the time, despite all our grandiose pretensions. Yes, we all like to carry that picture of ourselves as an inspiring Buddha of limitless compassion, showering out blessings endlessly, without any thought of earthly reward. Yet, the reality of love for most of us has been replaced by a shabby image that is both tarnished and calculating. An image that may be right there in your office, framed and symbolized in that picture of your wife and daughter, while you are busy committing infidelities, in all directions. Yes, there are rabbits springing up everywhere, making it seem like Father's day in Oakland – one of mass confusion!

Our whole aim here is not to sell you back on your ego portrait at bargain basement prices. The Course is not here to sell just another elegant frame of self deception. It is here to enable you to penetrate through to the real loving dimension, deep within yourself. You do not have to fake it, until you make it. Our goal is to bring back to you, awareness of that inexhaustible fountain of unconditional Love in which you were created, and still have your Being. This alone represents your fundamental reality. All else is ego delusion and subterfuge, that can only be spray painted on to masks.

HEALING THE DREAM THROUGH LOVE

True love is entirely invulnerable to all the evils of the ego, as reflected everywhere in the world around you. It is a love that is positively welcoming and one that knows you in your true essence. One that lets you stand revealed, for it sees truly and without any hint of distortion. It will enable you to see all in the crystal clear purity of a timeless light, that you had long forgotten. One that became hidden away under your mantle of ignorance and idol attraction. You may be wondering, at this point what snake-oil, I am attempting to sell you on, and what my true motives are? Why should I care a toss about you? Doesn't each just reap their own just rewards, as they continue on their own warped ways? There are many dark shadows that have entered our minds. We spontaneously impute evil motives everywhere. Yet there can be no progress, until we come to a point of trust. The motive for me, is that as I help you, I simultaneously heal the One-Mind, we both share.

You may think I am being forthright and superior calling myself a healer? Yet, we all possess the capacity to heal. Healing is natural, it is sickness that is an aberration. Yet, it is only our decision that determines whether we heal or not. Most of the time I am functioning as anything but a healer. In fact, more in need of it. At the end of the day, it is the veracity of the message that heals and not the messenger himself. Yet the messenger must be to some extent healed, if he carries a veracious message. Even the most powerful healing message is powerless and ineffectual, if it remains unheard and unused. Learning to remember yourself as unconditional love, is your real purpose here. Then you will find there is no self. The Self alone exists. So will all dreams fade from your eyes, as will memory and spacetime. But for the present they are still needed. They all serve as useful learning aids for you. Psychological crutches of a sort, that you can use to heal, until you finally need them no more.

As you are probably aware, those suffering from schizophrenia, severe alcoholism or drug dependencies etc. experience often the most interesting and frightening hallucinations. Yes, they are the grand masters, par excellence on hallucinations. They are the connoisseurs, that enthusiastically barter back and forth dream figures between themselves and no one. When someone first experiences a hallucination, they can end up feeling like a douche. It was as if the universe played a trick on you. One in which you were the only one fooled. Yet, it was not the universe, but your own mind that played the trick. The virus of your own beliefs had you fooled. Beliefs that remain buried deep in the underlying substratum of your thought. Beliefs reaching far into the unchartered realms of your unconscious. For this reason the hallucination had tremendous credibility and impact. The capacity to deceive your mind entirely. Its credibility is born from the power of your belief. Yes, your hallucination is a mental projection, in exact likeness to your beliefs.

It can be extremely hard to doubt the reality of that, which is before your very eyes. Others may be laughing, saying you are suffering from weird imaginations and distorted perceptions. One cannot be expected to grasp, at once that all those wonderful and fearful figures you see, were never there. Nor expected to know that all time, actions and dream figures are powered from within and are merely acting out your thoughts, wishes and fears. It seems a great affront to your mind and sanity, when you finally realize you made them all up. The entire fabric of your former reality becomes shorn. It is only then that the journey to real sanity and healing can begin. Yes the simple recognition, that all distorted perceptions are effects, arising as a consequence of false beliefs, transforms you. Then you see that the hallucination is driven by the power of your mind and its beliefs - conscious and unconscious. This alone it parades before your eyes. Clear understanding, a clearer lens of mind, changes your entire world. It pictures one, that sparkles now with a luminosity, that was never seen before. One that radiantly reflects the powerful transformative changes happening within you.

On a somewhat larger scale, but qualitatively no different, we do not recognize this world as your hallucination. That it is simply a distorted perception arising from distortionary beliefs. It seems to have substance and merit because it is shared and reinforced by a multiplicity of other dream figures, going back-and-forth. So it becomes transformed into a collective belief. Yet, there is nothing and no one, apart from this hallucination. All are embedded in its framework and give evidence and credibility to its existence, as bona-fide truth. Yet, all serve to steal you awareness away from your true Identity. All are figures you made up and represent just aspects of your greater Self. Do not mistake this for solipsism, which promotes the view that only one's personal ego exists. In stark contrast, the teaching here is that no such ego exists. It arises only in the mirage, of sights that are not there and sounds that are not heard. Fundamentally it arises from false understandings. These figures that populate your world are not "outside", and are not as you know them. Each has the light of the Holy Spirit in them, and is part of your Whole-Mind. Just as you are part of theirs.

A ZEN MASTER POINTS US IN THE RIGHT DIRECTION

The Zen master, Huang Po, once said "**The Perceived cannot Perceive.**" A full understanding of this statement, will lead to your Enlightenment. It will enable you to rise out of your hallucination. You must simply recognize, that all dream figures are apparitions of your own split-mind. Since you mentally created them, they are unlikely to tell you that they <u>are</u> dream figures. In fact they cannot tell you, because they themselves do not know. They are entirely likely to agree with your belief in them. They were after all generated out of your beliefs, in the first place. You loan them all the power they seem to have through your belief. Yet, Huang Po, is simply stating the obvious, which has now become hopelessly shrouded in complexity, confusion and delusion. He is simply saying, that all that is manifest and perceived has no power to think. All exists as reflections and images of thought, seen in the puddle of the world. A world that is not to be taken as real and self-existing in itself. Because an image has no capacity to think. Likewise "the perceived" has no active power of its own. Just as an image in the mirror has no power to see itself. It cannot see you - you alone can see it. You alone are its dreamer. You alone have the power. Yet because you have taken yourself to be a figure in this dream you made, this power has become lost.

Why is this not seen or known? It is simply because there is no one to ask and no one to tell. Finally to rub it in, you do not ask yourself. The lens of your mind has become too dull, conditioned, specific and time-bound to see what is obviously the case. So you have fallen into hypnotic identification with the dream figures you have made. The development of a collective hallucination is fascinating. Aspects of what is One-Mind become split-off and dissociated. They no longer recognize their essential unity, but consider themselves instead as independent minds. These aspects then hallucinate entirely different subjective mental worlds. Yet, each takes its own subjective world alone to be reality. These worlds have only partial overlap, for the minds that make them are not entirely in agreement on what is seen. Each aspect sees and projects its world from the lens of its own unique understandings, interpretations and accumulated memories. Since these are not agreed upon, between dream figures, accounts for each experiencing a different world.

Their time-spatial experiences start from different vortex points in the dream and the composite of their beliefs are different. This results in slightly different phenomena manifesting for each, and the illusion of different worlds. Each developing uniquely out of each dreamer's subjective thoughts alone. Were inner mental states and conditions exactly the same, both would possibly agree entirely on the world they see. Their interpretations and perceptions would be identical. What we call the sane in this world, are often just those sharing the same false beliefs, interpretations and ideologies. They agree with "other" dream figures, they themselves have projected. They do not question enough for themselves. So they are ready to bend to the court of "outside" opinion. Yet, this sharing of the false can only make us more integrated with the state of nonsense. We are all hallucinating here, to some extent, so long as our perception lasts. Those we label "sick", are often just those whose beliefs, are more deeply contrasted with our own. Yet these "unshared" beliefs, can be critical triggering beliefs, directing us on the path towards finding our real sanity.

REALITY AS THE HOME OF THE IMPERISHABLE

There must come a point, as we emerge from our muddleheaded confusion, when we realize that reality can have nothing to do with this world of objects and perceptions. The eternally valid cannot be this world of the perishable, where everything breaks down, wears out or seems to die. Reality must be the Home of the imperishable, the changeless and non-transient. It must represent a world far more potentiated, abstract, formless and deathless than the one we now perceive. It cannot contain any objects or things because objects are perishable and always impose limitations of some degree. Reality cannot be held limited or there would come a time when it becomes too frozen off and static - having accomplished all that it could be. What would it do then? Go back and play the same games over? Yet, with no longer any sense of accomplishment? How many times have you ever repeated the same jigsaw puzzle over?

No! there can be no objects in reality – that is for sure! Objects always represent limitations. We assign various capabilities and attributes to each. These then become their "magical powers", which determine their range and scope. It establishes the range of phenomena, they are capable of producing or interacting with. Yet, it is more accurate to say that phenomena produce the notion of an object, than an object its phenomena. A multiplicity of fields has arisen, from our various "magical beliefs" including science, medicine, technology, genetics, economics and so forth. These all make bold and certain statements. They take the worlds of the phenomenal and conceptual, to be exclusively real in itself, and the end goal. Rather than merely, to be used as a raft to take us to transcendental and the real. We so easily forget, that all the "magical and exotic powers" we bestow on the world of matter are mind-made. That the world remains a mention invention and fiction, formed in the exact image of our beliefs and expectations.

Reality and Knowledge must go hand-in-hand. Each is infinitely potent and has no boundaries or limitations. Knowledge and Truth must remain forever untethered, unbound and independent of all else. Those who know, likewise become unlimited. Their certainty means they are no longer handicapped by unreal phantoms and apparitions, born from their own minds. So they can be creative now in all directions. They enter the gate-less gate and disappear from the world of illusion. Yet, unlimited potency seems to be an abstraction, that is entirely alien to us. Particularly when contrasted and compared, with the very limited and specific world of form, we appear to inhabit. Yes, Knowledge has become merely hidden by our loss of capacity for abstraction and by our inability to fathom its limitless depths. The supra-conceptual remains far beyond our very limited modes of understanding. In the blindness and distortion born from our own mind's obsession with specifics, it potency seems lost and powerless.

Yet, its being untethered to any specific form, is what endows it with infinite potential, capaciousness and flexibility. It is what makes it truly creative, invulnerable, and deathless. For it is that content, which is immanent and transcendent of all form. The Absolute, knows nothing about our world. This remains our own private illusion. One born in that darkening obfuscation, in which true knowledge became lost. One which unleashed a vacuum in our Self-understanding, from which all untruths spread quickly as a veritable contagion. The ego propaganda machine has never stopped since. Never stopped cranking out illusions and misperceptions to blind our view. Nevertheless, appearances can never be transformed into fact. Appearances born out of habit energy, conditionings and false beliefs can go unquestioned, but this does not make them so. Yet, we appear to be living in this world and reacting to it, as if it is True "**Now**". The Course's response, is to have us ask ourselves, exactly who is this '**I**', that appears to be living in the world? Is it not an illusion that we ourselves have made? An illusion fueled out of all our ignorance, erroneous thoughts and beliefs, which then semi-crystallizes into a rather static, frozen and congealed image. An illusion, which then proceeds to distort what **IS** into what **IS Not**. Nevertheless, an illusion, we take to be both true and substantial.

One of the Course's key aims, is for us to correctly identify true Cause-and-Effect. So that we can reach to true understanding, undo all our confusion and make all false images disappear. In this undoing, we become empowered and healed. We rise above our state of ignorance and the powerful web of distortionary beliefs, that encapsulates our minds. All that which hooks us to the world of the relative existence. All that foolishness, born from our notions of being a personal "I", in a landscape of illusion. It is not just the Course that teaches this. Many other treasured spiritual teachings, down the millennia, have been propagating the exact same message. This quote below from the Lankavatara Sutra, also relates how the world of our perceptions, only arose under the influence of our numerous false beliefs, attachments and through he power of conditioning. The world nevertheless remains an illusory effect, produced from wishfulness and imagination. It should not to be taken as Absolute Reality.

> **"As to the first; he must recognize and be fully convinced that this triple world is nothing but a complex manifestation of one's mental activities; that it is devoid of selfness and its belongings; that there are no strivings, no comings, no goings. He must recognize and accept the fact that this triple world is manifested and imagined as real only under the influence of habit-energy that has been accumulated since the beginning-less past by reason of memory, false-imagination, false-reasoning, and attachments to the multiplicities of objects and reactions in close relationship and in conformity to ideas of body-property-and-abode."** ["The Lankavatara Sutra", Ch. VII]

OUR PERENNIAL GROUNDHOG DAY

In the movie, groundhog day, the actor Bill Murray is stuck living the same day over-and-over. Nothing is ever changing on the outside, but something radical is changing within for Murray. He starts becoming more considerate, even compassionate to those around him. He starts saving the "random" people he meets, in the course of his day. He knows the particular mishaps and accidents that will befall them in advance. Yet, it is this change, going on inside him that enables him not just to survive, but to thrive. It empowers him to overcome the hell and boredom of living the same day over-and-over. So he begins, at last to find true peace and self-worth.

This movie also very cogently reflects our own position. We too seem to be flying blind through life. Unsure how to appropriately respond to it. We are in fact continuously reliving the same instant over-and-over, until we learn to become more understanding, forgiving and kind. Only by becoming unconditionally loving, can we overcome and escape this seeming outward hell. A hell that each of our egos has imposed as a penalty against us, for listening to all its wicked ideologies and crafty schemes. It is true, that all our days seem to be somewhat different from each other. Everyday the set is changed and a new cast arrives. So a fresh crew of motley dream figures comes and goes, engaging us to join their scandalous charades or else launch on some holy crusade. We also appear to be getting older within the dream's context. Turning in our own unique portraits of 'Dorian Gray', before our very eyes.

But do we ever consider, that this entire virtual reality system, is being powered very precisely by our minds? That is a projected holomotion picture, that faithfully corresponds to how we ourselves are changing on the inside? Because the movie we see, but we fail to recognize ourselves, as the projectionist. We feel tired, worn down, uninspired and disenchanted and we then project these feelings to our bodies. It often has been far too long, since we last did something truly exciting, vitalizing and life affirming. How can this not show up in our outward image? The Course teaches us that there is a single meaningful script, running behind all the appearances, in our daily lives. This script never changes in its content. The script is for us to become more loving and forgiving. Only then do we escape the movie of perception.

Our mistake is thinking that the instant of '*The Fall*', from God's grace, was actually accomplished in reality. We have never fallen from God's grace, but we believe we have. So in terms of our experiences, it makes no difference. We will remain bound to our beliefs, until we believe them no longer. This is true of all beliefs. Our healing of the dream of perception, can only occur, when we choose to no longer believe the false. We do not need to believe in what is true, because truth is beyond belief. Truth becomes self-evident, once we drop all that is false. The belief that we can separate ourselves from truth and our Creator, is the problem that produces the entire world of appearances. Its ridiculousness is apparent to a sane mind. For we cannot ever be apart from truth and still exist. That we continue to believe we can, is why we appear to remain here in the first place. This false belief is what seems to bind us to this dreamworld, of the relative existence.

COMING TO TERMS WITH OUR AUTHORITY PROBLEM

In Course vernacular this belief is known as :- '*The Authority Problem*'. This is the single root belief that propagates all error. It is responsible for all our other false beliefs. It has a few fundamental components to it, namely :-

1) **That we have successfully usurped God's power of Creation**
2) **That we can exist apart from Truth**
3) **That we can be our own creator.**

This belief, that we have the power to self-create, is the reason we have lost awareness of our true Identity. The reason we have lost access to our true creative power. Because all true creative power, must first acknowledge its Source. It is its intimacy with its Source, that empowers and protects it and keeps it from falling into darkness. From its Source, does it receive that Knowledge, from which it derives all its power. Once we lost this intimacy with our Source, we fell into a dream of darkness. So we appear to rule now a pathetic kingdom of illusions, where everything is falling apart and where no lasting joy or meaning is to be found. From this one fundamental mistake, arose an entire world of unreality. So we seem to find ourselves now, in a world of illusions, that will remain forever insubstantial. Existing as hungry ghosts flaking about with insatiable desires. Not comprehending, that we have witlessly embedded ourselves as objects, within the frame of our own dreams. That nothing we perceive is really there.

> **"The essential Understanding is that in reality nothing is. This is so obvious that it is not perceived."   [Wei Wu Wei]**

There can never be any real solution for a problem that does not exist. We are still in the Kingdom, so the problem does not exist. Our expulsion from the Kingdom and separation from God has never happened in truth. Yet, we have the illusion that we are outside the Kingdom because of our belief in guilt. We (the Sonship), feel guilty, for believing we could usurp God's throne and power for ourselves. We believed this would bestow on us the specialness we craved. Yet, there is a healing solution for our illusionary problem which heals us of our belief in guilt. This solution is **quantum forgiveness**. Guilt's perfect antidote in the dream. Forgiveness gently awakens us, and in the light-filled dawn, we emerge from our spiritual chrysalises. Coming to the epiphanous realization, that we have always been safely snug at Home. Dorothy has never left Kansas. All our nightmares, never had any affect. So one clear day, we awaken to realize there never was a world. At least not the relative one, we perceive. What seemed to be, is no more. Instead we find ourselves enfolded in the warm embracing manifold of the Kingdom.

The truth is that our minds remain infinitely powerful. Yet we no longer operate, as if this were so. So powerful indeed, that each moment the entire world is manufactured fresh out of our thoughts and beliefs. This world we perceive continuously tracks our thoughts and beliefs, conscious and unconscious. Yet, this occurs so rapidly that most of us do not recognize it, and are therefore in denial of our breathtaking power. When a thought is sown often enough it starts to produce certain results. So over time, it becomes registered as a fixed belief. Beliefs then attract more thoughts and beliefs, that are in their likeness. Just like '*The Law of Attraction*'. Since perception, is just our beliefs projected, the result is that our perceptions start to crystallize into the exact likeness of all our beliefs. Thus reinforcing them. Our perceptions can therefore become very narrow-banded and circumvented because of our fixed beliefs. Hence the term tunnel vision!

It is also for this reason that the Course has written. "*It is not until beliefs are fixed that perceptions stabilize. In effect, then, what you believe you do see.*" [T-11.VI.1:3-4] Our beliefs aggregate further, to shape our experiences. Crystallizing into our worlds, perceptions and identities within them. They make us believe that the world formed in their image, is a fact. Having lost awareness of the awesome power of our minds and having placed ourselves in bondage to these beliefs, we then fall into the trap of victim-hood.

Victim-hood teaches us that we are for the most part powerless over the world, we perceive. That we are merciless prey to an assortment of haphazard influences and evil forces, far more powerful than ourselves. So we forget ourselves, as this world's sole inventor. 'The Atonement Plan', is Heaven's plan for our release from bondage. Through accepting Atonement, we regain power over the world we see and escape the hell we made. Atonement restores us to awareness, of our original magnificence and grandeur. It restores us to awareness of our true Identity as the '**Son of God**'.

Atonement undoes the fiction of a personal self. Yet, this fiction did not happen in a day. Instead it was manufactured carefully over eons by the voice of separation - '*the ego*'. That same voice, which believes in our guilt. This fiction teaches that each of us is a mind trapped and bound inside a body. A mind that is for the most part pretty powerless. A mind that must exercise constant vigilance, if it is ever to progress. A mind that must surround itself with a litany of defenses, to protect the little it has, from all those who would steal from it or otherwise detract from its power. Yet, this fiction, that is the ego does not exist in truth. It must become evident then, that all those thoughts and actions, motivated and directed by our complicity to it, must be accomplishing nothing. We are merely selfishly and venomously protecting an illusory fiefdom in the sand. So reinforcing this voice of separation and our own split-minds. Wei Wu Wei puts this very succinctly in '*Ask the Awakened*' when he says _- "Why are you unhappy? Because 99.9 percent of everything you think of, and of everything you do, is for yourself – and there isn't one".

The Course teaches that the ego cannot be real, because it represents a coterie of beliefs, unshared by God and by our Whole-Mind. Beliefs arising from its manifold reactions to its own distortions. A lone voice within, serving to reinforce these distortions. These beliefs represent the composite of all our wishfulness and fears - all our unwholesome desires. The ego is incapable of knowing anything, because it arose with the loss of Knowledge. Each ego is a private illusion. It represents only the individual thoughts, of one seemingly separated mind. So it meets all the requirements, of an hallucination. One that maintains the mirage of its seeming existence, through its invented notions of self-autonomy. Yet, its false notions of autonomy weaken us. They further isolate and bind us to a private world of our own making, which then seems to hold us captive.

All our thoughts of protection, care and love for the ego, must be redirected towards true communication. We must come to recognize, that our minds are forever joined together in holiness and as One. That we all arise from a single Source, whose reality is unconditional love. Once we come to recognize, that others do not exist outside us, nor us them and that we are all parts of a greater Self, the ego's reign will end. We will see then how it is a nuisance, impeding us on the path of our own best interests. So will it be disbanded and our greater Self will shine back into our awareness. Only then will we know that we are invulnerable. This Self is always present. However this Self becomes lost and obscured to our awareness, in our foolish dreams of ego self autonomy. Sane perception will wean us from the illusion of separateness, and from all our beliefs of victimization by an external world. So will we be restored to vision and see '**The Great One**' in all. See each as '*The Son of God*', and as part of our One and only Reality.

As we undo, the single error that is '**The Authority Problem**', and embrace instead the Atonement, our world will be completely transformed - then disappear. But first it will become an abode of holiness, joy, peace, clarity and hope. Its vagary and phantasmagoric elements, will be transmuted into ever purified perceptions. We will penetrate through to our true Being, and finally disappear into the sea of absolute purity, potency and perfection. The sea of immutable formlessness. Yet, this disappearance, is our real appearance. So we find ourselves merged, dissolved and blissfully alive in unitary Being and the powerhouse of the One-Mind. The Knowledge of the One-Mind is beyond all conception and perception, yet within our soft embrace. So do we wake-up, to find ourselves abiding in an eternal state of bliss, peace and creativity. Our true Home and eternal Reality, dawning back into our awareness. This final step that merges us with the Absolute and non-differentiated, is known as grace, and it is taken by God. This moment of grace, seems to be far into each of our futures, yet it has already happened. It would be witnessed, in the *'Here-and-Now'*, were our awareness not blinded, by the kaleidoscopic mirage of all our false identifications and beliefs.

OUR MANY FALSE BELIEFS ARE THE ONLY BARRIER

Yes, our present state of mind is the only barrier. Our beliefs place us firmly in a hall of ignorance where our vision remains obscured. We remain heavily conditioned by false thought forms. Deep in our minds, there is a place of complete peace and rest, one that retains no memory of this world. A place free of all dream fiction. Dream fictions that have been reappearing interminably, since the instant of the seeming fall. It is only the unreal and 'separated' part of our mind that entertains foolish beliefs. It is this part alone, which makes us feel that we are inhabiting the world. The real part remains as always in eternity, where it is actively Creating. However having become dream identified, we continue to interpose, a past that never was into our awareness. This then hangs as a dark cloud over ever-present truth. **We react in our dream fictions, as if the past were present and real Now.** Yet, it is exclusively our reactions to the many projected dream images we make, that is concealing the face of true Reality. Thus we fail to recognize through naked perception, that alone which **IS Here-Now**.

The *'Second Coming'*, is not about some new savior, emerging into the flux of the relative, to "save" us. It is merely the restoration, back into our awareness of an ever-present Reality, that is always Here. In the end no "external" savior can save us. We can only choose, to save ourselves by listening and attuning to higher wisdom. Then actuating this wisdom into our lives. Truth will come of its own, once we dispossess all that is false. If "another" were to save you, he would be implanting and instilling into you, beliefs in weakness and incompletion. Teaching that you are not Whole within. This would be a great affront to your reality and serve to disempower you. Your self-imposed handicaps would remain. Each must come to recognize, that the personal ego makes for a very poor counsel. That it is hopelessly obsessed, with just regurgitating the vomit of your past, into your present and all your tomorrows. It is the thought system that prevents our natural spiritual abilities and inner awareness from flowering to release us. It is constantly introducing illusory barriers, which function as a darkened overlay, interposed between truth and our awareness of it.

> **"Is it not possible that all your problems have been solved, but you have removed yourself from the solution?"** **[T-17.VII.2:4]**

Many horrific and meaningless videos will play over-and-over, like an endless groundhog day, until we choose the healing power of **the Atonement**. The purpose of these videos, is to remind us to forgive. So we heal our guilt ridden minds. The videos are purposeless in themselves, without the decryption key of forgiveness, which alone bestows on them meaning. Until we use this key, our false beliefs will continue to function, as blocking devices and jammers that cost us awareness of reality. **The Atonement Plan**, is purposed with training our minds, to competently distinguish the true from the false. Doing so, we are released from the many distortions of the ego, and come to retain only the Knowledge of Spirit. The past reinterpreted by the light of Spirit, relinquishes the false and restores us to awareness of our original purity. It is this which leads to our healing, while restoring us to the eternal present. The past purged and divested of all impurities is eternal. The eternal, is not really any aspect of time, but timelessness itself. Through Atonement, the altar of our minds becomes restored to its unblemished original radiance. An immaculate altar remains which alone knows truth, and which alone is truth.

THE ATONEMENT, AS A SPIRITUAL FILTRATION SYSTEM, WHICH AVOWS ONLY TRUTH

You may well ask, if the past does not really exist, how could it seem to be at all and why is it taken so seriously? In fact this is one of the best questions you could ask! The mind that believed, it could separate from God and usurp His Creative Power, seemed to become split into two parts. **(1) A Real part, which remains in God** and **(2) An illusory aspect, which believes that it can attack God.** The mind has therefore become severely dissociated within itself, a condition known as split-mind. Once the illusory arose, the real was lost, to our awareness. Reality is still present, but it has become so distorted by obfuscating illusions, that it can no longer be recognized. The mind therefore is confronted with a serious problem. How is it to decode the meaningful and true from all the fragmented and chaotic perceptions, that it perceives? There is no possibility of this, if it attempts to weave a meaningful tale from the entire ensemble, it is presented with. This is because the real alone, will only ever be true, and those unreal aspects born out of ego distortions, will always remain meaningless.

It is a bit like mixing vodka with orange juice. You no longer have the pure OJ anymore, yet what you have will make you mindless. You will find it very difficult now to separate the vodka from the OJ, by tasting this concoction. Yet its presence is most definitely felt, despite appearances. When illusions first entered our minds, it was as if illusions were placed now on a parity with truth, and capable of waging war on it. Yet, we no longer seem capable of separating one from the other. The real is still here, in all its perfection and completeness - just like the pure OJ is still there somewhere in the vodka. However with the apparent separation, we are now in the unfortunate position of needing to build a filtration system, that can reliably separate the vodka from the pure OJ. This is the only solution. This is what 'The Atonement Plan' is for. It is an extremely effective and simple spiritual filtration system, designed by the Holy Spirit. One in which we learn to question and dispel all effects arising out of the ego and its thought system. Thus we can restore to our awareness the pure OJ of truth. The Course puts it this way :-

> "By steadily and consistently cancelling out all its effects, everywhere and in all respects, He teaches that the ego does not exist and proves it."
>
> **[T-9.IV.5:6]**

In the meantime, we appear to be in a mind generated minefield of illusions. We carry with us everywhere, the darkness inherent in all those contradictions, forged from our erroneous beliefs. Yet, we do not realize this. So we seem to find ourselves in a spacetime existence. In this spacetime artifice, many contradictions can arise serially or even be juxtaposed. All of them, would be instantly and easily dispelled under the light of true understanding. Viewed from the frame of spacetime, both sides of a contradiction can promote belief in the very partial and biased picture, each presents. Each side claiming to be independent and the whole picture. Yet, these contradictions are merely artifacts arising from our poor viewing context. They represent our own limitations. Our lost cerebrational capacities for pure, expansive and abstracted thought-forms. So we are easily fooled and deceived by our myopic thinking patterns. We lose all clarity through the mental amnesia induced by apparent temporal separation. At the personality level, this leads to dissociation, and in extreme cases manifests as multiple personality disorder (MPD). All driven by our denial and subsequent loss of integration.

It is also the reason why our mind-states and emotions are so unstable, volatile, unreliable and consist of shifting thought patterns and energies encircling no fixed center. Our minds seem totally confused and endarkened by the rotational fields of contradiction, within which many competing personalities, are temporarily licensed to take control. Yet, these are all merely effects streaming from the original error. So we go about plodding, a seemingly endless path through time, learning meaningless information and undergoing futile ventures, in a vain search after idols. Idols are our mind's attempt to feel whole in the absence of God. They are compensations our minds seek, for the loss of awareness of our true Identity. So we seek for "specialness" and desire manifold "special" "love" and "hate" relationships, to support some meaning in our fragile lives. Through these we attempt to compensate for our perceived lack of self-worth, by greedily extracting it from another. So does each fractured and decimated ego seek to complete itself. It seeks to alleviate its guilt by displacing it elsewhere. Nevertheless, it still believes in guilt's underlying reality. Doing so, it deactivates from our awareness, knowledge of our completeness, timeless innocence and holiness.

Our only hope, is to re-establish into active awareness our own sense of self-worth, by not being afraid to go within. We must face up to the true source of our fears and bypass the Mad Max terrain, of the ego world. Everything that we need and Are is here already inside us. It needs no external proxies for its support. The plan of Atonement is given. The new adventure within will help shine light on all our false concepts, fear driven defense mechanisms and other strategies of self-deception. All untruths will be fried in the bonfire of self-enquiry, allowing our true effulgent Self, to shine back into our awareness. As the mists that shroud over our true Being disappear, the world of perception, will be correspondingly transformed and purified. This will usher forth a world of joy, innocence and increased self-worth to take the place of all the fear, confusion and lack of certainty, streaming from projected error. For errors undone through right understanding and forgiveness are powerless to affect perception or to victimize their maker. The pure OJ will be tasted once again - that is for sure! It is just a matter of having the right intentions and following inspired guidance. This then disavows all the mindlessness, induced by the vodka of the ego world. This voyage within, whenever you choose to take it, is the only meaningful voyage of the world, for it is the voyage out of it into the safety of Reality.

2. THE WORLD AS PROJECTION OF YOUR SUBJECTIVITY

Sometimes destiny throws a point of inflection on your path. The economy was not doing good. I had been stewing away in my apartment for many mindless months, feeling the four walls closing in, about to suffocate me. I had applied for many jobs and gone to numerous interviews, with no success. Sometimes I would do some yoga or go for a long run or hike to energize. Or head off on a road trip to break up the monotony. On occasion I would throw a party and knock back some of my vintage *'hole in the boat'* cocktails until delirium and the fatigue of alcohol set in. The game was over. My Silicon Valley dream had transformed into a nightmare. This was the point at which I had expected to be a millionaire. Instead, I had just enough money left to last one more month.

I started to sell all my furniture. I advertised on craigslist. So one Saturday morning it, was all taken away. My couch, and recliner had suddenly disappeared along with my prized brass lamp, pictures and ornaments. There was nothing left in the kitchen except some basic cutlery and a tea pot. The apartment had become so bare and characterless, making it even more miserable to live in than before. All I had now was my bed and some pillows. I would sit on the floor in the living room, with my back against the wall and no music system or TV to entertain me. I just wanted to clear my head. I walked downtown, but could not go to the Irish bar anymore because I was barred. In fact I was barred from every bar in town, except the Tied House. So I jumped on the Caltrain and headed to San Fran.

There, I started tossing them back at some random bars. Strolling out of one, I saw a homeless girl sleeping down an alley and felt immediately sorry for her. There she was down in this basement, of a building in the tenderloin, peering out through the black railings. Her aunt was dying of cancer in Oakland and she could not afford the train ride to go see her one last time. All she wanted was to bring her Aunt some flowers for her birthday. My heart, so long numbed and stymied by this ambitious culture, we live in was beginning to open. I said, that I would get an inexpensive hotel room and she could stay for the night.

Then another homeless guy came by. He was all bubbly and spirited and I immediately liked him. That did not mean I trusted him. Yet, he had charisma and seemed to be one of the characters in the neighborhood. He knew almost every street person we passed by name. His only complaint was that his boots were falling apart. He desperately needed some new boots. I said he could also crash with us. Next morning, I brought him to the shoe store to get him new boots. His eyes were beaming now with such exuberance and pride that it made me feel so grateful and empowered inside. Then we all headed to the gumbo shrimp factory to eat a delicious lunch. I gave them a little money and bid them farewell, knowing I would almost certainly never meet them again.

Heading back on the train, I was looking forward to just crashing in my bed. Unfortunately, the Caltrain wasn't going all the way, but coming to a halt at Palo Alto. If life throws you lemons, make gin and tonics. Yes, I would have a few nightcaps first, and obey the universal mandate. After engaging some genial folk in conversation at the bar, I felt pretty charged. I finally stumbled out and made my way for a taxi. Then at the last moment decided to get some pizza. Walking towards the pizza joint, I saw this colorful character spouting some spirited nonsense to all the fleas and drones hanging there in the square. They were walking by like sleepwalkers with absentia-dementia. He had so much gusto and humor and was a startling and welcoming contrast to all. He did not look homeless, but then I saw his green backpack near the fountain.

I assessed that he must be half-starved and asked if he would like to get some pizza. He agreed and was grateful. He ate it ravenously, as if he had not eaten for days. Seeing his intense hunger, I offered to get him another slice. He refused at first, but was finally persuaded by my persistence. He seemed unconcerned about everything. This to me was such a welcome relief and refreshing to find. I had spent so much of my life surrounded by an army of work obsessed pressure cookers, sweating over a thousand sweet nothings. Perfectionists, intensely absorbed with tiny little minutiae, yet who always seemed to miss out on the bigger picture in life. Yet, if you did not play in to their small-minded games, you were callously placed on the rack, and torn apart limb for limb. All they ever talked about is work, stock and politics. My mind was beginning to reverberate, with so many hellish nightmares, just thinking about it again. I snapped myself out of it, and said we would get some beer and vodka and he could crash in my place. So a short while later, he was sitting on the floor in my apartment, with his back against the wall. Taking large swigs from his vodka bottle which made James Dean look like a cultured priss.

I immediately knocked back a number of beers and fell asleep somewhere on the floor. Next day, when I asked him his name, he said it was 'Skywalker'. It turned out he had been in the military for many years and had worked in over a dozen companies in the valley. Yet, here he was deserted and sleeping in storefronts and alleys. Yet, he possessed too much integrity to beg a penny. I decided to bring him downtown Mountain View for one last meal, before I would drop him off at the bus stop.

Then my cellphone started going off. It was Trish, my out of control friend from New Jersey. She was hysterical. She wanted me to come out to New Jersey immediately to give her some support. I hadn't known her very well, apart from numerous phone-calls, at the most random of times. After all I had just met her briefly the Christmas before. I told her I would book a flight for the very next day. Yet I knew, I could not really afford this trip. It would have to go on the credit card. With this change in events, I decided to let Skywalker stay in my place, until I returned. At least he would have a roof over his head, for a week or so. Then I went to a friend, who was living in an apartment nearby. I gave him some money to provide to Skywalker, so that he could at least get the bare necessities, while I was out of town. I requested that he not give the money all at once, since I did not want Skywalker getting trashed on vodka for days on end, while starving himself of all essential nutrients.

In New Jersey, it was snowing heavily. I felt like I had arrived in a completely different world. Like something out of an Anne Rice novel. There she was circling about in her mother's clothes, who had recently died. It was as if I entered the Gothic museum to modern culture. She was beautiful despite her years and very engaging too, and yes she most definitely had the eyes of a witch. I felt, if I looked into them for a few seconds or more, I would have either a catatonic trance or enter some weird world, that I did care not to intrude upon. Yes, they were definitely engaging, even hypnotizing and they held me transfixed. They perforated through all the ages, instantly making me feel like I was hanging over some tremendous abyss, with just my finger tips. Feeling as if the carpet of all linear thought had suddenly been yanked and my species had become extinct, in these parts.

Her brother circling about as some real-life Quasimodo, only added to the atmosphere. He had been hit by a drunk driver, when he was young and he no longer had any good command of his faculties of speech and movement. It was painful to watch him eating - in fact positively embarrassing, especially if you are out in public. I could not imagine the pain, prejudice and exclusion he must have put up with over the last fifty years. He could only navigate the computer using one finger. Even this finger took so much effort to rightly coordinate, that he operated the keyboard like a woody woodpecker of sorts. Yet, his relentless spirit was admirable, and after six grueling long years, he had finally almost completed his Masters degree. Despite all his handicaps, he was all positive and game. He wanted me to take him to all the topless bunny clubs and bars. He was glad I had flown in. Glad he had found someone to ferry him about while he proceeded to cave in to all his vices. His sister thought this shameless and would never support his "interests". I felt like I had been strategically placed between a rock and hard-place.

So off we went to one, where he proceeded to get trashed on cocktails. He was sucking them out of a straw and heartily enjoying himself. Yet, some guy at the bar took an instant dislike to me. He was like a wolfhound gyrating up and down, just waiting to be unleashed. I decided it was time to go. I started ushering my friend away in his wheelchair. But this guy was already in a rage and decided to follow us out. He had a murderous intent and wanted to throw me off a ledge into the gutter below. But I held on tenaciously to the railing, and would not let go. I knew it would not be a nice landing and more than likely a death call. Finally he gave up his game of hatred, but not before delivering a few punishing kicks to my ribs. The pain from which, remained with me, for a long time thereafter.

Next morning, I called Skywalker to see how he was doing. It turned out he had not eaten in three days. When I inquired further, he indicated that no one had come by to give him any money or provisions. I immediately called up my friend and told him to make a visit. I was grateful that he did take good care of Skywalker from then on out. When I arrived back in town, Skywalker was still there.

He was lying on my bed looking pretty weak. Yet, I could sense that he was the very embodiment of integrity and honesty incarnated into the flesh. He did not know a soul and yet there was a positivity to him that I had not come across before. Not an ounce of bitterness or condemnation, just a perfect unconditional acceptance of life. A raw beauty and an endearing simplicity. Yet, I had so little to give him and was losing my place within days. My plan was to fill up my 3000GT with all I had left and head off into the desert. I imagined myself as some vagabond night rider, with little left to lose.

The day was coming fast. Just one last interview to hear back from, out of the seventeen I had done. That was all that stood between me and the desert. But first my downstairs friend wanted me to party with him in Bakersfield. I knew this would be my last fling before heading off. Yes, it was to be a night of great partying for sure. I soon became powerfully intoxicated and a legless drunk. There I was sprawled out spread-eagle on the floor, unable to make it the final few steps into my hotel room. My friends were trying to lift me up when an officer came by and said '*You either get her back into the room or she goes in my car."* Next day, I woke up all excited about life. I even had the appetite for breakfast and not the wicked hangover, that I would have expected. I was driving back up North, when I got the call saying I landed the job. I would not become a Mahavira after all, a meandering naked recluse stranded somewhere in the desert going through all sorts of penances and contortionist postures and pygmy dances. Instead I would be going to green Grass Valley and taking Skywalker along for the ride.

OUR WORLD EXPERIENCES ARE NOT AT RANDOM

You may be wondering why I bother to share, this brief vignette from my life, and how exactly it relates to the topic at hand? At that particular time in my life, I was obviously somewhat disconcerted at not finding a job, running out of cash and having to sell all my possessions. Yet, I still had food to eat and an apartment to live in. When I ran into those homeless in San Francisco, I began to see their immediate needs. My focus became deflected outward and away from myself. As a result, I became more expansive. I began to explore life more, through the eyes of others. I was entering new vistas of thought, new social, moral and humanitarian dimensions. My thought patterns were no longer contracted and toxic. With just a few brief encounters, I was able to readily transform my mind-state of grievance into one of gratitude. By entering a mind-state of giving, I was able to receive. So the whole series of experiences was a powerful learning lesson for me, on gratitude and miracles. Important healing began to take place, because I had made loving decisions, in response to all the information, that I was receiving from the world of my perceptions. Consequently, I was able to heal my inner fears through empowering the Voice of love within.

One of the powerful messages from the Course is that our perceptions are not at random. What shows up in our perceptions, always reflects our current learning needs. Experiences and events are there to present us with an opportunity to heal. This is what motivates and triggers them, otherwise they would not be appearing at all. Yes, there are always positive messages streaming to us from the world of our perceptions. Many healing opportunities coming our way, which we often feel powerless to decode and only see the value of in retrospect. Existence is never wrong. Nothing happens by chance or based on contingency, no matter how tragic, heartless or meaningless the event may seem to be. All such interpretations arise from the ego. All meaningless perceptions are driven by its toxic and fallacious thought patterns. When we no longer empower its thought, these meaningless perceptions begin to disappear.

The reason perception is able to respond to our current learning needs, is because it is a 'made-to-order' thing. There is not just one world, but many illusionary ones. Each hallucination gets projected from each mind independently. Each tracks both our instantaneous needs and special learning lessons. We see not in one way, but in a multiplicity of different ways simultaneously. We see through the eyes of our reason, understanding, intuition, memory, experiences, conditionings, expectations and desires concurrently. We see also through the eyes of our emotions, prejudices, biases, beliefs and attachments. All these different streams are being pipelined to us simultaneously and overlaid as a composite. They are what color and shape our world, into the many exotic and mundane forms it takes. They are the motive force that drives this holomotion picture. Yet, all is formed in the mind and it remains there. After a while, some of us, begin to realize, that it is really with our mind's eye that we see and experience. The mind does not play just an important role in our perception - **it plays the entire role**. It is what produces it. Perception is nothing more than the composite of our mind's projections.

Projection is the inner dynamic responsible for generating our entire world. Yet, it is one of the most deceptive of all mind dynamics. This is because, we are so easily fooled into believing that what is happening is independent of our own mind-states. When our mind's projecting power is denied, we gradually fall into delusion. Over time we begin to feel a heightened sense of disempowerment and failure. This is part of the cost of our denial. We become more reactionary and fearful instead of more commanding, responsible and responsive. Like the web of a spider, this world only seems apart and independent, yet it is actually spun from inside ourselves.

Our constant use of projection, is what alone maintains our world picture moment-by-moment. Yet, we are blissfully unaware of our mind's power, because we are too caught in the trap of worldly vices, identifications, wish fulfillments and fear based reactions. Yet, you should know, that your real mind is always active and never sleeps. Even when fast asleep, there is a part of you that remains wide awake. This part of your mind has been called the unconscious or subconscious mind. It keeps your respiratory and digestive systems working while you sleep. It maintains hormonal secretions, the endocrine and nervous systems and so much more. It is the aspect of mind that remains extremely vigilant, when you become drowsy and dull. It is that which remembers, what you have long forgotten. You seem to live out your entire life on the surface of this great mind, accessing only a tiny bit of its tremendous landscape of intuition and understanding. Even that portion is heavily filtered and conditioned to be in line with your beliefs. Yet, you spend all your life, dream identified with your self-made phantasms and easily forget yourself as this world's dreamer. Nevertheless, everything you see, everyone you see, all events and catastrophes, that play out in your world, are nothing but your own projections.

> **"Projection makes perception. The world you see is what you gave is, nothing more than that. But though it is no more than that, it is not less. Therefore, to you it is important. It is the witness to your state of mind, the outside picture of an inward condition. As a man thinketh, so does he perceive. Therefore seek not to change the world, but choose to change your mind about the world. Perception is a result and not a cause."** **[T-21.Intr.1:1-8]**

THE ILLUSION OF AN OBJECTIVE UNIVERSE

All that is projected, already exists inside us, as our own mental objects. The ideational content, that is the very essence of all we see is formed and shaped in the flux of our mind's inner processes. Formed in the exact image of our judgments, beliefs, filters, conditionings, visceral prejudices and senses of limitation. Unfortunately, almost all of this remains unconscious to us, and is screened to our momentary awareness. Nevertheless, this content gets projected "outward", as images and forms, that hold the key to our Self-understanding. For our underlying beliefs, are imaged in forms, that we can more easily relate to. This becomes our world. Yet, form always represents limitation, and a loss of power from true abstraction. Form only arises in a mind deeply asleep, and therefore in a mind at prey to illusion. Yet, our mind is never discontinuous to itself, nor to the world it perceives. It remains perfectly unified with all that IS, and to all of Mind. Our mind in its true essence is limitless in its potency and seamless in its continuity. Apart from it, there is nothing. For it is the Kingdom. Yet, this Kingdom has become completely obscured and shrouded through our defilements. And what are defilements, but the impurities of our incorrect understandings.

> **"Mind reaches to itself. It is *not* made up of different parts, which reach each other. It does not go out. Within itself it has no limits, and there is nothing outside it. It encompasses everything. It encompasses you entirely; you within it and it within you. There is nothing else, anywhere or ever."**
>
> **[T-18.VI.8:5-11]**

What appears as objects and phenomena "out-there", is nothing more than thought projection, of all spontaneously arising in the turbulent sea of our own subjectivity. The fundamental realization then, is that there is no external universe. Objectivity is an illusion. Not a single object has ever existed. Objects are like phantoms, arising from the sea of our own thoughts, both conscious and unconscious. These then get projected into the void, where they become imaged as your world. Objects and phenomena possess no independent existence, apart from those thoughts that power them, and give them all their seeming life. There is nothing external and apart from the mind.

> **"There is nothing outside you. That is what you must ultimately learn . . ."**   **[T-18.VI.1:1-2]**

If even a single object were objectively true, then all objects would be true, as would the space needed to contain and extend them. Yes, the conspiracy arising from our own ignorance, is so vast that we can no longer see its underlying mechanisms. That is why we are mostly in confusion, and do not really understanding ourselves or the world around us. In fact, not understanding ourselves, is also the reason our world appears meaningless. Once we accredit one illusion, we accredit all of them, and illusions soon proliferate to support one other. Accepting belief in a single falsity, is opening the can of ten thousand worms. You have just licensed illusions to infiltrate your belief system, where as poisonous snakes they slither about, keeping you at ransom to the powers of darkness and the so-called "objective" existence.

GOD BECOMES OUR PATSY

Now also, you have just made the illusion of your body, into a seeming veracity. So you begin to feel vulnerable. At prey to so many mysterious and magical forces, you ascribe as being "outside" yourself. Firmly identified with the body, you project this mistaken belief, also unto God. So is God held responsible for your body and for the entire world of your projections. He is held accountable for all the illusions, you made through your misbeliefs. Not liking what you made, you come to detest God, for inflicting this hellish world of vengeance and misery upon you. You play the victim, who digs their head in the sand, and you do nothing to cure your ignorance. Having made God into a vengeful and fearful One, you are afraid to go within. In the meantime, perception's enormity makes your shrink even more, from what you made. Its seeming endless scope for variance and its countless uncertainties frightens you. So you do not take any responsibility for it. Its chaos and never-ending madness, seem too deeply entrenched and irredeemable, to be your own. Too much for you to take on. Yet, you will not heal until you begin to take this responsibility.

Yes, God must be made culpable. He is made into our patsy. So enters the ego, who is only too joyous to assign Him blame. The ego casually ignores its own role, in the mass deception and comes in the guise of your savior and friend. Yet, it is indeed an evil portrait, one with the trembling fingers of fear and lips smeared with nothing but condemnation. One that audaciously dares to declare to God, what He must be and accuse Him for it. The world's random senselessness and mad ways, must now become part of God's greater Will - an exact likeness to what He has in store for you, in the realm eternal. This hellish mess of projected mental diarrhea, is now seen as His intelligent design, His final wish for you. So is God held forever suspect, in the ego's scheme. Now all those ego worms of thought, seem to creep up under the rug of God's omnipotence, to undermine and tarnish all. These bed bugs of the ego are soon enshrined into idols and seen as part of the fabric of our reality. Yet, God is not responsible for all the cruelties, random brutalities and evils going on in the world – this is your ego's masterful design. God knows nothing of this world. Objects, form, phenomena, and spacetime are all one illusion. To believe in one is to believe them all. Yet, if you deny one, you have placed your feet securely, on the royal road to wisdom.

It is the height of madness, to believe that God created both good and evil. Yet, through your projections, He becomes imaged and reflected through the distorting lens, of your own split-mind. So you see Him perfectly content to endlessly wage war on Himself, for all eternity! There can be no rest for Him, no way to STOP THE MADNESS and so end the vicious torment. Yet, He is also somehow supposed to be this fountainhead of unconditional Peace, Love and of unassailable Knowledge. Is this likely? Or is it instead the case, that this world you perceive, is entirely born inside you? Formed from your thoughts and misbeliefs, and never apart from them? Your own just reward, for all that you desire, believe and attempt to do. For it is assuredly nothing but a stage, in which your own thoughts are acted out. One in which you react to your projections, as if they were a thing apart. Learn to reason more and to fall into the trap of identification less. Your worldly identification, has made you a prisoner to merciless dreams. Those who project will be punished by their incorrect beliefs, until they wisely decide to give them up. Punished and enslaved by themselves, until they decide to relinquish all erroneous beliefs, that power their perceptions.

The Zen Master, Hui Neng once said, **"From the first, not a thing IS."** This is the ultimate truth and represents the Knowledge of all the Enlightened. Huang Po also echoed this same sentiment when he said :- **"Remember that from the first to the last, not even the**

smallest grain of anything perceptible has ever existed or ever will exist." Now that's the spirit. One of the reasons, I like Zen so much, is that it is so full of such wise aphorisms, which cut through all the bullshit and chiaroscuro. Aphorisms that really hit the nail on the head. Reflecting on such royal understandings, day-in and day-out, one moment when you least expect it, you will reach complete Self-Realization. Then you divest yourself, of this relative world of bondage and undergo that most beautiful of metamorphoses. One in which you shed the body of form, for one that is perfect, formless, blissful and deathless. Then you are no longer a prisoner of dreams. Sometimes it can happen, in a single instant on hearing such words. The simultaneously born, possess a deep metaphysical understanding, that can instantly penetrate the dream.

Directing our awareness to the subjective, we are reaching at last to the source of all forms and perceptions. This will give us unique insight into why they continue to arise. So we begin to see how all forms, concepts, symbols, actions and perceptions are mind-dreams we invest meaning to. All arise from our lower mind and its need of healing. They are all intricately tied up with, our subtle and evolutionary use of mind. Our subjective "inner" self makes everything we see. An a-perceptive witnessing, that is inclusive of our subjective awareness, is what finally releases us from all erroneous dualistic modes of experiencing. So we heal and transcend the duality of mind and form, and are enabled to enter the gate into formlessness. The subjective is not a physical dimension, but a vector into our essence. It always perfectly corresponds, to our own inner development and evolution. As all our inner beliefs are called into question, we become transformed and healed.

The world is powerless to give us wisdom, because it will always remain an effect. We must find wisdom inside ourselves. Our inner pioneering work correspondingly transforms and transmogrifies the apparent outside world, because these were never separate. The Zen Masters had a phrase for this understanding :- **"This being So, this will also be So."** The outer always perfectly corresponds to the inner. This is a lion's roar that cuts the head on the foolish notion that causation is temporally driven. Once we fully realize this, we are free to choose again and so change our entire world. Whatever is happening now is never the result of some past event, but the direct outcome of our present state of mind. Truth has no room for anything but truth. It cannot uphold any time-based and event driven causality that you subscribe to.

Past events are not cause of present effects. Rather all effects arise exclusively, out of present beliefs and present states of mind. Time therefore is powerless to withhold your release – only your present decisions determine this. Yes, present decision is so powerful that it can vaporize your entire world. You can recognize through vision, this moment the truth, that is everpresent. So are you freed from the shackles of time, along with all skeletons inherited from the past. God's justice does not punish you for past mistakes. In fact it never punishes you at all, it only ever blesses. But you can punish and handicap yourself through your present bad decisions. So you reap the harvest of hell or heaven based solely on these decisions.

Once you connect to the power and understanding inherent in your true Identity, everything changes. For we surely act and behave based on what we think we Are. Everything we think we are, attracts like beliefs, which then produces the world we see. Not comprehending true Cause-and-Effect principles, you react and play the victim and sow the futile seeds of wasted effort into the field of time. So you cross your fingers foolishly thinking time will give you all that you want. As your inner subjectivity deepens, the projected phenomenal counterpart that is the world is correspondingly purified and transformed. The only solution to the myriad problems, you see as endemic in the world, is to correctly place their source firmly inside your mind. That is where they are, whether you accept it or not. Thus you come to recognize the power of your mind, decision and begin to take full responsibility for your world.

This is the decision to grow-up spiritually and not remain a child. It is a healing understanding that heals you and all that seems apart. You have stopped reacting and scapegoating. You have stopped placing the source of your misery outside yourself. Now there is hope at last for loving extension in place of projection. Extension of forgiveness, compassion and true understanding in place of ragged fear-based projections. Projection is what makes the world, but it is the power of extension that undoes it. Projection seems to separate you from the world and from all those around you. Through it you set up invisible barriers that are totally unneeded. Yet, the dream's counterpart of extension reunites you with all. Through extension you teach and share only what is true. Extension arises out of Love and undoes all darkened images on the screen. It is through the power of extension that you come to recognize that you are already at Home. For it heals all apparent dissociation and all that makes you believe you are a thing apart.

3. SEARCHING FOR A PLACE CALLED HOME

"His disciples said to him, When will the Kingdom come? It will not come by watching for it. It will not be said, 'Look, here!' or 'Look, there!' Rather, the Father's kingdom is spread out upon the earth, and people don't see it."

[The Gospel of Thomas]

We have lost the capacity to value, what is in front of our eyes. We take everyone and everything for granted. We place them in our chest of mannequins, cardboard cutouts and matchstick toys, that are our hangovers from childhood. In they all go, as set-pieces. We are done with them for now. In fact, we are completely bored and stifled by their presence. Now they can sit next to the golliwogs and clowns, and half-stuffed teddy bears, where they will remain for all time. We need to move on. Our eyes voraciously consumed by new wishful desires jet-stream towards our projected futures. Yes, we see all people and events mostly from a purely utilitarian perspective. If we have no immediate need to use or exploit them, into the trash-can they go.

So we find ourselves surrounded by a cemetery of static objects, that have lost all meaning for us. We have given everything and everyone all the value and meaning, they will ever hold. The mystery has been beaten out of us, far too soon. All natural childhood wonder is long buried, before it ever had a chance to flower. Our cherished fantasies were misplaced. Replaced by a soul crushing world of spiritual decadence and the stifling grind to pay the bills - a wasteland of sorts. Yet, as we move onwards now towards our uncertain futures, we peer out through deadened eyes. There is the pension to worry about, and the nappies for the kids. We need to gather some more acorns for our nests, before the winter of our efforts begins to perfume our weary bones with the poisoning fumes of brittleness and atrophy. Yes, we see these deadened soulless eyes, all around us in the marketplace. It seems to be the collective pandemic virus of mankind. Yet one that has gone completely unnoticed. Our consciousness and thought processes have been subjugated and streamlined into the interests of serving the large corporations. Now we finally realize that RIP and rigor mortis are setting in. Is there any chance to extricate ourselves from our self-made hell? Any chance for one last dying gasp? We must find something fresh and novel to quickly invigorate and excite ourselves again – to make us feel alive, one last time.

There is no mystery in reaching the Kingdom. It is right here in front of your eyes. It is the greatest open secret that has ever been. A secret that has been photocopied a million billion times over and diffused into every crevice and cesspit of humanity, to the point that no one notices anymore. Yes the mass propaganda machine has worked. No one sees or values, what is all around them, because it either has become far too close or is taken for granted. In any case, we stand powerless to decode it, with the utilitarian eyes of our egos. It is only because we have misjudged and poorly evaluated, everyone and everything, that we remain blind. We have cashed everyone in, for the worldly pearls that we would seek.

The journey of the world, is but a journey inside oneself. The entire purpose of the journey, is merely one of gaining right evaluation. We do not know how to properly esteem and value anymore, which places us in hell automatically. Even if we climb to the top of Everest, we will start making more misery for ourselves - pronto. Like an Alexander, we will weep our buckets of tears, because there will be no more summits for us to conquer. The ego is the very personification of restless discontent. So it keeps us continuously on the move, seeking out ever new exotic fantasies. Yet unbounded happiness comes naturally and spontaneously, only to those, who know how to treasure, what is right in front of their eyes. Those who can see with a purity and innocence, lost to the rest of us. Those who have retained the mystery, and learned to see with new eyes. Those who never strive to separate themselves from the present moment, but always see it complete, in all its luminous radiance and splendor. Seeing it, as a never ending outpouring of the wondrous and mysterious, from a realm they are powerless to fathom. For we are not bound to physical reality, nor locked within its dim scope. As we learn to part the curtains of conditioning which veil the Eternal Now, we will step into the sacred realm of our Whole Selves.

As mentioned, the entire phenomenal existence, is nothing more than a seeming objectivization of our subjectivity. The world and our thoughts, are not different. Our thoughts are cause, for which it is the effect. Our only mission is to leave truth behind in the refrigerator, while cleaning out all the moldy leftovers, we have placed there since. Our fictional selves are composed entirely out of dream fabric and need to be purged. Only then, can we successfully awaken. Our final gift to truth, is the disappearance of our fictional selves. Along the way, many learning devices will be strategically used, to turn the dream back on itself and on you its dreamer. Yes the gears and camshafts of all the machinery, that drove us deep into the hell of the relative existence, will need to be reversed, if we are to successfully travel outside this wormhole again.

Some of the learning devices, we will artfully employ on our holy crusade include spacetime, symbols, forms, the body, consciousness and perception. Their purpose is to heal us, of our need for them. So are we freed from the handicaps, they represent. Then is it revealed to us, in full psychedelic multidimensional splendor, the reality of what we really Are. When we reach the target, there will be no one to witness it because perception itself will have disappeared. Disappeared back inside the dreamer's mind, where it has always been. All the time, you were just a sleeping giant. Now that you have awoken, you are mystified and in awe.

The ego is the only barrier to our awakening. Yes this puff of smoke, needs to be vaporized and eviscerated from our minds. Consumed in the bonfire of purifying knowledge. Yet the ego cannot be dispelled, so long as we continue to subscribe to its network of beliefs. This is the only barrier to our natural awareness, as the Christ Consciousness. So we become a pure awareness, which entirely heals us, of all our beliefs in separation. An awareness, that no longer peeps out at the world, through the rusty corrugated, dirt smeared screen of our misbeliefs. We said before, that one cannot solve a problem with the same quality of thought that made it. So we must migrate to higher ground and reach to that crisp thin mountain air, which alone can suffocate the ego. This higher level of consciousness alone, can provide the transformative context and illuminating perspective, that can solve all our problems. For it is one grounded, in the bedrock of our deeper intuition and truth. Yet, this dismal world will seem to continue, so long as our thought remains impure.

DEVELOPING A MIRACLE MINDED AWARENESS, AS OUR HEALING RECIPE

A miracle-minded awareness, represent the only panacea needed for healing our minds. This alone lets the light through. It clears away all our misconceptions and misperceptions, presenting us with a totally different thinking approach. A worldview that is truly holistic and altruistic. As we arrive at this higher ground, in which our ego is fried, we begin to work legions of miracles. By denying no one, we naturally empower into our minds *The Law of Abundance* - a fundamental Law of Truth. Activating this Law into our lives, we are purged of all our foolish notions of sacrifice and limitation. For it is only ever, our endorsement of the toxic thoughts of the ego, that blocks our natural spiritual abilities. These sink us in the swamp of selfishness, ingratitude, fear and contraction. So do we imbibe, all those sulfurous fumes, from a world which slowly poison us.

Once we made the decision to deny our Creator, we lost sight of the Christ Consciousness. The Knowledge and Power inherent in our Identity, became forgotten. Not using our power freely, we morphed into a very ugly and despicable character in a dream. A troll mindlessly navigating about psycho-planet, raising hell everywhere it goes. Our denial led to dissociation and thus was impurity stirred into the mix, contaminating our natural awareness. As Our Whole-Mind is always in full and instantaneous communication with truth. Yet we polluted the waters, by adding in, something extra - *'our beliefs in the unreal'*. This rendered us completely impotent and inefficacious - incapable of using our God given power as Mind, in its natural capacity. So the governing equation of our mind now became, **mind = Mind +Illusion**. (or Alternatively written; **Split-mind = Whole-Mind + Illusion**)

The part of our mind that retains false beliefs, became capable only of generating illusions. This part is known as our lower mind, and also as the ego. This part only appeared, after Adam fell asleep in the garden. Born from our belief in separation, it serves to reinforce it. Yet, only Mind alone, can be shared. This is our "higher" Mind, and one that is perfectly unified. It is in tune with the Knowledge of Spirit. It empowers miracles and knows nothing of dissociation. It is our innermost tabernacle and our holiest of places. This Mind still possesses the power to Create, in the exact same likeness as God. It cannot distort, nor does it experience itself as split. It sees all with a perfect transparency and is aware only of the Eternal. The Eternal knows nothing of our worldly thoughts, for what can it know of defilement.

Unfortunately, our minds entertain now, much that is false and non-existent. It depicts our obsessions with the unreal and hallucinatory. It reflects not, our Real thoughts, but for the most part only those idle thoughts of the ego. In its present condition, it is powerless to create anything of true value. Rather it leads us astray and bring us on a meaningless voyage deeper into the phenomenal. Wei Wu Wei expresses this understanding very beautifully and succinctly when he says. **"Whole-mind has no "thoughts," thoughts are split-mind."** [Ask the Awakened]. Our Mind remains immaculate and incorruptible and it bathes in the light of Knowledge. It knows nothing of transience, spacetime and the phenomenal. It alone is what remains, when all our illusions are undone. Reaching to its purity, is finding ourselves at Home again, with the Holy Grail at our lips. Yet, our innate purity still depends on our practice of forgiveness, to be known.

> **"What *seems* eternal all will have an end. The stars will disappear, and night and day will be no more. All things that come and go, the tides, the seasons and the**

lives of men; all things that change with time and bloom and fade will not return. Where time has set an end is not where the eternal is. God's Son can never change by what men made of him. He will be as he was and as he is, for time appointed not his destiny, nor set the hour of his birth and death. Forgiveness will not change him. Yet time waits upon forgiveness that the things of time may disappear because they have no use."

[T-29.VI.2:7-14]

Right now we find ourselves "living" on the wrong side of the tracks. Illusions have already entered our minds and clouded them over. Our one power of escape, is in judiciously exercising our power of decision. It is this alone, that can free us, of all apparent bondage to illusions while strengthening and increasing our lucidity of Mind. It can bring us into harmony with the Kingdom and function as the healing touchstone that diffuses true light, on all we perceive. So does it correct all misperceptions, arising from our false beliefs. The world of darkness and contradiction disappears. We find ourselves illuminated with a fragrant, potent and healing interpretation, that both frees and empowers. We look out now through a clear, light-filled and distortion free lens, that reflects our increased integration and harmony with truth.

A COURSE IN EXISTENTIAL DIALECTICS

When we look out at the world, it is hard to deny the many good and selfless deeds, being accomplished every day, as well as the many great ingenious advances being made on behalf of 'progress'. We are surrounded by many acts of kindness, compassion and many illustrious examples of unselfishness. An essential goodness seems to pervade human nature, that is seen all too clearly by those with eyes to see. Our efforts are often greatly rewarded and miracles are easily witnessed, by those who do not hide behind the blindness of denial. Modern day luminaries, that do not attempt to explain everything away through the many magical formulations of rationalism and scientific theory etc. There seems to be an intelligence in nature that truly humbles us. We are awed by the power of its miraculous simplicity and efficiency in motion. Wellness and abundance are often very evident. Many awesome events occur regularly, which simply stun us into silence. Taking all such events and happenings collectively we can consider them operating under the general '*thesis*' of '**the Good**'.

Soon however it becomes evident to us also, that there is much that is nefarious, seedy and insidious going on in the world. We find glaring contrasts, disparities, gaps and inconsistencies in the general thesis of 'the Good'. Stuff we cannot easily sweep under the carpet, if we are to still maintain our sanity. Yes, there are numerous elements that contradict the '*thesis*' of omnipresent good completely. This includes all those wars, famines, genocides, coups, murders, abuses and atrocities that speckle and bedazzle the cultural milieus, in which we seem to live. It includes all those acts of meanness, unmitigated viciousness, coldness and thoughtlessness. The presence of sickness and suffering seems undeniable. Temptation is rampant. All compelling evidence that cements our firm beliefs in injustice, scarcity and sin. Evidence that functions as a prime motivator, for the blind worshiping of some of our most venerated gods - particularly those of judgment, fear, sin, sickness and death.

Fear is a god that seems to arise from the ashes of the world we made. A powerful force that holds us at ransom and one that we feel we must prostrate before on bended knees. For it speaks of a world that is surely there. Looking at the vast spectrum, of its many diverse effects, how can we have the impudence to say, "*we ourselves created this beast"*. This monstrous hydra-headed entity, which catalogs all our hells under its cloak? Nevertheless, taken together we can merge all such evidence under the collective banner of 'evil' or **'the Bad'**. This can be considered the ***'anti-thesis'***, by which the world operates. For many, the predominance of evil is considered, to be the complete theory in itself. They attempt to umbrella all under this *'anti-thesis'*. They impute all varieties of human motives and actions, as governed solely by this *'anti-thesis'* of evil. Thus they justify their firm commitment to the god of evil using such rationalizing phrases as "T*he survival instinct"* or *"It's every man for himself"*. This is their store front, a remodeling of their ideology and one that reflects their attempts, to make their heartless decisions seem more palatable for general consumption. For in the end they are going to behave coldly and selfishly. They will seek to justify, all their evil actions, as necessary in the interests of self-preservation and success.

Dazed and confused, we do not know where to turn. We may oscillate furiously between "*thesis*" and '*anti-thesis*, yet seem unable to make up our minds. For heaven and hell are both decided, on the fall of this dime, it seems. Where will we place our chips? We desperately desire to make one side or the other into the complete picture, so that we can find some measure of peace. We then want to judge everything in our worlds, through the lens of thought, our chosen belief system alone endorses. Yes, juxtaposed together, they make for a pretty meaningless picture. They place us in an intolerable situation. Moreover we separate our mind from the picture that we see. The picture becomes a thing in itself, representative of a real and self-existing world that is actually out-there. So we perceive a war going on outside between good and evil, between the Christ and the Anti-Christ. A war no side can win.

As with Hegel's system, the healing of the world can be considered as taking a course in existential dialectics. We can only heal when we discover the magic bullet, of the ***'Synthesis'***. The synthesis places all on a more transcendent framework and context. One in which, resolution at last is found. For this advanced perspective sees all, that is entailed in both the '*thesis*' and '*antithesis*'. This is what the Course is. A synthesis that successfully resolves all aspects of our perceptions and misunderstandings. It eliminates all apparent contradictions and enables us to become integrated, unified and healed. From its higher perspective, "*thesis*" and "*antithesis*", can be seen clearly now as special cases of the "*synthesis*" much in the same way that Newtonian physics is a special case of relativistic physics. Yet, as we know, it is relativistic physics that completely enfolds and transcends the theories of Newtonian physics, not the other way around.

The '*Synthesis*' presents a completely different picture of the world we see. It agrees that there is great conflict and confusion pervading our minds. This conflict and confusion arises it declares, because there are really two inside of each of us. Each painting an entirely different picture, of what we are into the canvas of our perceptions. These two present diametrically opposing understandings, interpretations, methods and goals. The first speaks on behalf of the timeless, and sees only the good. It sees nothing, on the level of form and recognizes only truth. It looks to content alone and find evidences of the Love, in which it has its Being, everywhere it looks. The second is born in time. It can never be made part of the fabric of reality and this is its despair. Looking out through the soulless eyes of its despair, it can witness only a tattered world born of evil and separation. Seeing only form, it becomes obsessed with it. Yet, it can never recognize or understand the meaning and content behind each form. Yet it aggressively seeks to protect its existence by whatever means possible. So it is responsible for all illusions and distortions that arise to obfuscate our vision.

The "synthesis" fully recognizes, that each seemingly separated mind perceives a battle going, on in their world. A battle that is tearing them apart and seems to place peace forever beyond their reach. Yet it teaches also that this battle is not happening in truth. It arises only because illusionary beliefs have interposed themselves into one's thought patterns. Forging a world that is in their likeness. Yes the battle is only occurring, in that part of your mind, that has lost access to truth. The problem is, that you have capitulated into believing in both truth and illusion. Yet, the real can never be destroyed and the unreal, can never be made into reality. The synthesis teaches that lasting peace cannot be found while you continue to believe in both sides. It says that all darkness and contradiction are caused by the *anti-thesis*. From its higher perspective, we begin to see how this *anti-thesis* of evil arose entirely with the separation. This alone is what seems to relegate Whole-Mind, into our experience as split-mind.

This *anti-thesis* may not have any basis in truth, but it has a very powerful basis in illusion. As a composite it is representative of the thought system of the ego and of our lower mind. Yet all effects and illusions arising from the *anti-thesis* remain unreal. They are powerless to affect reality in any way. We need to refocus our minds to cherish and avow only the real, while simultaneously divesting ourselves of all that is false. False beliefs retained through fear, are the only cause of all our illusions.. All illusions must be purged through reinterpretation in the light of truth. Found wanting, they will be relinquished from our mind, so that the Eternal alone remains to shine in it - as it always has. Yes, it is fear-based beliefs alone that support the '*anti-thesis*' of evil. Yet fear only ever arises, through a lack of love. The healing cure then, is for us to become more loving.

For example, suppose your are peering into a limpid pool of water on a bright sunny day. Suppose you can see clearly many different colored fish swimming about in this pool. You notice all the details, on the rocks and of the underwater plants below. Then some clown comes by and accidentally spills a bucket of colored dye into this pool. As the dye freely circulates about, everything goes out of focus. You can no longer distinguish anything clearly anymore. You cannot distinguish a fish from a rock. Yet, you know the fish and the rocks are still there. Unfortunately you will only see them clearly again when all the dye has been removed. The dye in this case is representative of our *anti-thesis* of evil. To reach again the clarity and purity that can witness the eternal and true, it is not a question of improving ourselves. We are already perfect. Nor is it one, of adding some new beliefs, abilities or powers. It is just a question of clearing away all our false beliefs. These alone cloud our perfection. Eliminating them restores us to vision. A vision in which the truth of the Kingdom, that is all around us, can be seen and known once more.

Our journey is one of constant reinterpretation, of the mind's understandings, experiences, and perceptions. One simply learns to distinguish and remove all aspects that are false, so one can penetrate to the Truth beyond. Truth is beyond belief, but not beyond reality. In the correction of error lies all our healing. This is an existential correction, that changes us and our world, as we progress. Yet all change, only ever happens at the level of illusion. Atonement stands in sharp contrast to the theories and mind-games of philosophers who may know legions of ideas intellectually but are not changed by them. Instead now we imbibe ideas into our being, by putting them first into practice. So we gain lasting conviction, at our deepest levels of their ultimate veracity.

Having actively integrated them, we become part of the solution. False ideas, now are seen as representative of our prison-house and bondage. With each successful integration, one is born again, in one's experience of themselves and their world. This may be called conscious evolution. Finally healed of all distortions, the lens of our perception comes into direct contact with truth. With our complete integration, consciousness itself disappears. This correction of errors, works progressively as well as retroactively. This means, it heals both the future and past together, obviating whole sections of time, that would otherwise need to be played out. Since these sections of time, no longer serve the purpose of learning they simply disappear. Time's purpose is simply to provide that space, in which we can choose to correct all errors.

THE MAGIC WAND OF FORGIVENESS

Imagine for a moment, this great long carpet that seems to go on endlessly in both directions. This carpet spreads out into the infinite past and future. Appearing upon this carpet, are all your memories and experiences, all your past skeletons, all your future aspirations and "experiences". It is quite the carnival and motley spectacle, as you can well imagine. This carpet may be called the fabric stream of your guilt. It houses all those despicable characters and events, which are either still retained in your active memory or have long since been forgotten. It holds all those symbols and concepts, you learned along the way. All that you have yet to learn. It holds your entire future, as yet unknown to you. This carpet is the event stream of your entire passage through time.

Your practice of forgiveness is like waving a magic wand. Each time you wave it, you cause some of these characters and events to disappear from it. So the carpet rolls up, just a little more. Soon, you begin to glimpse its end in both directions. When your forgiveness is complete, the carpet will be completely rolled up and your dream of time will be over. You have always searched for your Home. You feel it in your heart but cannot find the words to describe it. For the heart has wisdom, that the mind has long forgotten. The heart knows there still exists a Home, that can quench all your anxieties and fears. A Home of bliss and unassailable peace. Yet the heart cannot verbalize this Home anymore. So you do not know which direction to take and what decisions to make. For you have lost sight of the one remedy that alone can heal. This remedy is one that seems no longer applicable, to the world you seem to live in, and the world teaches it not.

Your Home itself is beyond words, but hardly beyond meaning. It is simply throbbing with meaning, life and joy and it engages in unhindered full-hearted communication with all that IS. Your Home comes into sight, as the carpet rolls up. So you cease to be obsessed with the many shiny trinkets and skeletons appearing upon it. You want them gone for good. You have become like the bull in the china shop, that cares not a toss for all this mindless junk. Your Home stands at the Eternal Now, silently awaiting for you. It only becomes revealed, as you remove your focus and interest away from all that junk. Away from all those attractions and investments, that are unworthy of you. Your attractions to guilt, sin, judgment, condemnation and attack. Your investments in idols, sickness, suffering and specialness. So do you remove all distorting symbols and beliefs, that one very powerfully seemed to disconnect you from your Source. The successful evisceration of guilt from the fabric of your belief, exterminates all skeletons, which are then seen no more. With healing, all that is false loses its power-base, in your mind and simply disappears into the nothingness, from which they came.

As you continue to use your magical wand of forgiveness, you are simultaneously healing both past and future. This healing goes way past your active memory or future projection. Then occurs the realization, that all was illusory dreams and miscreations projected from your unhealed split-mind. Feverish dreams, that served as reflections of your ill-health and sickened state-of-mind. As your evil dreams disappear, you become embraced into a more meaningful context of being. For you 'the dreamer' have developed an ever more expansive and evolved consciousness. Your thoughts have become transmuted and purified. You have reached a luminous awareness of Reality, as it **IS,** unsullied or corrupted by all the appearances of time. Dreams disappear, as you cease to identify with them. Then one fine day, you 'the dreamer' remember your Self and awaken. You have discovered within that clear, untarnished and tacit understanding that brings you to your Home. You have stumbled on the touchstone that brings you the holy place, that precedes all thought. Then you no longer identify with the dream, nor as the dreamer. You function now as Mind, that no longer dreams but is Creative instead. Thus is the Son of God re-born back into active awareness. The great sleep that descended upon Adam is over.

Yes, with a complete letting-go of all these false understandings, you come to stand again at the eternal instant. You are restored to awareness of your wholeness and completion. You no longer plod heartlessly through the meaningless horizontal dimension of time, but escape the hall of ignorance and penetrate through to the vertical dimension of the eternal. This movement from the horizontal to the vertical dimension of being, in not a linear shift but a quantum leap. The eternal exists apart from and out of time. Yet, it can still be accessed from within time's illusionary manifold. Just as a hole punched in a piece of paper, does not really exist in it, yet is accessible from within it. You just need to know where and how to look. Each aspect of Mind holds a window to all of it and is completely unified with all.

For example, imagine for a moment, a large sphere composed of many semi-translucent windows. Within its center rests the eternal flame of truth. Yet, many of the windows may have become so foggy or smeared by ignorance, so they can no longer witness this flame. It is certain that if you are embracing the thought system of the ego, you may find yourself at such a window. Only dimly or partially reflecting the flame of Truth, that lies within. If this window is dark enough, you may deny the flame, at the center altogether. You may even deny you are part of this perfectly unified sphere. Yet, other windows nearby, neatly polished and glistening from purification have become almost perfect reflectors of the Truth within. They pass on their knowledge of the light they so gloriously reflect, to all those who are ready to listen. All windows are joined together as One reality and all are inheritors of the Knowledge it contains. All are integral to the One-Mind, that is symbolized by this sphere.

Likewise, each of us has the capacity to become both a perfect reflector and creator of Truth. Our dust and grime, just needs to be cleared away. That impure overlay of false belief needs to be removed. The world is over and the Kingdom of Heaven is 'Here-Now'. This Knowledge will come at different times to every mind, or should I say to every aspect of Mind. The Course teaches this moment is determined by each of us. It happens when we become willing to embrace the Atonement, which expedites our progress out of the time and out of the relative existence. Truth remains undifferentiated and is tasted the same for all. It is not open to partiality, contingency, individual predilections or arbitration. As each looks upon the Truth each becomes it, and loses their false identity as the darkened window of the ego. Each becomes perfectly harmonized with the non-separated state of the One-Mind, and is fused with the reality of unconditional Love that always remains within the sphere.

4. IDEAS LEAVE NOT THEIR SOURCE

Ideas leave not their Source. Reflect on this statement over-and-over, for it holds your entire key out of slavery. It contains the metaphysical essence of all religious systems and one that speaks of your deathlessness and indestructibility. Your being is not as any form. Rather you are that which creates through thought. Your being is not dependent on thought, yet through your creative thought, is it witnessed. As an idea, you are entirely unassailable and invulnerable to the storms of life. Here is the statement of your complete empowerment and liberation from the dream. One that dissolves all beliefs in an external world. Absorb it in totally and you are enlightened.

Your conviction in its veracity will implode your entire world, in an instant. You will have discovered your essential Self - your original face, the uncreated, unborn and undying. Understanding this open secret and all yogic Siddhis and miraculous powers come naturally to you, for you will have understood your true essence as Self and seen the true metaphysical basis of the world. This thought exposes all object orientated beliefs. It ends your belief in spacetime, since you recognize now that spacetime, and all it presents, exists just as a series of thought projections. Spacetime and perception are thoughts that do not function independently of your mind, and they have not left it. Likewise it exposes and weeds out all phenomenal and time-based notions of causality.

You arrive at an intense alert awareness, in which time is rendered meaningless, and you see again with naked perception. As Adam once did, in the garden of Eden. Spacetime and perception come to be recognized now, as simply learning devices reflecting your current psychic-evolutionary progress. Learning devices born from within. They are like a toddler's training wheels formed from the genomes of your inner body. Space is essentially spaceless. There is no "*out-there*" out-there. All is spontaneously arising from within. All is effect, arising from the sea of your subjectivity and present decision. You are, *"The miraculous awareness, in which all things happen."* What is in your awareness and perception, at any given moment, just reflects your current state of learning. Objects, no more exist independently from your mind than you exist independently from God's. Your manifold reactions, to your own projections and wrong-minded thoughts is ultimately what kills you each dream. Just like the dog found dead in the hall of mirrors, in the amusement park – you also die of exhaustion, from barking at so many ugly reflections you make. You wear yourself out through your own circumventing thoughts and misbeliefs. Now is the time to take back ownership of your world. You need to admit responsibility, for all that you see and all that seems to happen. As the Course teaches :-

"I am responsible for what I see.

I choose the feelings I experience, and I decide

upon the goal I would achieve.

And everything that seems to happen to me,

I ask for, and receive as I have asked"

[T-21.II.2:3-5]

You were needlessly fearful of a world without. Now you know all fear is produced within. Now you have reached the understanding needed to finally release yourself. Fear has no basis in reality. God still is Love and only God IS. Understanding that **"Ideas leave not their source"** [T-26.VII.4:7] releases a new mystical and timeless fragrance into your world, that both emblazons and dispossesses it. Finally the spring of true hope has bubbled back to life, from the cauldrons of nettle soup you had made to nourish yourself, but only turned you green. After much futile wandering, you have found the deep, subtle and elusive elixir that reveals your immortality. There is no hope in the world, because it has never existed! There is hope for you because you do! You have always existed, though not in the form you now see. Become this knowledge in its essence and you cease wasting time and effort in political activism. You cease being an incendiary pundit relentlessly advocating for social change. You stop chartering your Greenpeace ship madly around the world's waters pandering after oil spills. You see the uselessness of all object orientated approaches, towards reaching to true peace and progress. You stop trying to solve problems at the level of effect. You know now, that the world will never change, unless you change first. You need to be the instrument that drives all change.

All problems evolve from a fault-line that has developed deep within us. A fault-line that we no longer see. The many effects emanating from this rupture include our mindlessness, greed, recklessness, belief in separation and "special" interests. Mindfulness alone is the lasting cure. You are the cause of all perception. With cause identified, who bothers analyzing and dissecting effects! Improvements will happen automatically as reflexive states of your inner insight and healing. The real solution is in integrating back with your true inner essence of mind. Through the purification of mindfulness, judicious decisions and actions spontaneously follow. Good and responsible decision making cannot be coerced on you, or it will become rejected. Thus propagating increased spitefulness and self-destruction.

Freedom cannot be found through coercion, being its polar opposite. Yet, through a dismantling of all your current conceptual beliefs you will undergo meaningful transformation and change. So you come in contact with the formless and all-pervading Self, and reach the firm foundation of Truth. You are no longer scribbling idly now on the cave wall, moving shadows from one place to another. You are releasing all shadows and barriers to the light. It is only because light cannot shine freely through all those distortions and obfuscations you have interposed, that these shadows appear at all.

ALL IS IDEA

You may think this statement, *'Ideas leave not their Source'*, is preposterous, outrageous, laughable and ridiculous. It may carry no meaning for you. But ask yourself this **'Where do ideas come from and where do they go?'**. They are hardly spatial entities to be collated neatly in PO boxes until they are needed again. They are more like spontaneous apparitions, arising in the sea of your awareness. Your awareness in its essence is formless and non-spatial. Since all ideas arise in it, they must remain at this formless and non-spatial source. Now, your next step is simply understanding that **All is idea**. If you can take this step, something tremendously sacred is possible. It will be like the ultimate 4th of July for you. All your inner fire-works, flares and rockets will go off all at once and sputter across a world, that is no longer the same. For once you take these two necessary steps, it is as if you have witlessly stepped on to a land-mine, in which your entire existence implodes. Your beliefs in spacetime, objects, phenomena, sickness, scarcity, loss and even death are all now gone. These are no longer seen, as self-existing realities in themselves, but merely parts of the fabric of your belief. Their illusory nature has been explored and exposed, at their very foundations and underpinnings. There is no real world for them to ever happen in.

Death too is just an idea. An idea that has unfortunately become associated with bodies. No one can die, because the pure radiant idea that each of us is has nothing to do with the world of bodies. Bodies remain miscreations of mind. They never had any reality. They are vehicles of separation, which we as the ego made to hide from God. All the Course ideas, and its complete thought system can be inducted from the potent understanding that "**All is idea, and ideas leave not their Source.**" Here is a clear and entirely unambiguous statement, of what you Are. You are an idea possessing limitless potency and potentiality. You contain perfect knowledge and are an idea that is unified and whole, and capable of seamless communication with all Mind. How then can you be a part of any physical world?

Ideas do not walk around in bodies, but bodies can certainly appear to walk around within ideas. So long as your mind continues to entertain false and distortionary beliefs. Yet, this body just represents one of the many ideas you believe in and so it seems to be. It is part of your own ideational matrix, which then crystallizes the world of separation into seeming fact. Now you know all bodies, objects and phenomena in your world, are nothing but fictitious and fabricated entities arising out of your own mental invention. Through them you experience this false artifice of separation. So does your identity become forged from dream fiction.

As idea, you remain in complete communication with God, who is your greater Source. Forgetting this you fall into endless hells. The hells of sickness, sacrifice, loss and death are obvious and glaring. Yet, there are many subtle hells that evade your radar. For example, with the advent of scientific materialism, as the new international creed, much of our attention has been diverted away from discovering our true essence and deeper reality. Its arbitrary laws and formulations, are designed to bind and limit us to false images. The modern day obsessions with science, technology, bioengineering, medicine and genetics etc. can be considered the blind worshiping of false gods. These gods seem to offer us many dazzling inventions, comforts and healing remedies but once again, their complete power is borrowed from the reservoir of our own mind's ingenuity and belief. They are believed because they are created by belief - yet this important piece of trivia is glossed over and politely ignored.

OUR TREASURING OF IDOLS MADE FROM DUST

Our ego desired deities remain castles of sand. They are mental surrogates and substitutions that shield us from recognition of our true mind power. Our power seems to become displaced to the external world instead — projected into its various laws and phenomena. Prostrating humbly before the feet of our invented gods, and continuously devoting our mind and efforts to satisfy them, does cost us dearly. Because we live out our lives only on the surface of mind and never reach deeper. So we become far too distracted and spaghetti brained. Yet we think, that we will drown or suffocate in the swampland of our deeper unconscious. We ignore the laws of true cause-and-effect and often reverse them. We place our existence on a false foundation and build from there. Yet what we build is arbitrary, shallow and meaningless, as are the laws and principles we use to promote them. They cannot save us from death, nor make our lives meaningful. All the comforts and cures they appear to offer are transient. They make us feel us shabby and so our bondage seems all the more absolute and inescapable. Yet these will remain our chosen gods, until we are ready to question them at their foundations. After all what else can we expect, when we have sold out on ourselves?

Are these the idols that you seek? Through these, do we hope some day to make ourselves complete? Any attempt to make ourselves complete from the without must fail. It will always be a futile misadventure that attempts to weave the tapestries of illusion into something meaningful and lasting. We do not need to strive to make ourselves complete, because this is already the case. Yet, this becomes denied through any outward seeking. Our completion can be known only from within. For example, the big bang theory posits that the objective universe started from a fixed beginning in time and this 'spacetime' universe has been expanding ever since. So one naturally asks just for laughs *"What is this universe expanding into?"* We get various responses that say *"It is expanding into vacuum, empty space or nothingness."* But this nothingness, cannot really be a nothing then, if it is capable of receiving an expanding universe. It must be on the same order of reality as that, which it is receiving. It cannot therefore be really separate from the rest of the universe, which invalidates the theory of an expanding universe. Nor can the big-bang be expanding out of a nothing. Because any nothing, that can create the phenomenal universe, is not really a nothing. So let's dismiss all such foolish theories and beliefs. In the physical realm, they sound plausible and sound, but in the metaphysical realm they are seen as pure nonsense. As we probe further, we see that the physical realm itself is pure nonsense. It has never existed.

Even the premise, that time had a beginning, proves time itself must be an illusory entity having no real content. Because at some point, it was not there and therefore it is not real. It is simply a mirage. It is not to be taken as a self-existing reality. Truth does not appear, nor disappear, nor is it contingent on anything outside itself to support itself. Any Taoist or Zen practitioner, worth their salt sees these understandings as self-evident. Yet objectivists cannot really peer into the abyss. Their questions always stop short of meaning. Their own metaphysical basis of operation, is far too shallow, precluding real insight and vision. We continue to see some physicists starting with the premise that objective existence is a self-evident fact. But is this a fact, or merely a biased and prejudiced belief? A sacred cow, one hopes to enshrine into a god, in order to remain within one's comfort zones?

Many who follow the thread of this bias then proceed to teach that the nothingness of empty space, isn't really a nothing at all. That a vacuum has weight and texture to it and enough energy, in one square foot to fulfill all our energy needs indefinitely, if harnessed correctly. So can we agree then that it isn't really a vacuum then? Which by definition is a space that is void. Yet no one has ever found a space that is void. It is purely a hypothetical entity. A concept but not a reality. One would have better luck tracking down the Easter bunny on a Saturday night. When will they give it up? They are merely using their own biased beliefs in phenomenalism, to prove the phenomenal. Weight and energy are still phenomenal beliefs.

I often laugh thinking how many professed Atheists claim not to belief in God, and yet their No-God comes packaged in the form of a Dawkins. Yet, I would still prefer an honest atheist over a dishonest believer, any day of the week. Let us briefly explore then the primary premise on which objectivism is based. Namely that of an "objective" spacetime. Let's trace this ray to its meaningless end. You know, that cul-de-sac where you get dumped off late at night and will sign just about anything to stop the waterboarding treatment. Objectivism postulates two theories pertaining to spacetime. (1) Spacetime is an "objective" reality that was born with a bang and is destined to come to an end. (2) Spacetime goes on indefinitely. Let's be clear. If spacetime comes to an end, then it never had any real existence at all. This is just a revamping of the big-bang theory, in reversed form. One that makes spacetime into a phantom, not to be taking seriously. Since what comes to non-existence, has no real existence. The second possibility for spacetime that objectivism proposes, is that it goes on forever. This however is a theory that can never be proven! Because it would require a witness at the two extremes of infinity and no such witness can ever be found. Because the presence of any witness would invalidate the premise, that it goes on indefinitely.

Apart from this, if spacetime went on indefinitely, it would present a picture of itself as completely barren of purpose. Does a spacetime fabric that endlessly creates and destroys universes (with no end purpose in sight), seem reasonable? It would be like some mad builder mindlessly erecting buildings, only to demolish them a while later. There is no room for God in such a purposeless universe and if we were bound to this universe, no hope for us. Proofs that spacetime is objective in nature, can find no meaningful validation in the phenomenal universe. This is because such proofs would then be part of that self-same context, they are attempting to prove. Akin to putting the cart before the horse. Therefore you cannot use a phenomenally based proof, to prove the nature of spacetime as objective. Because spacetime itself, is the higher basis, for which the apparent "objective" phenomenal existence is downstream.

Similarly a field of logic, cannot establish incontestable proof of the veracity of its own initial premises. Because it was born and molded from these premises and can never therefore rise above them. These premises are its foundation and determine its range and scope. The ultimate veracity of a context (whether this context be spacetime, phenomenalism or logic), can only be found from outside that contextual fabric. Likewise its falseness or limitation can also, only be known from outside its own context. Thus we can certainly know for ourselves that spacetime is a mind generated illusion because our underlying reality lies outside spacetime. We can transcend the illusory manifold it seems to impose on us, because our true existence is high above it. For it is born in us, and not us in it. We can know this for ourselves through having the "right" inner experiences. Certain visionary or drug induced experiences can make it known to us. The presence of psychic-mediums, channels as well as experiments conducted in remote viewing, remote healing, precognition, retrocognition etc. prove spacetime's unreality out.

The key premise of objectivism, is that spacetime exists

independently of our minds. Most swallow this carrot whole, and turn this assumption into a fact, while ignoring that it is but a biased and prejudiced belief. There is another possibility for spacetime and one that has gone unnoticed, not because it is far away, but all too near. So near to ourselves, that it is in fact part of us. The new possibility does not need us to capitulate to the premises of objectivism. We find instead we have no need to entertain these false beliefs at all. This new possibility, proposes that the fabric of spacetime is entirely mind-created. It is no longer seen as a purposeless place steamed by its own arbitrary volition. It serves instead as our own mind-made virtual reality. A holodeck that provides the classroom, for our minds to heal. An illusory space, we can use to evolve back to awareness of our original perfection. This classroom is necessary to purge our minds of all our false beliefs and limited understandings, so that we can once again become aware only of the eternal.

The reason this possibility is mostly rejected, is because our first-hand tactile experience of spacetime and its contents presents the illusion, that it is for the most part independent of our mind and its thoughts. This is because we appear to live in a world, that seems chaotic and random and beyond our direct control. Yet, this is just a powerful deception that is stubbornly believed in, in much the same way that for millennia we continued to believe the sun revolved around the earth. That is we are so lacking in awareness and asleep, that we do not usually recognize, the direct connection between the power of our will and intention to our direct perceptions. These have become so atrophied in us, as to be rendered almost entirely ineffectual. Destroyed for use, by the mind pollution that is the ego.

Many then are ready to wholeheartedly gobble down the primary premises of objectivism, based on the unreliable witness of their own eyes. Yet the senses can be the greatest and most deceptive of liars. Believing in the tale they speak, we proceed to get progressively lost in the phantasmagoria of words, forms, symbols, concepts and equations (generically illusions). Yet in the end, can any choice of words or symbols make foul things fair? We easily forget that we are merely playing mind-games, built up from the evidence of our senses, while avoiding penetrating through to naked reality at a deeper and more metaphysical level. We do not endorse the inner view, only the outer ones. We look to the phenomenal but not to the noumenal. Yet the noumenal is the mother to all that is phenomenal, and yet in no way dependent on it. Just as a mother can exist without her daughters, but her daughters cannot exist without their mother. Or just as silence can exist without music, but music cannot exist without silence.

Nevertheless, we see these "lost in space" attitudes showing up in other fields. So we see A.I. (artificial intelligence) experts, and neurologists etc. hovering around the phenomenal world, like flees over a pile of dung, searching furiously within its scope for the genetic algorithms and markers that delimit how thought and memories are formed, stored and manipulated. Searching for a holy grail of sorts. Looking to find the "OM" of intelligence and masterful decision embedded in the world of matter. Then they hopelessly try to figure out the primary mechanisms by which the 3D world is encoded and decoded in the imprints of brain tissue. Yet, this is even more futile than a psychologist attempting to map the individual pixels in a Rorschach inkblot map to the psychological states of their patients. The games must go on or else we will have to open up more prisons and lunatic asylums. Better to keep these guys in the luniversities for now, until we can think of something else to have them do.

Our Denial Enables Empty Ideologies to Proliferate

Denial has a very subtle and cunning power. One that often leads to a proliferation of empty ideologies. It is only because of the many tantalizing gifts ideologies promise, that denial of their true content, is seen to be attractive. For example, take the ideology, on which Nazism gained steam - that attraction of being included as a member of a 'Master race'. Seduced by the power of this attraction, many fell blindly into denial of all the inhumanities and atrocities, they were committing in the name of Nazism. Then there is the ideology of democracy, that states, it is a government of the people, by the people, for the people. We all know this Utopian concept, has long since died. In reality, it has morphed into a government of the super-rich, by the corporations, for the corporations. Yet, we are attracted to the belief that we still have power and say - that our vote can change things, both at the top and at the bottom. Thus the empty essence offered by the ideology goes denied and unchecked.

Then there is that hypnotizing elixir, called *'pursuit of happiness'*. Crafted somewhere in the matrix, I would imagine. An ideology that is short and sweet and has a power of attraction. Yet, it is designed to keep the middle class subdued as minions on minion farms, fast asleep and caught up in dreams of future self-aggrandizement. Yet stress and anxiety is all they reap from their monumental efforts. Since life is just a succession of present moments, when you are sold on a dream, you lose the prize of your reality. You engage instead, a mad and frantic game of *'seek but do not find'*. When will we accept, that we are rats in the cage, running on a ball that will never go anywhere? We will never make it to the food just beyond our reach? That is why it has been strategically placed beyond our reach.

Then there is the wonderful world of the Internet, with its endless supply of mind churning facts, tweets and superficial online personas. Yet, we are attracted to its offerings. We are sucked in by the allure of becoming some special image in a cyber-world, of being finally listened to or of just going viral. Yet, there are many weeds surrounding the soil of this fast growing ideology. We are in denial of the fact that we are just being tagged-and-bagged. That we are making ourselves vulnerable to phishing software, cyber-theft, cyber-profiling and data collection engines. We leave a cyber footprint everywhere we go that can be very damaging.

Other hells, include the ever increasing encroachment of materialism and consumerism. Consumerism hemorrhages each of us. It sells us on a vast bodily identification. It then proceeds to imbue in us, belief in needs we do not have. It does not care to teach us, that we are a mind that is powerful and free. It offers a plethora of industries that sell us on a host of bodily needs, most of which are specifically invented to maintain its own dog-n-pony show. These industries sell us on a host of fictitious medical and nutritional concerns, so that it can then merchandise to us certain remedies and drugs. Then there are those institutions that provide borrowed money, inducing us to become increasingly stressed, enslaved and firmly tethered to the corporate machine. A vast amount of our mental and physical health issues arise, from endorsing and buying into consumerism. So does the rat-race propagate. We are made to identify with the body, instead of our boundless nature as spirit. We are made to feel constrained and limited to a tiny spacetime fragment – a horrifying caricature of ourselves that disavows all our former glory. We then make the additional boo-boos of projecting bodily limitations to our mental world. An often unnoticed ego reversal of cause-and-effect.

THIS HOLOGRAPHIC UNIVERSE IS POWERED BY OUR BELIEFS

We know from the theory of holography, that holographic images appearing in 3D, are not really "out there". The object "out there", is an illusion that arises simply from illuminating a plate containing the interference pattern of the object, with a laser known as a reference beam. Now visualize, for a moment, your mind as a plate containing numerous interference patterns, generated out of our many false beliefs and mental distortions. Then when this plate becomes illuminated by our natural light of spirit, what is projected out there as the images, that form our perception, is nothing more than an faithful representation of all our false beliefs and distortions. Collectively these distortions can be considered the ego. They gives us the illusion of inhabiting a 3D world, in some 3D body. We see objects and movement in this illusionary 3D space, known as the world. But it has only one cause - our own rigorously held mental beliefs - our movements of thought. What appears out there, is just the projection of that special interference pattern of belief, embedded in our minds. It is for this reason that the Course teaches the more profounder understanding of true cause-and-effect, namely :-

> **"It is impossible not to believe what you see, but is equally impossible to see what you do not believe. Perceptions are built up on the basis of experience, and experience leads to beliefs. It is not until beliefs are fixed that perceptions stabilize. In effect, then, what you believe you *do* see."** [T-11.VI.1:1-4]

Modifying our beliefs, is the only progressive action we can take to undoing this illusionary holographic landscape we witlessly navigate. Our beliefs can be changed, by drawing on a deeper wisdom within. By questioning our beliefs, we work directly on the only cause this world has ever had. We cannot gain wisdom, by looking at the screen, because this screen contains nothing but the projection of all our mistaken beliefs. In overly identifying with the projection, we forgot to self-remember. What we see often makes us fearful, so we do not go within. Yet, fear is maintained by our refusal to do just that. We need to reach to those root understandings that will both free us from fear and enable us to transcend this world.

Rigorously held false beliefs, on the inside give rise to miscreations on the outside. False beliefs form into very dense, obfuscating and distortive interference patterns on the plate of our minds. We must navigate to the Source of Truth deep within, where the ego dares not to go. We must go beyond the plate of our belief, to direct knowledge. Reach the spiritual light, that illuminates all. We will gain lasting conviction, in the efficacy of what is learned, through the application of its healing thought in the field of our dream-lives. Since **"Ideas leave not their Source"**, we know where to go to find salvation. We can escape from the multiplicity of evils seen in the dream, not by denying them, but by truly seeing how they came about. The effects of evil are not your responsibility, but the undoing of their cause is the gateway to your release.

The body is one of the images on this plate. Yes it remains only as an idea in your mind. You see the body, not because it is real in any way but only because you want it to be so. Your continued desire for those temptations of specialness and pleasure, continue to power your belief in it. You want to live out your ego desires. You do not really want to relinquish your desire for specialness. The body wonderfully facilitates the break-downs in communication that support your specialness, while simultaneously reinforcing your beliefs in vulnerability and limitation. You have a vested interest in the body, that you dare not declare. You have used it always as a vehicle for maintaining private interests and private thoughts. Once you relinquish specialness, sin and temptation and decide to communicate fully and limitlessly with all, the body will diminish in importance and soon be lost to your sight. This body is made by you. You made it into a seemingly independent self-functioning object in your world. One that now tells you, how you feel. You think the world and the body are different beliefs, different realities, but in essence they are the same. This is like thinking the apple and the tree are independent of the soil below them.

Just think how ridiculous it would be to have a body, if there were nothing else in this world to be perceived. Just visualize for a moment your body suspended in empty space, in a world with no objects, no sounds, nothing to smell or touch. Then see how purposeless the body becomes. You could not maintain your illusions of having a body for long. Now you can see that the body and the world are one illusion. Each supports the other for they are interdependent and support the apparent reality of each other. When you move your hand or feet, or roll your head or eyes, this is because of psychokinesis. It is not really action at a distance because, as already indicated, there is no distance. Movement is one of our magical beliefs, part of our dream fiction that is deeply imprinted. Yet you do not see, that all seeming movement is the product of mental action. The illusion of movement is just your thoughts and mental scripts precipitating into the canvas of your perception. Yet you are so unconscious of these inner powers, that you mislabel them now with such glowing terms as reflexive action, involuntary response and autonomic nervous system functioning. As if a label, can successfully capture or explain the fundamental dynamism involved. Labels delude and make it seem that the body and its actions are apart from your mind. You still believe ideas, **do** leave their Source. Your deep conditioning makes it so. So you begin to think of the body as a thing, in itself, one governed by its own centralized intelligence. Once you truly recognize that all which seems outside is really inside, your psychokinetic and self-healing abilities will greatly improve.

5. TAKING OFF THE BLINDFOLDS

The first time I met Dr. Gobbler's Knob was when we were both working in London during the 1980s'. We had both been assigned to a demolition team. When we got off work, we would tour the city and its nightlife always partying late and hard. Sometimes we would crash out in the torn out buildings we were working in, picking some non drafty spot to strategically place our sleeping bags. At other times, things would go astray and we would end up in some unexpected part of the city, such as Turnpike lane, Ruislip, Brixton or Camden town. Usually waking up in a house full of hippies, punks, socialites or just degenerates and drug-addicts. Then next morning, we would try to piece together how exactly we got there, from the fragments we remembered. If the natives looked safe, we would go through the usual wake-up checklist. Making sure there were no broken bones, bruises or scars. Then work down the priority list of wallet, clothes, jacket and glasses. If all checked out OK, we would go searching for some coffee. Since we had no car, many nights we would end up taking the last underground train back to the sites to sleep. If we missed it, we usually were left with the choice of walking for miles or doing a runner on a cabbie.

The Dr. had a number of very annoying habits. He liked placing his hands between the merging sections of the tube doors to hold them open just as the train was about to depart. Then the train would have to wait a while longer. Then he would repeat step A. This really worked like a charm to piss off all the downtown yuppies during peak hours. He seemed to be annoyed by the success of others. He said success smelled. I responded that it was failure that smells, as any homeless guy living in the sidewalks and sewers can easily tell you. That is if you can get close enough without spewing your guts out first. Yet he remained pigheaded in his loathing and contempt for all those born with silver spoons in their mouths. All those who had it easy.

All the posters and pinups of the celebrities and models that he could see everywhere, positively enraged him. All those advertisements of the good life that were slapped to every open space, felt like an insult. He had never had a taste of that silver spoon. He had to work for everything he got and never seemed to catch a break. He even had to take out a loan, for the privilege of working long hours in those noisy and dusty building sites. Sometimes he would be so covered in it, that he came out looking more like Al Jolson. Then after his first week there, his apartment was robbed by a juvenile druggy named Matthew, who shared a house with him. All those aerosol cans lying everywhere should have been a hint, and must have finally got to Matthew's head. The Dr. was infuriated when he came home from work to find everything gone. He said whenever he caught up with that prick, he would dispense a little piece of street justice, of his own. Meanwhile he had lost his room in this house, after getting into an argument with the landlord. He had warned the landlord prior of the danger of housing delinquents, with those who were out working all day, but the landlord had done nothing.

As the train shot through the tunnels, he would be bombarded with lethal doses of this shameless stuff. There they were silently mocking him in their designer suits and dresses, sipping cocktails while he made his way in dirty maggoty clothes to put in another fourteen hour day. As far, as he was concerned these models, celebrities and musicians in the posters had never done a hard day's work in their lives. They has got instant success through their looks, connections and shameless self-propaganda. They would never know what even a single day of demolition work was like. So one night after drinking quite a bit downtown, we entered the Bond street station. Immediately he began to vent and fume, like a bull in an arena. He felt the imposing presence of all the posters, glaring at him from every angle. All insinuating what a miserable failure he was. Who were they to judge him? Staring at him with such conceited looks, frozen in time?

He was livid. He set off on a mission to tear them all down. He immediately jumped down onto the tracks and started to go deep into the tunnel, ripping down one after another. I was beginning to get extremely anxious, despite being toasted myself. Any moment another train would arrive and he would become road-kill. I was starting to have visions of him rolling around inside one of the wheels, his beady eyes whirling about at hundred of rounds per minute. Then as a bumble bee, splat on the front windscreen of a fast moving train. I doubted he would have enough time to get out of the tunnel in time, and make it back onto the platform. It all seemed like a dark episode out of the twilight zone, only it was for real.

Now, I could see the train coming. The light deep in the tunnel was already showing and I could hear the whistling sound on the tracks. I implored him, to get the hell out of there. He started running like a striped ass ape and managed to cling on to the edge of the platform and pull himself up just in time. Then we boarded the train and headed back to the demolition site to sleep it all off. He had this most self-satisfying grin of deep contentment written all over his face. *At least I managed to get that bitch,* he finally spurted out. Shaving her head, he said, that was just a cunning marketing ploy. The contagion of her shameless self-propaganda machine, should be stopped in its tracks.

I was somewhat taken aback. I said people shave their heads for a million different reasons. I had done it myself once, after failing miserably in my first attempt at cutting my own hair. A project I had witlessly initiated one night, after coming back from the pub. Disconcerted with my efforts, I had finally thrown my hands up in exasperation and it all come off. My mother was in a fury next morning, and commissioned my father to deal with me. I was not looking forward to it one bit. My father was like one of those sleeping giants you do not want to awake but prefer to tiptoe around. But when the time came, he could not and would not do it. Inwardly, he was proud of me. He had always wanted to shave off all his own hair, but said he never had the guts.

I then related to the Dr. that some people shave their heads, because their bald-spots are driving them nuts. Others, like monks do it to signify their withdrawal from worldly investment. They recognized that the ego can use hair for pride, while a shaved head helped remind them of their selfless nature. Others were probably just exercising their God given freedom. Maybe they didn't want to be bundled neatly away as some stuffed animal, only to finally suffocate later from asphyxia, condescension and the highly conservative vomit of "high" society squares. The Dr. remained however supremely unmoved by all my illuminating digressions. He said, this was all just gobbledygook, jabberwocky and highly loquacious nonsense, that I was trying to force him to consume. He said people always do things for a reason, even if their reasons are grounded in insanity. Many, he said, shave their heads and do acts of weirdness as clever and cunning marketing ploys. They want to soak up more attention and flattery from other egos. Why else do something so outwardly visible, unless you are simply an attention grabber? She could just as easily, have cut off a number of her toes or tattooed her nipples and breasts with Xs' and Os'. No she wouldn't do such nonsense, it held no marketing value. It could not be made part of her public display case, unless she walked around nude.

THE PLANETS AND COSMOS ARE LIVING OFF OUR PSYCHOLOGICAL ENERGY

The Dr. definitely held a number of outlandish beliefs. He would try to convince me that the planets were sucking us all dry to the bone. That they were feeding off all our psychic energies. I asked him to explain in more detail. He progressed by saying that we were all just like colonies of bacteria to mother earth. She was living off our efforts. Using us, just to get her back scratched or a deep massage. But once we got up to no good, she would sneeze us all off, and start out fresh. That, which would be the end of our civilization, would merely be a cold to her. He said the scientists have it all ass backwards. Often they make us feel like planets are pretty dead and inert. At best, they see them as highly interconnected systems - the Gaia principle for example. But at root, they look at them more as storage lockers of resources, personal bank accounts that we dare not deplete. But these planets are very much alive, he said. Supreme living organisms, laughing their asses off, at our ignominious follies.

Yes, one hundred years in our lives is like a bare second or less in the life of a planet. That is why we entirely miss the show, of what is really going on. If we had time lapse photography and took a photo just once every 100,000 years, we would see all the mischief these planets were getting up to. We are like nothing to them, he declared. Just like those millions and billions of cells, organisms and creepy-crawlies living in our bodies, are like nothing to us. All our skyscrapers and cities and great architectural feats are simply like Lego toys printed in nanotechnology, as far as these planets were concerned. When mother earth gets a scratch, there is going to be a great earthquake or tsunami somewhere, that can knock millions of us out of the game. That is her way of taking care of business. That is her Kleenex.

Venus to him was like a young girl, still bubbling with cauldrons of vitality and exuberance. A little innocent and naive perhaps, but after all, the daughter in the household. Maybe a little high maintenance at times too. She needed to be watched over by the rest of the planets until she matured some. Uranus and Neptune were the big older bros in the household and they always remained somewhat stolid, unmoved and aloof. They had learned to look on all her vibrant gyrations and colorful impassioned ebullitions, with a cold, austere and remote look. Mother earth, on the other-hand was proud of her younger sister.

But Saturn, was a cold self-absorbed pretentious prima-donna, always wearing those flashy-dashy rings as jewelry. Yes, Saturn was gay but he hadn't quite come out of the cosmological closet yet. So he hovered about us quiet and calculating with his dark Saturnine personality, waiting for his opportune moment to unleash a tirade of bitchy psycho-dramas. Great Mama the Sun was finally starting to lose a little of her former vitality. A little of the flush was gone from her cheeks and she looked now positively etiolated. She had already developed her own liver spots, which we referred to as sunspots. She may end up dying young in a fatal accident, and then she would have to either gobble us all up as her last meal, or else slingshot us all off into the cold and icy cosmos, where if we were lucky we would end up as comets.

MORE CONSPIRACY THEORIES

To the good Dr., conspiracies were everywhere. All about us, he said, there was hidden information and open secrets easily decoded by the wise. Most of us however, just did not possess the right vision and discriminating perspective needed, to stand up and take notice. We were all wearing halos around our heads. These were really nothing more, than the dark nebulous clouds of our denial. So we were being duped at all times by our wishes and wants, by all those scripts we wrote into the screen of our lives, that we so desperately want to make true.

He said, take this prohibition on certain drugs for example. What do you make of it? What do you think is behind it? What is this self-righteous motivating force or power that is sealing tight the cookie jar? We see almost everyone getting locked up and criminalized for the simplest of offenses and the taxpayer having to foot the bill. In response, I said there were a lot of bad drugs out there, that lead to self-destruction, disease, theft, broken families and ravaged communities. Bad drugs that seem to shut down the prefrontal cortex and make us go berserk, so that we stomp on car roofs in the middle of the night and behave like crazed gorillas. We can't just flood the markets with such stuff. If everyone was on heroin, right now, there would be no revenue from taxes and nothing at all would ever get done.

Then the Dr. glared at me, with the most vile and contemptuous eyes, I have ever come across. Suddenly, he very derisively grunted out *"You don't have a clue what is going on, do you? Your mind is pumped chock-full with media BS. All your opinions were given to you. You are just an automaton approximating a human being, witlessly navigating your way about on psycho-planet. A space-cadet floating about in a lunar landing module or inter-stellar space propulsion vehicle, provided to you by the government and the media. Earth calling Sharon, come in Sharon! You have just bought those mass-produced eyeglasses, that come with all the special filters."* Then he said, if you look closely and astutely enough, you can see the truth. But for that you will need to take off your eyeglasses. You may feel dazed and myopic for a while, even overwhelmed, but eventually clarity will come.

Then he proceeded to say, that it was all a matter of motivation and control. Big centralized governments, large corporations, plutocracies etc. all retain their power through control and subjugation. They leverage people on their needs and misfortunes. They do not want real progress and freedom for the individual. This is their greatest threat. Instead they want to keep things frozen over, hermetically sealed and sewn up from all angles, so that they can preserve the existing Status Quo. Thus they remain as top dogs - the supreme Authorities, who think it is their God given right, to mercilessly whip us about. They give you a dream of progress and upward mobility and that is all.

The truth is they want you to remain firmly indoctrinated and suckered in to all those ideologies, that they mass produce. So that you remain in shackles, from the cradle to the grave. They don't want you to exercise an open mind. An open, flexible and impartial mind is a dangerous thing, from their perspective. You can see such attitudes prevailing in China, North Korea, Russia, Syria, Sudan, and so many other places. In the end, they think, freedom is a dangerous think, when placed in the hands of gorillas. It is a shut mind, that catches no flies and so the thought police are always out. They want you to remain numbed-out and zombified. When you can no longer remember your own name, then you are good to go. That is why you see alcohol everywhere. Every supermarket has become like the church to this great god of the masses. So many aisles dedicated to alcohol, just like the sanctum sanctorum of a temple. Each time we enter a supermarket, we should go down on our bended knees and pray for absolution, or at least delirium. Maybe if we are truly blessed, we will be canonized with the D.T.s. Yes, alcohol is the miracle drug for the government. It is what enables them to retain their big bad bear-claw footprint, in every mesh and alley. Angry drunks and drug-addicts provide the justification for increased police forces and military presence. It provides justification for increasing the strength of the judicial system, and has lead to the expansive proliferation of jails, human warehouses, screenings, biometric tests, and all sorts of other programs.

Without alcohol, government would be lost. It would be relegated to a ghost sitting behind a large control box, full of obsolete technology, like in an old star trek movie. Trying to boost us all into hyper-dimensional spaces in the transporter by overloading the power thyristors. No, without alcohol, the various authorities would hardly be able, to manipulate even a single puppet on its strings. Understand alcohol, and you will understand also, why it is that the great Oz does not like all those drugs, that truly open your mind and give you a full swig of your freedom. Yes, these are kept, under lock and key and strictly prohibited. No scientific or research studies of their benefits, is ever allowed for covert reasons. The danger is that once, we have a taste of our true freedom and unity, we may become too open-minded and altruistic and less ambitious. So governments feel, they would soon lose all control. We can see for ourselves that in all those countries, where alcohol, sex and everything else "joyful" is prohibited, all sorts of extreme groups breath underground. Only to come out of the woodwork later to have their own 4th of Julys. Yes, a smart government caves, to at least one vice, for its citizens to enjoy. This places the soother in their mouths, then we can get our revenue stream and control by criminalizing all else.

That genie, which promoted an evolution in our consciousness, was let out of its bottle in the sixties, and see how many human rights revolutions that kicked off. All those sickening chants of love, freedom and equality day-after-day. It was all a little nauseating perhaps. But there was more freely expressed love and progressive change, in that one short decade, than in entire centuries prior. So the genie had to be put back into the bottle, and it firmly capped, until we could learn how to tame this beast.

Then the Dr. pointed me to war monument in the middle of the town and said, *"What do you see there?"* What I asked? You mean the war monument? Isn't it delightful? Isn't it great to honor those who fought for our freedom and gave their lives for our country? All those completely selfless acts. Many coming home severely wounded and shell shocked. Destined to suffer out the rest of their lives. Yet they cannot even rest satisfied, with their own acts of tremendous courage, because of survivor's guilt and ongoing PTSD. Then I started reflecting on Winston Churchill's praise and apotheosis of the RAF, for their strategic win in the Battle of Britain. He had said, *"Never was so much owed by so many to so few."* My uncle, Batty had fought in that battle, and his body was never found. He had been an Electrical Engineer too. Was young and intelligent, but he never got to have a life. Yes, never got to screw a woman, voice an opinion or own anything more than a shabby bicycle. He paid dearly for his brief life, and was probably blown to smithereens somewhere in the air over Belgium.

My father thought about him often. He remembered shining his shoes to glowing perfection, on the day he was leaving for duty - never knowing he would never see his brother again. For many years afterwards, he cerebrated on the remote possibility, that his brother may just be suffering from mental amnesia. Living happily somewhere, unaware of his past and that he would walk in the door, once he came to his senses. Suddenly, I was getting a little more emotional. I felt I would lose it and breakdown. I started thinking of Skywalker. He had enjoyed it so much, when we went to Arlington national cemetery together. There lay buried, two of his uncles, who had died in WWII. One was involved in the Murmansk run and the other drowned in Panama. He was so proud of them and felt he should have died too in Vietnam. Skywalker had also served in the South Pacific, the Philippines, Japan, New Zealand, Pago Pago and Adak Alaska, during his peace-time service. He always wanted to see the grave of the unknown soldier and now he had. I said part of the final indignity, of being one of the unknown soldiers, is that you had to share a grave with so many other unknowns - like sardines in a can, for all time.

Skywalker Taking it Easy

Then the Dr. said to me, that this may all be well and true, but you only seem capable of looking at surfaces. You never go more than skin deep. All these glorious memorials and statues, that our nation treasures, are hardly placed here at random. There is a deeper message here, for those with eyes to see. When a nation is populated everywhere with war memorials, know well it is trying to justify its military machine. Yes the massive defense budget spending on powerful arsenal and new technological initiatives serves but to empower the various vested interests. Overt acts of aggression and brutality become morally legitimized, by ennobling them under such glowing terms as honor, liberty, patriotism and courage. Yes, many glowing euphemisms, keep all our ideologies in place, so that the rottenness at their core is never seen.

Spew out enough euphemisms, he said and people will pay top dollar to buy real estate in hell itself. One statue or memorial, on its own means nothing, but taken as a collective, the picture and the message becomes very evident and clear. He detested these monuments so much, because he resented been told who his heroes should be. He said, you won't see you or me up there, as the prized central piece of some town, oxidized into some sickly green and covered in bird shit. No because we are not the heroes, but the anti-heroes of the dream machine.

Our Lost Illumination and Misdirected Energies

Now he said, pick a few notes quickly out of your pocket and tell me what you see. Exactly, he said - Washington, Jefferson, Lincoln, Hamilton and Jackson, all sticking their ugly coconuts into my face – all politicians and mostly past presidents. If you are lucky enough to ever latch onto, some of the higher denominations, he said, and you will also see Grant, Franklin, McKinley, Cleveland, Madison, Chase and Wilson. Not a single note is imprinted with the face of one of our artistic geniuses, writers, inventors, entrepreneurs, scientists, humanitarians or peacekeepers.

There is a not so subtle message, going on here that is impossible not to read. That the government, is to be the power and the god of our nation - our supreme being and authority. Towards which we need to bow down deferentially and devote our complete admiration, lives and energies. It is a power we should be fearful of, but also respect - not so different from a godfather. No wonder we see our education so poorly funded, and ranking one of the worst among developing nations, and even in the world at large. No wonder, so many American artists and inventors usually starve to death or go mad, before they become noticed at all. Not that many are. Most of our significant artists had to become expatriates, because they remained completely unknown and unappreciated, on their own soil. Hidden from sight, like lepers or the untouchable Sudra caste.

One thinks of the likes of Henry Miller, Ernest Hemingway, F. Scott Fitzgerald, Henry James John Sargent, Mary Cassatt to name but a few. As early as 1887, Henry James had remarked, "It sounds like a paradox, but it is a very simple truth, that when to-day we look for 'American art' we find it mainly in Paris." I could go on digressing into street names, stamps and other areas, but if you take a look at Europe, we see a completely different story. There they prize their great artists, writers, musicians, philosophers, mathematicians and inventors. Take Paris, for example. Look at some of its major street names. These include Rue Dante, Balzac, Hugo, Cervantes, de Vinci, Seurat, Verlaine, Ampere, Arnauld, Descartes, Euler, Foucault, Fresnel, Galilee, Huygens, Leibnitz, Legendre, Laplace, La Grange . . . I could go on, but this will do. It has completely shaped their societal orders, culture and mentality. Imprints all they esteem and affects how they direct and invest themselves as a nation.

Such nations see the arts, as the means of expressing the sublime, the intangible and the mysterious. The medium for illuminating those hidden aspects, that confer on life its full splendor. All that which is blunted, or obfuscated from view, in the conditioned and work obsessed mind. That, which may not be perceived, but can most assuredly be felt. For it resonates with the deeper undertones of our being and the subtle inner chambers of our unconscious. True, it may not be readily quantified into material wealth and power, or stratified into various laws, codes, statutes and so on. All that is the dominion and sole focus of the worldly man. Thus it is often too quickly dismissed, as being of no consequence. Yet, even though we cunningly exclude and bar it from our conscious minds, it still exerts a powerful presence. It can help us decode the many enigmas and hidden dimensions of life. All that makes life worth living. It can empower us, to be far more than that, we currently experience ourselves to be. It carries the seeds of our enlightened futures, and it can enable us to experience our realities psychedelically, holistically and multi-dimensionally. Harnessing its power, we can elicit the latent and lost, into the world of the manifest. Without its information, we would still be locking horns like Neanderthals and fighting it out with clubs. Come to think of it, we are still doing that, only now our clubs have become a little bigger, and our weapons far more subtle, duplicitous and deceptive.

First there are those overt weapons of destruction, such as guns, blades, drugs, scuds, chemical weapons and nuclear devices. These are here for our betterment, for damage control and for keeping the peace. They make us better and safer Americans, able to sleep soundly in our beds at night. Yes, we can have the sweet beauty sleep, of a hot blonde that just witlessly stomped on a cockroach, before going to bed. Was this cockroach from the middle east – I do not know! Then there are the more insidious weapons, such as privacy erosion, mind programming, media bombardment, strategic cyber-attacks on financial systems, stock-markets and other nations. Information extraction and profiling weapons. Soft weapons that accumulate everything about us, every nuance of our lives, every tasteless action, every random thought spouted out, on some social media site.

Yes, this giant distributed electronic mirror is everywhere we go, gazing at us faithfully, dazzling us with its limitless capacity to depict all we have long forgotten. Our buying habits, health issues, crimes, interests, vices, social relationships, divorces, alimony payments. It is all there in black and white, should we ever hope to escape from the chains and manacles, that have been firmly placed upon us. We cannot erase the slate, should we ever be tempted to make meaningful progress in the present. This great slate just keeps on growing and growing and following us about like last night's nightmares. Accumulating more-and-more dark messages, that it will forever hold against us. Yet, messages it speaks out loud and clear for all the world to hear. It is a face of wrath and implacable vengeance, a Medusa of sorts, that holds us forever in check. One that looks only to balance its books, not to empower or heal.

The Dr. went on. It is not just our artists that are stuffed in the closet and given no food rations or voice. You see this also with all the great thinkers of the past. All the great metaphysicians, philosophers, existentialists and mathematicians, to begin with. They are usually long dead, before their ideas are even heard at all. Yet these, just like the artists have a very strong mystical bond and they stand at the gates between the world of the formless and potential, and the world of form. They steer the world and evolve it, infusing it with life and hope. They carry the world upon their shoulders and function as catalytic agents, who can harness the nonmanifest into existence. They have the vision to see the higher operating intelligence and the power to elicit the undiscernable and unnoticed. It is they, that can decode and transmute the higher meaning of things, into very potent crystallizations. Yes, they can summon the phantoms of higher operating modalities, out of the void, like rabbits from a magician's hat. Rabbits we would never have seen, or known of otherwise.

How many dumb-asses walked by the apple tree, before Newton looked up into the skies and declared the sun and the cosmos to be our bum buddies? He saw them as inextricably linked through those magic rays of attraction? Yes, if we focused just on the visible, we might think the sun was just going about its business. Galileo had already declared the earth and other planets to be, like a set of mantra beads for the sun. Silently spinning and whirling about its neck, as it made its mystical incantations of OM! OM! OM! The metaphysicians and mystics alone can bridge the gap between science and mysticism, between the world of the seen and that of the unseen. They are never seen above ground, because they work only at the foundations. They are not fooled, like the rest of us, by the world of appearances. They are so top dog! It is as if they have stepped off the ladder in the clouds, and entered into the celestial void. They work with that, which cannot be symbolized, because its scope and potency, is beyond all symbolic representation. A world beyond sensation and not readily perceived, nor even open to intellectual analysis. A veritable dark matter, which nevertheless has light at its core.

GUILT, THE ILLUMINATI AND VARIOUS PISS-POTS IN THE BOONIES

The Dr. continued, saying when a nation is speckled everywhere with the most ornate churches, know well that it is trying to mitigate its guilt. That is why the Conquistadores built so many beautiful churches, in the territories they ravaged. These were masterpieces constructed from all the gold, silver and marble they plundered from the Inca temples. A culture they brutally massacred. These churches were decorated with the most stunning paintings and statues. Sometimes these are sixty feet high or more. You can see them everywhere in South America, where the Conquistadores invaded. Some of these great churches have catacombs beneath them. These were used for torture and peonage, far more than for burial.

And in Rome, he said we see Vatican city with all its gold reserves. This the federal reserve of ancient times. The treasury where all the gold and wealth extracted from across the empire was housed. So this church was built on a foundation of subjugation and extortion. When times were lean, there was the selling of indulgences, to ramp up profit margins. Just pay the man and you can erase your crimes and mortal sins forever. Much like it is today then, with savvy lawyers getting their rich clients off the hook for brutal murders and overt acts of financial fraud. Such churches were an affront to the Dr., almost as assault to his sense of morality. He said where true religion is practiced, there is was no room for pomp and glory, no choice jewels sprinkled generously over the fingers and no ornate vestments inlaid with patterns of gold. Yes, there are no unholy artifices needed to intervene between God and ourselves. Our spiritual altar is within, and found in the silence of our heart.

Now he digressed to another topic. He started divulging in detail his own unique collection of paranoias. It turned out, he had an extreme paranoia associated with living in a small town or village. He said, one loses all rights of anonymity in such places. In cities where thousands of scurrying souls crash into one another every moment, there is far more anonymity. But these pisspots in the boonies attract gossipers who want to listen in on everyone's secrets. Malicious gossipers who are downright evil, who continuously blackball and besmirch everyone with the dark brush-strokes of their egos. Yes, they twist and distort all they hear and see, turning their neighbors into the very portrait of the Anti-Christ in motion. Tiny little things and minutiae become amplified out of all proportion, sometimes leading to murder. The mob effect can often kick in, due to a profusion of corner bar whisperings. If you are not physically tarred and feathered and ousted from the town, you will psychologically feel you are.

He said beware and extremely vigilant in each, for all such places become infused with all sorts of collective neuroses over time. They are loaded with all sorts of invisible poisoners, that seep in through the thin porous membrane of your mind, causing you to cave in to so many neurotic misbeliefs. So you become imbalanced through various exclusions, biases and over-amplifications. The filters are now on, which darken your entire worldview. Filters, in which you come to believe, almost anything. You feel diminished in some way, but cannot place the cause. You are definitely not the man, you were a year before. All your confidence is gone, as is all your 'Joie de Vivre', replaced by a bitter sarcastic troll you cannot relate to anymore. He said I did not pick up on such things, because I was living in a warped reality distortion field, of my own unique custom design. He said, don't kill the messenger! Don't blame me because, I can perforate the canvas and see through this bleak hall of appearances.

He proceeded with his full frontal assault on my cerebral cortex, decimating the cozy landscape, I had once lived in. He started saying that there is much we think we see, that is not there, and much we don't see, that is. I could not make out the Dr. at all. His tone of being was entirely different from anyone, I had met before. Sometimes, I felt he was like a Richard Feynman character, "*Half Genius and Half Buffoon*", or in his special case, "*All Genius and All Buffoon.*" Yet, a part of my mind was entirely revulsed by him, like he was some insect that need to be squashed and crunched under my feet. A human virus, or Gollum figure, perpetually flailing and rummaging about in the jungles of mankind, raising Dantesque infernos in a teacup and emanating his volcanoes of incendiary rage.

His unique tragedy, was that nobody listened to him at all. And in this, was most veritably like, the Cassandra of ancient times. They shared this unique tragedy. Everyone went calmly by him, and about their business like automatons and machines, running their corporately implanted software scripts. Yes, all were like figures from Noddy's toy town, who just didn't get it. I thought for a moment that the Dr. needed to be flung to the walls, or exterminated out of his misery. I wanted desperately at times, to move onwards free and unimpeded - to go back and swallow the blue pill quickly. Yet, it was too late and I was beginning to feel sorry, that I had ever listened to him. My innocence was gone, my purity was lost in the warped soul sucking sphere of his darkness and negativity. I wanted them back. They were my teddy-bears.

He wanted, so desperately to convince me, that this world was run from behind the curtains by the illuminati. Yes, this was no Lego-land story to him. Instead everything was punctuated with insidious investments and malicious intents. Everything had colorful overtones and undertones imbued in its foundations. He rallied against all of it both emotionally and viscerally, like a tragic Don Quixote figure. I, on the other-hand could be accused of a cold clinical and analytical detachment, even of a certain aloofness. I was like an emotionless flatfish forever witlessly setting off land-mines in the hearts of others, then rocketing the tomb of my soul, into the austere unfeeling cosmos, like a captain Spock. I couldn't give a flying fuck, if the earth suddenly fell out of its orbit – hardly worth getting out of bed for. On the Titanic, I probably would have slept it through.

Yes, the schools had knocked all shows of exuberance and life out of me long ago. Flatlined all my emotional responses and left a cruel, cold and clinical portrait, they now proudly wanted the world to know. At least that was my own story to myself. The other possibility, far less appealing, is that I had been this emotionless flatfish, from the very beginning. That I was stillborn at birth, lobotomies percolating through my entire inner psychological makeup and showing up like Swiss cheese. I who had always preferred a bottle in front of me instead of a frontal lobotomy. One thing was for sure, I always felt in jail and an utter alien in my body.

A jail strategically placed in the center of a circus arena. Every day the animals would come by in the classroom and heave and shove, and try and engage me in their antediluvian games. How could I tell them that I had discarded that costume millennia before?

TAKING RESPONSIBILITY, FOR THE WORLD WE INVENTED

So was ours a shared world then, or one of startling contrasts? Did the Dr. and myself inhabit two completely different universes? I put this thought in my pocket for now. It was a trinket I would keep, until it held some value. Only many years later, when I had stumbled upon the Course, could I rightly evaluate this trinket, from new angles and with fresh eyes. The Course had brought to me many incredible insights. It never pussyfooted around, but went first for the jugular. That is, it went right to the root of things and gave it to you straight up. It attracted me because it wasn't interested in making worthless compromises. I knew in my heart, truth could not be cut up, just to accommodate every beggar and bum in the village. It could not accede to all those with special preferences, contingencies, conflicts, moods and mental vacillations. It was not an 'A La Carte' menu, that changed by the day. Would truth come then, as some great underground earthquake, together with bolts of lightning? No, not at the phenomenal level, yet it would most certainly rattle our world picture, at its very foundations. That which we thought we understood, would be seen as merely the confusion, of our own self-made ignorance and we would penetrate to the greater reality beyond and beneath this screen. Yes, myself and the Dr's worlds were completely different. We each had generated our own special universes, with each faithfully tracking our own pet peeves and predilections.

"I have invented the world I see"

[W.32]

Yes, spacetime was most certainly a mind-born illusion whose only purpose was to facilitate our healing. Yes we had become too dumbed down, through listening to our egos across the millennia. Thus we no longer possessed the capacity to take in the whole picture at once. Remained as children, playing games of make belief with our special toys. Yet unwilling to give them up. Like a little girl, tenaciously clinging to a filthy torn up doll, that she has fallen in love with. Yes, this doll has a name and a personality, special eating preferences and a fatal power of attraction. It can become a moody bitch too, if her hair is not done correctly. Yet is seen as so alive and real to her, that she cannot bear to be torn apart from it for long. She prefers her dream fiction rather than facing the painful truth, that it is completely lifeless. All its seeming life, talents and characteristics have been borrowed through projection. So we all cling to those imaginary toys and beliefs that we have come to cherish. We feel awareness of our completion would divest us of all this.

Yes, somewhere along the line, wholeness seems to have got blown up into millions of meaningless and disconnected fragments. Examining the fragments in isolation, we cannot make any sense. We flounder hopelessly about moving from one piece to another looking to exploit each for our own special interests. So is the real value in each part lost to us. Such is the legacy of our pseudo-serial adventures and experiences in time. Yet what smashed this perfect crystal? Why does it no longer reflect perfect thought? Why has all become dark? Who are all these horrible and fetid creatures walking around, through the cracks of our own distortions? Was the crystal ever whole? It seems unlikely. Yet, chief Big Bear did vouch for its wholeness, one night, under a psychedelic peyote induced trance. He said all fell asunder, with the coming of pale face. How will we ever manage now, to put this Humpty Dumpty back together again?

Maybe he is still whole, and yet we do not know it. It is us that are broken!

When we no longer recognize ourselves, as this world's inventor, we become its victim instead. It is as if we got hit-up with a date rape drug, one night and woke up in a completely different state of mind. Feeling this intense migraine headache now, it is as if we are suffering from brute force trauma. Victimization became our most relished form of passive entertainment. We entered the fight club of mere mortals. The best show in town. So we go about idly blaming others, for all the bad things that seem to be happening to us. We feel so unlucky, due to our being continuously whacked about by random and incidental events, that are knocking us out of the game. We were the ones, after all, who started out with such pure and noble intentions. If it wasn't for the deeper conspiracy that has us in its bull's-eye – wouldn't life just be grand?

Yet, when good times come and fortune lands in our laps, we attribute ourselves as the architects of our own good fortunes. Aren't we such creative, inspired and self-motivated souls? The ego lives it large in such times of plenty, and is almost sweet to us for a moment. We after all, are ardently transforming ourselves into the very man-gods of its desires. The good-time friends pander at our feet and worship the crumbs that fall from our table. They want to steal our magic recipe and pluck the diamond out of the dough. It is only in the bad times, that we think we are in no way responsible, for the bad luck waves that have suddenly blown in for us to surf. Aren't our loyalties most divided then and so totally one-sided? That is they are always directed towards ourselves, and that which serves our own best interests?

I know it can be hard to internalize, but all the great disasters in your life, were caused by you. It was you, that caused all those failed relationships, sicknesses, afflictions, tragedies and disasters that you looked upon. Knowing this, would make you go mad, you think and yet it is its denial, that has made you so. You feel that no one can tolerate such pain, such accountability. So we choose to fall into denial, of our own mind's power. Put simply then, either this world is born inside us, or it is without? There can be no in-between on this. The ego preaches that it is outside, while the Course teaches it is within. Yet, have you the willingness and strength, to recognize that this world, is arising entirely from your subjectivity? Accepting this is empowerment! Can you accept that you are, the only cause of all that comes your way? That there is no outside agent or event, with a toss of power over you? This small distinction is yet extremely potent. One, you were too busily consumed with ego propaganda, to notice. You were too engaged in projecting your own internal conflicts, onto the screen of the world and reacting to these, as if they were self-independent events. But remember our mantra, *"All is Idea and Ideas leave not their Source."* Remaining a victim then, can only be the decision to remain immature. Have you grown up enough to take responsibility for all your decisions, feelings and their manifold effects? Or do you continue to scapegoat the entire responsibility, for your misery to the 'without', whenever it suits you?.

Yet, the Course reminds us, that we cannot be unfairly treated. All that happens merely represents our wish. Maturity is simply accepting responsibility, for the world we see and for all that happens to us. This world is nothing, but your own mental interpretations and beliefs projected. All effects seen, are spawned from our own thinking processes and inner states of conflict. The world is the natural offspring of our denial of truth. Perception is nothing but the mirror of our learning. Our failure to acknowledge this, will not clear the muddy waters. We cannot heal, until we first take responsibility. Otherwise we just strengthen poor decision making habits, lending increased conviction in this hallucinatory, schizophrenic and meaningless universe that but seems apart from us.

THE HOPELESS AND DESPAIRING PLANS OF THE EGO

I gather how you feel. If all this is true, you say, then how did I get myself into this inescapable mess? Why are there so many parasitic, dependent beings hovering about, trying to steal all my energy and resolve? Diffusive presences, with nothing to give but their hatred and torment? How can this all be my fault and my choice? I have found myself in such dark situations many times. The ego rants and raves waiting for its moment to strike. Rocket fuel sputtering next to a fire. It is a painful voyage in the beginning. Yet until you begin to take at least some baby steps, you will never regain power over your projections, and quench the real source of your misery. The baby steps will enable you to proceed further in the right direction. Soon you will find, you can heal and that miracles are coming your way in abundance. You are no longer being mercilessly tossed about, but gaining in power beyond your wildest imaginations.

> "My holy brother, think of this awhile: The world you
> see does nothing. It has no effects at all. It merely
> represents your thoughts. And it will change entirely
> as you elect to change your mind, and choose the joy of
> God as what you really want."

> **[W.190.6:1-4]**

Perception is what you take yourself to be. Your Being is what you Are! Perception is always an effect, rooted to your beliefs. It is the reflection of your inward conscious and unconscious states projected to seem without. Yet all arises in perfect correspondence, to your believed self-identity and state of learning. The truth, of what you are has already been established and is unchangeable. It is on this key point, that the startling contrast between the ego and the Holy

Spirit becomes very apparent. The ego preaches that the world is what it is, that it is never going to change in any meaningful way. But that you can make the most of a bad situation. It counsels you to escape much of the turmoil and pain through crafting for yourself an invented self or image. This image can be tailored and custom designed, to exploit all the dream's weaknesses. So you set about crafting the self that you desire, limited only by your own powers of ingenuity and imagination.

The Holy Spirit simply reminds you, that you need not fear the world, nor escape it. You were never in it. The Self that you Are, is changeless, perfect and immutable. The world will change, for the better as you draw nearer to this Self. It will disappear, when you are One with the Self in full awareness. Until then it remains a learning device, that you can use to reach this Self. Your Being is not contingent on your level of learning, but right learning is what elicits the reality of your Being, back into your awareness. Realize then that you Are the infinite and the timeless. Call yourSelf by your real Name - **The Son of God**. Or you can call yourSelf the One-Mind, the Buddha, the Sambhogakaya or the Void, it makes no difference to me, because names are powerless to affect your reality.

> **Jesus said, "Why do you wash the outside of the cup? Don't you understand that the one who made the inside is also the one who made the outside?"**   **[The Gospel of Thomas]**

Sometimes we feel like that our whole lives, have been wastefully spent trying to push a gigantic snowball uphill. We feel frustrated and exhausted and just want to give up. It seems unwise to continue working against this law of psychological gravity. Such is the dark frustrating despair of all those, who blindly follow the ego's recipe for success, because they are working against the laws of truth and therefore against their own best interests. The dim distorted reflection of what we Are, as it appears in our consciousness is not always a pretty sight. It is an image, that has become darkened by the many storm clouds of our conditioning, and by our false identifications. One severely distorted through persistent actualization of erroneous understandings into our lives. The web of falseness has become so entrenched, into the fabric of our thought, that we can no longer clearly see, meaningfully evaluate or nurse any hope of transcending our prison-house. Even a little progression now and the would be nice, but this seems unlikely to happen?

We feel limited and worn down by the dinosaur of false knowledge, on our backs that is blinding us into senselessness and confusion. This is the thought system of the ego. This erroneous thought system cannot be repaired or even over-hauled. It needs to be entirely uprooted, removed and seen for the rotting tree that it is. The ego's thought system is ass-backwards, and confounds you with infinite regressive loops of contradictory and irreconcilable logic. Simply put, it will induce in you dullness, mediocrity, savagery and a chronic fear prone condition. To attempt to succeed with the ego, is like a dog attempting to pull itself up by grabbing its own tail. The nebulous cloud formations of this depressing and self-diminishing thought system are without any saving grace. Composed of a potpourri of shiny trinkets, that seem so effulgent in the darkness, but whose entire lack of substance becomes expressly evident, in the greater light of day.

So long, as you remain in compliance with the ego, you feel yourself hopelessly clutching at straws, a hostage condemned forever to collecting coke cans on the beach, and missing out on the sun of knowledge. You remain always center-nowhere and circumference-everywhere, foolishly substituting outside opinions of what-you-are, in the place of first-hand knowledge. So you blend the cocktail of your own dream fictions. Outside opinion is raised into your god, and you grovel about through the huge feet, deceit and gravitas of this monster, to find yourself a dishonorable grave. You are reduced to a powerless imp in la-la-land. Reduced to a passive minion whose total reactionary mode of functioning but feeds and empowers, his own fearful slave-based projections. Is this what you want? To become a futile wanderer in the lonely parched desert of a dream, searching in vain on the plane of the screen, for that perfect method of meditation or self-inquiry that will awaken you from it? Only to see many frightening projections arising, whose only goal is to focus all your attention to the screen and away from the projectionist? Yet, it is only by looking directly into the mind of the projectionist, that all your apparent problems can be resolved. Because here alone they were made. Thus do you migrate your awareness from the plane of effects and reaction, to the plane of cause and meaningful response.

THE ONE ALTERNATIVE

There is just one alternative, to this nonsense. Enter his royal highness, the Holy Spirit - yippee! He presents to you, a thought system that is diametrically opposite, to the one you are engaged and feel victimized by. One that presents, an entirely different picture of what you Are. A complete different interpretation of the world of perception. You cannot blend both stories in your mind, for long or you will feel torn apart. These two concoctions can never be meaningfully mixed. Any compromise on this, is but a thinly veiled attempt by your ego to retain its traction in your mind. It is attempting to persuade you to retain some conducive aspects of what it sells. Yet, to accept any part of the ego's thought system, is to retain it all. A compromise may seem palatable in the beginning and provide some quick and immediate satiation, but this compromise will end up costing you your life. For when you direct your attention towards the worship of nothingness and falsities, you make all illusions seem true. You have chosen death, by your decision to embrace the absolutely contradictory and irreconcilable. This is the tiny crack through which the whole world of ugliness enters. It becomes the spawning ground of all illusions and all distortionary beliefs. No! It will have to be the red pill or the blue pill. Your choice on this, will determine everything - your salvation or your continued bondage.

Choosing the thought system of the Holy Spirit, is the decision to know reality. Through it you learn, that you have always been center-everywhere and circumference-nowhere. With it, you take the plunge within and find the light that seemed hidden. The light of your true Being. You take the backflip, into the existential void and free-fall into the mouth of the eternal volcano. Here you are fried forever, of all false content, and freed from the maddening clutches of illusion. You no longer view things from the surface, and as seen at the mouth of the volcano, but from its center and heart.

At its heart alone, its true content lies. Here alone is essence. You become a nothing in this fire of purification, and are instantly reborn as the fire and light of the volcano itself. You die as your phenomenal, time-bound self, only to be reborn as the noumenal and timeless Self. You disappear from the world of time, only to find yourself at Home in Eternity. With your newfound vision you easily distill the true content behind all appearances. So perception stops spinning its wheels and comes to an end. All that false content that overlay your mind, which was keeping you blind, has gone up in smoke. You tell now of a vast throbbing, blissful aliveness that is unquenchable and never ending. It had simply become forgotten in the darkening corridors of time. And this newfound Reality was always but an instant away and ticketless.

6. I Am the Light of the World

When I Shine,

The World Shines!

When I am Clouded Over,

The World Grows,

Dark and Despairing!

I Am that Light Which,

Can Never be Extinguished!

One That Remains,

Radiant, Indestructible,

And Immaculate Forever!

The Light of All Things,

and the Spaces,

Between Them!

The Sun, The Stars,

And The Moon,

All Exist Inside of Me!

I Am the Light,

of the Comets,

And Far Reaching Galaxies!

Storms, Earthquakes,

Hurricanes and Tsunamis,

All but Reflect my Moods!

Thunder and Lightning Strike

From Deep Within My Heart,

Bringing the Urgent News,

That it is Time to Awake!

All Appearances

Bow Down to Me,

They Know That I Am,

The Source of Their Light!

I Can So Easily Shine,

All Appearances Away!

Birds Sing in Me,

Junkies get High in Me,

Lawn-mowers Mow Me,

Snow Addicts Snort In Me,

Rockets Launch in Me,

Nuclear Bombs Explode in Me,

Spacecraft Fly in Me,

New Life is Born in Me,

Flourishes and Dances,

For a While,

Then Grows Sick,

And Dies in Me!

For I Encompass All Things,

All Comings and Goings,

I am the Illumination,

of Perfect Knowledge,

Thought and Understanding!

That Light From Which,

All Inspiration and Intuition Streams!

The Light of Your,

Dream and Nightmares,

Visions and

Miraculous Perceptions!

I Am the Source Of All,

Strength, Abundance,

And Peace!

All Worldly Idols,

Are Nothing Before Me,

For I Am That,

Which Dispels All Notions,

of Sickness and Sacrifice,

Famine and War,

Suffering and Death!

For I Am the Death of Death!

And the Bonfire,

Of All Illusions,

In My Light,

All Appearances and,

Dark Dreams Disappear,

I Am the Light,

Of Your Enlightenment,

And The Recognition,

of Your Holiness,

That Sacred Light that

Sees all as Brothers,

As they Were,

Before Time Began,

And As they Will,

Be Known Again,

When Time is No More!

I Am the Light,

of the Eternal,

Streaming into the

World of Time,

At the Portal of the Now,

The Light That

Sources all Miracles,

Holy Instants and Revelations!

Simply Uncover This Portal,

And You Will Stand Revealed,

In the Perfection,

You Once Were,

And Still Are Now!

In the Home Where,

You Once Knew Peace,

Before Time Came,

To Intrude,

Upon Our Joy!

I Am the Light of The

Heavenly Garden,

That Can Never be

Destroyed,

Only Forgotten!

That Light which Illuminates,

And the Only Place,

Where Your Heart,

Will Ever Find its Rest!

7. ONLY GOD IS

Jesus said, "I am the light that is over all things. I am all: from me all came forth, and to me all attained. Split a piece of wood; I am there. Lift up the stone, and you will find me there."

[The Gospel of Thomas]

D r. Gobbler's Knob was back on a venting feast. He said, "*You say, God is all around us. Where in the hell is He then? It all sounds like wishy-washy, hocus-pocus crap to me. Next you will want me to start putting crystals on my head and articulating the Gayatri Mantra. Bring Him down here in a form I can understand and I will wholeheartedly agree with you. I would like to see Him show up incarnated as a crate of Guinness or as a bottle of Jameson whiskey. If He is as omnipotent as you say, let Him free me this moment of all my current miseries, get my boss of my back and pay my rent. Once I see all my problems resolved, I will gladly jump around in an orange suit, with a full Japa mala of mantra beads swinging at my neck. Would that make me Kosher enough to join your motley crew?*" Yes the Dr.'s needs were shallow and meretricious indeed. That is, he was attracted to the simple, often vulgar temptations in life. He was always flailing about, drowning in the teaspoon of his small-mindedness and missing the bigger picture. He was a parochial soul, if there ever was one and he could never glimpse the universal. Also he had a nasty tone to his personality, an extremely expeditious way of always threatening a hollow-point to your coconut and unsettling all one's emotions and composure, in just a few choice words.

I immediately retorted that God does not appear in forms that are just to our liking because that would be just promoting idolatry. If he were to appear in any special form exclusively, this form would then quickly become our new idol. Then His presence would become unseen in all other forms and we would proudly proclaim, He cannot be there. Thus would we transform God into just another slave of our pet likes and dislikes and seek to limit the unlimited. We would just be projecting our own biased judgments and preferences before truth? Rather, He must remain always immanent and transcendent to all form. Nor, I said can He free you, because you are already free! That is how He Created you. You alone are the one that continues to make your miseries and bondage. If he pays your rent, and takes care of all your problems, He would be attaching importance to the illusory. So you would never become aware of your true power and freedom. You would not be willing to give up this body, which you made to hide from Him. You would remain mentally impotent, a child throwing perpetual tantrums and expecting everyone to clean up your slops. Is this what you want?

Dr. Gobbler's Knob however was still not happy. He proceeded, "*You want me to embrace the reality of God! Yet how can I embrace that which I don't know? I cannot even embrace those who I do know. In fact, it is a deeply rooted instinctual habit of mine to hate everyone on sight, even when I find out later, I had nothing to fear from them.*" Then I said, that it all comes down to what you want to be true. This will automatically determine all your rationalizations, justifications and actions. If you do not open your mind at least to the possibility of God, you will not know Him because your blinders will be on. And you will default to embracing your ego instead. This is the paradox that keeps Atheists in fuel for life. In fact, you don't need to embrace Him at all. He is here whether you embrace Him or not. His reality is not conditional on your acceptance of Him. All you need do, to know Him, is to relinquish all your special attachments to your ego. Then you will ask no more questions and demand no more proofs.

We are all deeply hypnotized by life, I said - this is our fundamental problem. We are always busy scurrying frantically about like a mound of ants waving our antennae at each other, sending toxic signals into the airwaves. Then threatening lawsuits, if all does not go our way. Yes we are all fast asleep with our eyes open. In our dream, we keep on wondering to ourselves "*What is this dream that I must awaken from?*" I do not see it anywhere. All I see is this regular monotonous soul destroying life going on all around me. It is chewing its way into my bones and wearing me down. I see all those sick brutal parasites hovering about who give me no rest and plague my every move. They seem hellbent on my destruction, on reducing me and taking everything I've got. Yes it is all a desperate fight for life-spaces here in psycho-planet and the jackals and hyenas of the world are closing fast on any carcass. They are opportunistic of any hint of vulnerability.

Yes, the truth is that the dream is so close that we can no longer draw any meaningful distinction between it and ourselves. We don't really know ourselves. We have made far too many assumptions, caved to so much nonsense and we have lost complete sight of our Self nature. That is why we cannot draw any meaningful distinction between ourselves and the dream. We have sold ourselves on the images we ourselves have made. And the dream landscape is vast indeed, covering every aspect of our thoughts and perceptions. It envelopes all our experiences. It forms the fabric of our entire lives, our loves and hates, our illusions of grandeur and specialness, our thoughts of being attacked and mercilessly hounded. There is no aspect of our consciousness that the dream has not infiltrated. It breathes out from our every pore. There is no hidden shrine or concept we hold dear within or without where the dream is not. In fact consciousness itself is part of the dream. For without the dream, consciousness could not be maintained.

The awakened are not conscious of anything, because there is no *thing* to be conscious of. So they remain as an awareness, that is absolutely potent and all-encompassing and one in which no *thing* is.

The dream is the mystery of ourselves unraveling before us. In the dream, all appears to be effervescent and bubbling with life, mystery and misadventure. We see an ominous place of frightening and fragmented perceptions, seeming to hold us captive within its tiny scope and petty ways. In this dream of littleness, we have forgotten ourselves. So we willingly peep through a keyhole on bended knees willing to sell all of worth to purchase idols made from dust. These mountains of dust that we pay homage to become our sacred altars to madness. Yes the greatest minds of every generation seem to imbibe this stupefying perfume. Only when we have finally fallen into absolute despair and are prepared to awake, will these idols disappear into the nothingness from which they came. Then we will know that we have always been at Home in God. Asleep yes, but we had never left our Home. All this chaotic bustling and frenzy of frantic activity which has been going on almost forever is simply the feverish dreams of mind asleep. It is as if Adam had imbibed a lethal dose of Ambien, Lunesta or Trazodone that has knocked him out for millennia.

We are like a swarm of bees thinking we are doing something tremendously monumental, novel and world transforming, but we are simply drugged and hypnotized by meaningless activities. We have lost our mind's natural awareness. We choose the dreams meager offerings over our sanity and reason. Yet, the dream must go on, until one golden moment finally arrives when we no longer cherish any dreams. Only then are we ready to hold all dreams to ransom and see not one offers us anything of substance. We have tried many and reached nowhere. Yet, we foolishly think we can succeed with the new hottest ticket. It will end up like the rest and be like a futile selling of ice to the Eskimos or sand to the Arabs. We will see it brings us nothing but bitterness, disenchantment, despair, sickness, disaster and failure. The lack of substance of each dream becomes abundantly clear seen in the rear view mirror. Yet, each seems to have substance and allure as we approach it anew. We beg for its gifts and sell ourselves at its altars. Yet, nothing of value we find. Like the mirage of water in the desert, it can delude but it can never satiate for its waters do not contain the life giving gift of healing.

> "Anything in this world that you believe is good and valuable and worth striving for can hurt you, and will do so. Not because it has the power to hurt, but just because you have denied it is but an illusion, and made it real. And it is real to you. It is not nothing. And through its perceived reality has entered all the world of sick illusions. All belief in sin, in power of attack, in hurt and harm, in sacrifice and death, has come to you. For no one can make one illusion real, and still escape the rest."
>
> [T-26.VI.1:1-7]

Isn't it a wonder that our minds are emblazoned with such an unquenchable thirst, yet somehow we always remain unfulfilled? Each seeks desperately to get out of the hole he is in. He will not rest until he has found the fountain of wisdom and peace. Only then can he relax in the hot tranquil springs of pure Being. In the meantime he continues to entertain the idle notion that there is yet one more dream that needs to be explored. That this one will bring lasting satisfaction, despite all the rest having failed. So we move from life-to-death and death-to-life, yet nothing fundamental has changed and no meaningful progress has been made. Only in that instant, when we become absolutely despairing of all dreams, are we ripe for awakening.

ENLIGHTENMENT AND INNOCENT PERCEPTION

The few that are enlightened, did so during the a serious crash-and-burn episode in their lives. They became rigorously aware of the futility of this dream-world, at a very visceral level. Now they remain frozen, when viewed from a higher perspective. The cobwebs of illusions no longer cling to them. They no longer project more dream fiction along time's meaningless corridors. They remain now in a deep stillness and as an awareness that embraces the infinite through the portal of the timeless present. They no longer carry worldly trash to obliterate their view. Instead they remain naked and unknowing in their newfound purity, having purged themselves of all illusions. It is this that bestows on them the eyes to see.

Theirs is the innocent perception. Their original face has been reborn into active awareness. Yes, truth was always here hidden in plain sight. Hidden just beneath our masks and all that surface carnage that came sputtering out from our conscious dumping grounds. But now masks are done. This is the real death then and the real rebirth. For it is the death of dreaming and the death-of-death. All other deaths were but a continuation of dreaming, in yet another form. The meaningless content always replayed itself - the stage alone was all that ever changed. Now the machinery for spawning illusions and projecting false hope has been finally arrested in its tracks. The belief in any power or rescuer outside is gone. We have come to the Source – the infinite well of beatitude. We have realized that all paths offered by the world are paths leading to nowhere but despair. Remaining in this absolute despair we have at last stopped cranking out illusions. We have allowed truth a window of opportunity to reveal itself. And it comes of itself naturally wherever it is made welcome.

Enlightenment destroys everything, you thought you knew. You have collided with the infinite and are now awed by the magnitude of what has occurred. It cannot be said to be an experience, rather it is the fundamental backdrop to all experiencing itself. Everything has flipped outside in. You have gone from a world of objects to a world of thoughts. The world, you now realize never occupied any space. Since space itself was always but a projection of mind. Now you see the universe taking on all your mental colorings, as you think them. With this initial shock there comes a great unsettling. You have penetrated directly through to all the grandeur, magnificence and splendor that all your illusions and self-beliefs had concealed from you. You do not know where you stand in the new scheme, because phenomenalism has died - it was seen to be a mirage of split-mind, that it no longer there once mind is healed. You see that the world was always spontaneously arising from within you. In your heightened state of awareness you can see it now completely disappear, in a halo of heavenly light, *The Great One,* in your very presence, but not as any form. You are Him and He is you. He enfolds everything within and everything that seems without. In fact there has never been any within and without. Unlimited now are the paradises you can manifest from the knowledge that has become reborn in you.

Knowing yourself inseparable from absolute Truth, you come to a great unconditional peace. It was but your vain wishfulness and chasing after naught that had left you bankrupt. Because you were dream identified and so awareness became lost. This death that is Enlightenment can only happen once. All others deaths have been happening in seeming an endless regression since ancient times. This death is not a death of your body but a full mental implosion of your world. Caused by a subtle but potent flip in your self-understanding. You suddenly find yourself back at the instant of the fall knowing nothing meaningful and worthwhile has happened since. Even though in dream-time millions of years seem to have flown by. All was just smoke and mirrors and you had incorrectly identified with images in the glass of perception.

What was real in the past remains real in the present. All is Here-Now. Nothing has ever happened. Nothing not in the present, will ever Be. Everything truly in the present, always IS. This is the Law of the Eternal and a condition of its Reality. You have become the '*Alpha and the Omega*'. A perfection that can never be tampered with, nor destructed. Nothing can be added to you and nothing taken away. Yet to others you still seem to be living through a body and moving towards some uncertain future. They see you through their own blindness and beliefs. You know that neither the body nor the future exist, nor time and the apparently physical. There can be no diminishment in you ever. All glory is forever yours.

Enlightenment is merely the re-dawning in your awareness of what always IS. The Knowledge that only God IS. That you exist forever in unconditional peace and it can only happen in the exact present moment - **The Now**. Because this is the only vortex point, in the great fantastical parade before you, where the real cuts the illusory. Here is the meeting place of the eternal and the world of time. You must die then before you die, and your death must always be exactly **Now**. Then you enter the gates of truth and your body is transformed into the body of the Nirmanakaya - the dream body of the Buddha. Now you have become the hole in the paper resting at this portal between time and eternity. The breathing ground of all miracles. Those in the relative world may still think you are on their plane, because they are projecting their own darkness as an overlay upon you. Yet, you know your physical existence is but a dream.

With the death that is Enlightenment, God happens. Up to that instant, God was just another dream. Some miraculous omnipotent presence to be believed in, but ultimately not known. A Santa Claus of sorts. You were too involved in self-definition and in architecting your pitiful pile of dust to engage in more futile ventures and meaningless charades. All your progression was illusory. Now you have returned your awareness to God. Now you know that your unwise investments formed a self-made conspiracy and delusion that was holding you blind. God calls us always from the endless present and awaits our return. In His infinite patience, He silently awaits for us to put all our childish games away. He wants us to come to the inner altar where we exist as light, truth, knowledge and unquenchable bliss. To meet Him **Here-and-Now**, we must first meet His condition of peace.

Peace is the condition of the Kingdom and arises only in the perfectly harmless and trusting. Those untarnished by the deviant world. Those who will protect what God has made with love and appreciation. Those perfectly satisfied to be as they were Created, rather than that tawdry image, the ego has made of them. Yet, you are welcome to play around here as long as you want. One day you will see that your feet are torn and that the thorns of life are stacked against you and sticking in deep. Broken winged you will stand there moaning and dispirited cursing your body for the vitality, it has lost. Angry animals crowding around you in the arena, turning against you, opportunistically carving away the little that you have left. You will then shrink from this world, seeing that despite all its complexity and inventiveness, you remain joyless, fragmented, lackluster, depressed and despairing. You will feel its emptiness creeping upon you, hollowing you out but cannot word this great abomination you feel. This great humiliation. Your dignity in a diaper. Wet and pungent and a little salty to the taste. You just want to go Home now, that is all.

8. THIS WORLD IS NOT GOD'S CREATION

"The world as you perceive it cannot have been created by the Father, for the world is not as you see it. God created only the eternal, and everything you see is perishable. Therefore, there must be another world that you do not see."

[T-11.VII.1:1-3]

O ne of the most deeply rooted teachings and features in many religious systems is their stubborn unrelenting insistence that God created this world. They see this as His work and one for which He must be held accountable for at all times. This foolish and fallacious belief is the reason for the intense feelings of confusion and abiding futility that has hovered over mankind's consciousness down the ages. It is impossible to know God, while simultaneously believing He made this pile of junk. Because the knowing of Him is this world's disappearance. The erroneous belief that God made this world makes Him fearful, unintelligible and retaliative. How then can He be the God of Love? Instead we want to freeze all our communications with Him and condemn Him for what we both see and feel.

This world is not a holy sight but something entirely tasteless and festering, a merciless depot of many mindless cruelties, brutalities and an abiding sense of hopelessness and despair. Nothing can be clearly understood once we succumb to the foolish notion that God created this world! No further progress can be made! Because this belief places good and evil, creation and destruction, life and death, Christ and Anti-Christ on an equal footing. Both become real and are assigned almost equivalent power. Each constantly battles the other side for dominance. All of a sudden we think there is a real place where truth and illusions can meet to wage their eternal wars upon one another. Having accepted this belief, it is as if we have fallen down the rabbit hole and now like Alice are left perilously trying to weave something meaningful, magical, hopeful and worthwhile out of the many meaningless fragmented perceptions and cobwebs that adorn this world. Freeze from all such unguarded and fanciful thinking. Freeze from all such nonsense. If there is one certainty to this world, it is :-

> "God made it not. Of this you can be sure. What can He know of the ephemeral, the sinful and the guilty, the afraid, the suffering and lonely, and the mind that lives within a body that must die? You but accuse Him of insanity, to think He made a world where such things seem to have reality. He is not mad. Yet only madness makes a world like this."
>
> [W.152.6:2-7]

Einstein feared the findings of quantum mechanics. Its implications were enormous; that *"God does play dice with the Universe."* These findings presented to him a random arbitrary world without any meaningful justice and order, one run by happenstance alone. This he refused to believe. He was right. God does no play dice with the universe. He may be playful and creative but He does not gamble - except for maybe the odd game of 3-card monkey. In fact, God knows nothing of the universe we perceive. He knows nothing of the perishable, the sickly and the dying because illusions have no place in reality. Illusions cannot enter God's Mind. This is our own supreme fuck-up, yet one we consider our ego masterpiece. Time will remain always powerless to make any illusions real - in fact its only purpose is to relinquish them. Each illusion is just part of the fabric of a vast hallucinatory network experienced only in the dreaming mind of God's Son. The dreaming mind is the world - the awakened mind is God. Only the mind of the dreamer has any connection to God because this alone was Created by Him. The memory of God still remains in our minds as is the Knowledge, He gave. Yet this has been lost to our awareness. The mind of the dreamer is Whole-Mind + error. God only bestowed Whole-Mind and we invented error for ourselves. When all error is removed, mind is restored as Mind. Then the world disappears. But once error is believed, we lose all awareness of truth. All we see is a scrambled jigsaw of a gazillion pieces with no obvious meaningful relationships. Yet, hidden within each piece, truth remains intact waiting to be revealed to eyes ready to open. Error is sole cause, for which all illusions are effects. Sole cause for the relative existence, we see. Mind + error = split-mind = dreaming mind.

9. PERCEPTION AND THE DREAM NATURE OF EXISTENCE

Jesus said, "The Father's kingdom is like a person who wanted to kill someone powerful. While still at home he drew his sword and thrust it into the wall to find out whether his hand would go in. Then he killed the powerful one."

[The Gospel of Thomas]

What is all this talk of killing and swords? Is Jesus advocating that the Kingdom is reached through violence and blood spilling of a more powerful enemy? This is how your ego will naturally interpret this saying. This is because the ego interprets everything literally. It cannot rise about words and specifics. It cannot decode the powerful metaphors and deeper messages hidden behind words. Yet, Jesus is merely using words symbolically here to represent a higher understanding. One not easily decrypted by examining the words individually. The great Tantric Siddhas used this technique almost explicitly. They couldn't be bothered hiding their greatest teachings from the masses. What? steal around in the middle of the night trying to hide their teachings on papyri made from banana leaves? Not for them!

Instead they did something utterly revolutionary. They wrote them down directly and made them open secrets. Yet, they wrote the words down in a fashion that their meaning would not be apparent to an impure mind. That is they wrote them down as metaphors. The impure mind would be tricked into receiving a totally incorrect message. Its own evil motives would preclude it from accessing the decryption key that alone can unlock the true message. The meaning behind the words could only be successfully decrypted by a higher mind, a purer form of consciousness. A mind of altruistic and of noble intent, not one trying to exploit the teachings for selfish ends. The lower mind trapped in its web of biases and distortions would implement too narrow-band a filter to capture the true meaning of the message. It is as if one had modulated two different messages onto a single digital pulse-stream and then sent this bitstream out on the airwaves. The ego with its very narrow-banded filter would always pick up on the wrong message. The real message would bypass the ego's filter. Yet, the truly open mind that does not have any biases would possess a very broadband filter and could easily decode it.

Jesus never advocates using any form of violence in thought, word or deed. He knows that what you give, you will receive. The sword symbolically represents the sword of discriminating wisdom. Because real wisdom is uncovered only after you first learn how to ask the right questions. This sword can easily cut through all falseness and duality. 'While still at home' means being absolutely centered and in a pure state of awareness. You are calm and unruffled and in a deep meditative state. Your inner eye of "Shiva-Netra" is turned inwards on oneself. Pure awareness is non-identified awareness. It is therefore not identified with any form, attachment, obsession, thought, emotional state, memory or desire. This places you in a powerful state of capaciousness and super-mental fluidity so as to receive all that which your identifications normally block. You are feeling quiescent, silent, aware, empowered and in harmony with yourself. The wall is representative of illusion. You can also consider it the wall of perception, the screen of Maya, or the void. This wall you must successfully penetrate beyond, if you are to reach beyond appearances to truth. It is the formless passive mirror into which we project the apparent outside world of form through our thoughts and beliefs. It witnesses the various transformations and transmutations that make up the inner volcanic activity of our minds. These all appear as reflections on this wall. The wall thus witnesses the mind's incessant activities in a very direct manner.

It would be a great mistake to think of this wall, as some abstraction. Everything you see in this world is part of it. Your hands, your body, the helicopters flying by in the starlit night, the neon signs, the business men with their briefcases sporting intense lascivious looks on their faces as hookers drag on behind them are all part of this wall. As are all the stars and galaxies and the TV show you are currently watching. The discriminating wisdom of the sword gives it power to cut through all those foolish beliefs, strange notions and ideologies that you have been sold in the marketplace. Thus you will be able to uproot them. As non-attachment and non-identification increases, you become able to reach beyond the wall. So will the real world be revealed to you. So you come to know directly that the screen of perception never had any true existence. It merely depicted your mind-states and their unreal content. Your wishfulness and idols show up on the wall as do all your false beliefs, fears and expectations. The wall was never apart from your mind.

Remaining continuously aware of your thoughts, you increase in self-awareness and your thoughts come less-and-less. Now thoughts come more like lonely clouds, in a clear and serene sky. Yet the wall of your perception is composed of nothing but these. By not investing mental energy in the various frightening and powerful figures and symbols you see outside you, you come to know they have no independent power apart from you. Non-investment means remaining as a non-identified, non-complicit and non-reactive awareness. Yes, all their apparent power was established through your investment. Relinquishing this investment, they soon lose all their force. No seeming external figure or event need be feared because none exists apart from our own mind. Salvation, freedom and the end of darkness comes from within.

Killing the powerful one signals the end of the ego's reign. For the ego is very powerful in illusion where it exercises its great skills at craftiness, denial and self-deception. It has a powerful capacity to circumvent the important while binding your attention to the marginal, relative and worthless. It wants to keep the knowledge of your true inheritance well guarded, hidden and out of your reach. This is does through its various temptations and mind distractions. Yet by weeding out all elements of wrong-mindedness from your thoughts, you can regain awareness of your essential purity and reach back to your original and immaculate state of Mind. Mind as it was Created by God. Mind which retains no foreign, unwanted and unneeded elements to darken it. Thus does the Real world become reflected once again back into your perception. Thus the mirror of mind, that is perception is restored to its original formless essence and purity. You are placed now in a readiness state for revelations and final release. Ready to end perception and duality forever and bring back eternity into your awareness.

"The real world can actually be perceived. All that is necessary is a willingness to perceive nothing else."

[T-11.VII.2:6-7]

ZEN AND THE ART OF DREAM MACHINE MAINTENANCE

Once, my back wedded to the solid cliff,
I sat silently, bathed in the full moon's light.

I counted there ten thousand shapes,
None with substance save the moon's own glow.

The pristine mind is empty as the moon,
I thought, and like the moon, freely shines.

By what I knew of moon I knew the mind,
Each mirror to each, profound as stone.

[Poem By Han Shan]

Han Shan echoes the true relationship between purity of mind and one's perception in his very simple, lucid and penetrating poem further below. Once the moon's light illuminates, manifold objects are seen. Many diverse shadows and phantom shapes seem to spring to life. Yet, all these phantom shapes arise as a consequence of the moon's light. They have no reality apart from it and no self-nature of their own. Without the moon's light, these apparitions would cease to be seen. Their seeming existence is contingent on darkness, apart from which they have none. All their apparent motions and changes in texture and shape are a result of the distortionary effects of the earth's atmosphere and the wind. The moon represents the single true celestial light high up above irradiating the world of darkness below. The moon's light remains pristine and pure at its source for here it is unimpeded and undistorted. It is simply shining equally and unconditionally on all without any preference. It is not presenting any biases on where to shine, nor introducing any obstructions.

Similarly the clear pristine inner light within us is the Knowledge of Spirit. This light remains pure and unimpeded at our Source. As it illuminates the world of our perceptions, the distortion of our false beliefs gives rise to the wind of our mental movements and judgments which then distort and toss everything about. Thus giving rise to many diverse forms, shadows and false appearances that show up in the world we perceive. Collectively all these false appearances arise from the lens of our wrong-mindedness. Reality remains always formless and pristine, yet this reality can only be known when we illuminate without distortion through the natural light of Spirit. The light of Spirit is without hindrance so long as we do not oppose it. It does not have to be created – it already self-exists. It sees nothing on the level of form and so it brings us to our true perceptions. It brings us into awareness of the formless One that is all around us. Everything that seems to exist only does so, because of impurity and distortion. Yet, there is a real world and true reality that exists beyond appearances that Spirit can guide us to. As the Course teaches, *"The Holy Spirit is the Christ Mind which is aware of the knowledge beyond perception." [T-5.I.5:1]*

There was once a female Zen master named Chaitanya. One day, she was carrying a bucket of water from a well and was watching the moon's reflection in it, when she tripped up and fell to the ground. Since all the water was gone, the moon's reflection was no longer visible. She then turned her eyes upwards and saw the real moon. In that instant, she was enlightened. She had realized that the bucket carrying water was akin to mind and its thoughts. Recognized that the entire world of perception was being forged, fabricated and distorted by her thoughts, before being presented to her awareness as perception. These thoughts in her mind were functioning as intermediaries between truth and her awareness of it. They were shaping her experience of truth into something totally alien and distorted. She was never biting into the real enchilada, but having to go through the middlemen of thought.

Her many false understandings, incorrect interpretations, wishes, attachments and fears were akin to the water rippling in the bucket. As a result of the incessant rippling and rocking motion of her thought, the real moon of truth was being shaped, twisted and lessening in clarity. The real was being transformed into the false through these distortions. This then gave rise to the world of false appearances, she saw. Similarly, when we are too caught up, in this vast web of our own mind's distortionary beliefs, we cannot ever hope to glimpse the real world, that is beyond these appearances. The moon of the real is constantly undergoing shape distortions, transformations and obfuscations because of the rocking motion of our minds and the fluctuations of our thoughts. In that moment, she had understood that the real was never contingent on her own individual biases, beliefs and predilections. It was independent of her perception and thoughts. It could only be known by a mind, that was healed of the ignorance of all false and obfuscating beliefs.

Only this Mind can illuminate with the true light of Spirit. The solution is not out-there in perception but in-here in ourselves. We must reach to the faultless understanding of the infinite all–knowing Spirit. Only this Mind is motionless, pure and radiant. It cannot distort for it holds no contradiction to itself. So it rests in eternal quiescence and does not rock about capriciously as do all ego thoughts. Reaching to the light and letting it through, is simple a process of unblocking its path outward. We must remove all false understandings which function as obstacles that impede its outward progression.

So what is the origin of our dream machine? Part of the story is that most of us do not believe in unconditional love, peace and happiness. So we become willing to settle instead for conditional love, peace and happiness? Take happiness for example. We cannot even think of happiness without attaching some outer objective or hope to it. Our happiness must always have some form attached to it. So is it always a conditional happiness dependent on external proxies. We crave fame and notoriety and so are willing to engage in endless plastic surgeries, charades, games of showmanship and shameless self-advertisements to reach our end objective. We want that dream house in the Bahamas and are willing to sell out on all our values and ideals and the wellbeing of those around us to accomplish our dream. We want to be the top athlete in our field of endeavor and become willing to do whatever it takes to reach our pinnacle. We will drug our bodies with every wicked concoction known to man, to temporarily stimulate and boost our performance. So we sell out on all those who believed in us and rob other promising athletes of their rightful accolades.

Yes, the dream machine is injected with much wickedness, venom and callous disregard. We want to manipulate those around us and force them to change to meet our demands - forgetting completely they are existentially impelled to follow the dictates of their own self-natures. Yet, our voracious appetites for manipulation knows no bounds. We are no longer satisfied controlling all that others do, we want to change who they Are. Yes, we go in for the kill, searching for their fatal flaw and critical vulnerability, that Achilles heel by which we can completely unravel them. For our goal is to heartlessly subjugate all into mere backslapping flunkies to serve at the altar to our own special selves. We want to smell them out, find their weakness and then tear them apart leaving only the shell or carcass for the dogs. We would leave them with no emotional center, barren of all self respect, ideals and integrity. Rotting corpses, dead on the inside, lost to themselves, no longer possessing any capacity for laughter, love or joy - fit only for the morgue now. Is it any wonder then that we are not happy? For it is certain that our happiness is a monstrous beast that is both blind and cruel, one that enjoys that carnival where it gets to feed on all its anthropophagous delights.

So it is, we go about our lives, making dress rehearsals for our happiness in front of an invisible mirror - pandering to the lion of our own distorted self images and its insatiable demands. We have given up on the ghost of true happiness, so long ago and feel we would not want it anyway. So we flounder pathetically in our efforts on how to go about it and end-up looking so shame-faced before the world. We have become something else now, creatures of sloth and indulgence, sponges that have soaked up all the world's poisons. Mummified gimps that have assimilated every wrong idea, every tarnished notion, every fad sold. Our minds percolate now only with the seedy rivers of bile, sweat and amniotic fluids and those noxious clouds of gas bubbling over in the marketplace. The ego neurons are having a feast because we have willfully transformed this ever-defiled space into a den of sacredness. We cannot even look at the moon and stars without attaching our own special investments to them. We want to rope them down and make them our pandering subjugates and foot pillows. The Course teaches us there is no way to find happiness in this world, because the world itself is an unhappy place. It was born out of error and reflects nothing more than our futile attempts to attack God and have things our own way. It therefore has no value or understanding worth redeeming and all its paths lead nowhere.

We cannot pawn in anything we find here. Eventually each of us is most expeditiously manhandled from the store to try his luck another life. This remains but a place of hide and seek, a coven where we can cast our spells on the witless while searching for that specialness we feel God denied us. A place of indulgence and temporary pleasures, all of which are tragically cut short to exact an equivalent amount of pain. The scales of illusion need to be balanced at the end of day. Their net worth must always sum to zero, signifying the emptiness that they are. Our desire for specialness comes with a heavy price-tag. It costs us exclusion from our brothers, our healing, right-minds and truth. Through it we lose sight of our invulnerability and become pitiful figures of sand spouting out our vomit and pomposities, while inwardly thinking ourselves marvelous and absolutely majestic creatures. We think ourselves living gods, but remain just pope-the-dopes. We mentally ejaculate all our verbal diarrhea to an audience of one. Or maybe there is some ragged toothless lady in the audience, who has not left yet that gives us an evil snarling look as she shuffles her way out in her moldy attire.

The Course teaches in contradistinction that all true happiness is to be found only in the direct realization that we are not here. This realization changes everything. When we fully understand and embrace it into the core of our hearts, we are meaningfully transformed. No longer satisfied to paint or smear another pretty face upon this mannequin, or to accessorize it with a costly wardrobe. All those Herculean efforts invested in filling in the cracks of a high maintenance zombie will be expended no more. And all the time the greatest treasures were buried deep inside our coconut.

"How else can you find joy in a joyless place except by realizing that you are not there?"   [T-6.II.6:1]

THE PRISONER'S DILEMMA

In Plato's allegory of *'The Cave'*, Plato is aiming to have us grasp our real nature as mind. He wants us to escape our prison-house. Wants us to understand how this bleak world of appearances only arose from the darkness of our own ignorance. Like the prisoners, we too are all huddled and bound together in our shackles and chains, sitting in a dark underground space. A space devoid of real light. A space devoid of the knowledge of Spirit. We have been down in this dark cave for millions of years. So long, in fact that we have forgotten, we are in a cave. Like the prisoners we believe that the multiplicity of strange shapes, shadows and distortions that are showing up on our cave wall are real in themselves. We call this life. So we articulate our entire dream fiction out of the shadows and phenomena of the unreal. We do not see that our tiresome dream fiction is just a reflection of a belief system that has been projected onto our cave walls.

Ultimately our attempts to make our shadows meaningful cannot succeed and so we remain joyless and confused. We do not recognize that we are blind because almost no one has ever seen the light. As enough time passes we forget our blindness entirely and seek satisfaction instead in the hallucinatory universe each of us makes. Every now and then, one of us prisoners, finally escapes from the cave. He walks out into *'the Real world'* and embraces the sun of Knowledge. Blinded by its tremendous light he finds it difficult to adjust at first. He has become enlightened and is just beginning to grasp the enormity of it all. Trying to understand the monumental implications of all that is seen in this newfound light. In that moment he recognizes that everything he knew up to that moment was empty and illusory. He was just being presented with a world of shadows which only ever seemed real in the absence of light. But now he has uncovered the true source of light and knows what is seen by it alone is Truth.

Unfortunately none of the other prisoners will listen to him. They think him quite mad. He is saying that the shadows and forms they see are not real and entirely devoid of substance. That their seeming presence and existence is contingent on a world where darkness and distortion rule. This shadow-world can never make any sense and has no hope. Hope is only found by uncovering the real light within and reaching the Sun of Knowledge. Much in the same way that Jesus teaches in the Course that *"There is not thought in all the world that leads to any understanding of the laws it follows, nor the Thought that it reflects."* [W.134.13:2]

Back now in the cave it is hard for this prisoner who escaped to get excited about shadows anymore. Like trying to get excited about a magician's tricks once you know how they are done. All the magic has disappeared. Once you have penetrated the trick to its core, it loses all its former majesty, wonder and brilliance. It sits there unfrocked and utterly lame. Sitting back there now in the cave he has the reward-less task of helping the other prisoners escape. He realizes his shadow watching days are over. These abilities have become severely atrophied due to a lack of interest and focus. Ironically, he feels more handicapped in the cave now than before and eager to leave for good. He cannot launch any enthusiasm for shadows, but unfortunately this is where the other prisoners wholeheartedly invest themselves.

Moreover, he cannot find any common thread or language by which he can articulate the meaningful world up above. He finds he is limited to using extremely archaic and limited forms of communication, such as words, symbols, images and forms to explain to them the world of light. The shadow world does not possess an adequate context by which he can port direct knowledge and visceral understanding of the Real. Because this context was born and made out of darkness. He feels bound by very limited concepts and those lifeless ideas that perfume this deeply conditioned space to explain the supra-conceptual and wordless Reality. There is no way for him to transfer his experience and higher understanding. Each needs to discover it for themselves. Like the prisoners, most dreamers in the relative existence reject the Enlightened. At best, they bundle them in with all those eccentrics, ill-adjusted misfits and crackpots. Since most are deluded themselves, they do not have the necessary credentials to distinguish authenticity. The situation is worsened by the fact that the Enlightened will not reinforce the thought system that rules the world. They will not sing lullabies to keep one asleep. Their noble aim is to awaken the world and set it on fire using the light of true understanding.

In Plato's allegory, the prisoner who has escaped is Socrates. He has become illuminated and has entered the gate of truth. Rediscovered his original essence of Mind. The Source of all Being and 'non-Being'. This pure essence of mind has been called Buddha-mind or Bodhicitta. It is essentially empty and is divested of all that false and trashy content that has become overlaid through millennia. Accumulations built up in the worldly mind-conditioning shelter. This mind in its essence is unimpeded, radiant and pure and sees instantly through all false appearances, which then disappear before it like mists before the Sun. The cave, on the other-hand represents our accumulated ignorance and the shadows reflect nothing more than our current mental handicaps. Our failure to evolve past all contradictions formed from misbeliefs. In the end Socrates is deemed to have too much light, penetrative insight and kinship with the unknown. He does not fit in well with the Status Quo and is considered an unsettling influence. His illumination had rendered him too dangerous for the ruling elite. So they accuse him of corrupting the youth of Athens and sentence him to death by poisoning. Socrates of course knows there is no death, just a dream body ceasing to function in a dream. Yet, his pure essence of mind remains inexhaustible, boundless and invulnerable and will go on unimpeded.

> **"Perception is the result of learning. In fact, perception**
> *is* **learning, because cause and effect are never**
> **separated."**   **[M-4.I.1:2-3]**

When we wake up in the morning, we are just substituting one dream world for another. The forms of the dreams may change a little but the essential content goes on the same. The mind of the dreamer hasn't changed in any fundamental way. As its dreamer, we naturally believe what each shows because each dream reflects our beliefs. The dreams of the daytime may seem a little more substantial and less variable. Their aspects may seem a little more solid because of our familiarity, our conditioning and all the filters we impose. This reduces the variation and makes the transitions seem less exotic. But as we reflect on our life experiences from five, ten or even fifty years ago, we easily see that none is more substantial now than the dreams we had last night. Any dream which seems more substantial is often due to our excessive attachments and deeply rooted psychological issues. Our dream lives then are not so different from traumatic experiences, in which we continuously relive certain chosen nightmares at the expense of present reality. The world of our imagination can indeed seem more substantial through repeated emphasis.

HYSTERIA, TRAUMA AND PTSD

In one of Oliver Sack's books, "*The Man who Mistook his Wife for A Hat*", he delves into the case history of one of his patients named Gianfranco. Gianfranco had grown up in the Italian town of Pontito and his early life experiences there had a tremendous emotional impact on him. His entire psychological functioning was affected. He became obsessed with his early memories and experiences to the exclusion of his present day reality. It was like the video of his life had stopped and was now just replaying over and over the same old material. In ways, it is similar to those diagnosed with hysteria, trauma or PTSD. Often people with such afflictions take in just enough of their outer world to stay alive. The inner world of their thoughts and emotions can become obsessed upon to the exclusion to all else. So does the world of "regular" perception disappear from view. Yet even in these inner landscapes they can become very narrow-banded. They cannot successfully edit past their traumatic experience, nor can they integrate it. So it hangs there as a disconnect that they are powerless to blend with the rest of their lives.

It is like part of their minds is functioning as a quasi-independent center that is cutoff from the rest. An invisible barricade now envelopes some area of their mental real estate that can never be breached. No probing thoughts are allowed in without their security clearance. It is like any secret and covert government program but it is all happening within their private worlds. Groups of thoughts and emotions become islanded, clustered and frozen off from everything else. Unreachable and unable to engage in a healthy interflow with the rest of their organism. Instead these are hermetically sealed off and relived over-and-over. This becomes their sacred turf and yet it holds the key to their entire liberation. In the extreme, the mind of such a person can become polymorphic in nature. That is they deal with their world by splitting up in a number of distinct personalities, each specifically tuned and honed for addressing a certain range of issues and conflicts. Thus they can exhibit symptoms of multiple personality disorder (MPD).

Consciously they can know what is happening. They are able to digest and deal with their material at the conscious and even supraliminal levels. But at the subliminal levels, the trolls of devastation and self-destruction go to work. Demolition teams are called in to their underworld, bulldozers and forklifts start to tear away at their very foundations. Collapse is imminent and they have a deep mortal dread. They find themselves threading on thin ice trying to keep their emotional selves intact. The first evidence of this great underground destruction starts to show up in their changed behavioral patterns. They may no longer engage in their former hobbies, nor go out much anymore. An apathy has set in that they are powerless to decode. Nor can they trace its roots. They may become obsessed with acting out certain behaviors, or engaging in rituals. In the case of those suffering from extreme hysteria, ideational obsessions can become so powerful as to induce symptoms that mimic neuropathy, paralysis or stroke, even though no physiological damage is evident.

So Gianfranco continued with his inward visions of the Pontito from his youth. He was deeply invested in the emotional experiences of his early life, which were constantly being recreated as his present. This had become the surrogate mother of all his perceptions, moods and thoughts, substituting completely for his present day existence. We often mistakenly believe that we are in a different situation, that our dreams and perceptions have a semblance of reality and truth to them. Yet they are all carefully built up from the residual of all ours fears and obsessions. Thus we filter and shape the world of our perceptions from a very diverse spectrum of potentialities. All is dream until we wake-up. Enlightenment is nothing, but waking up.

Then we recognize all was dream. In an instant a very broad-banded recognition dawns that leads entirely to the disappearance of all dreams. For they were always on the same order of reality and entirely devoid of any substance. They just reflected our mind's unreal content.

TAKING RESPONSIBILITY FOR OUR DREAMS, AS THE MEANS TO LIBERATION

Dreams are our perceptual temper tantrums and ineffectual protests against Reality. Our choice is always simple. It is one between dreaming or awaking, illusion or Reality, spacetime or Eternity, the ego or the Christ Mind. When you awake, you will realize that every dream was spun from inside you. You were doing this to yourself. You were the director, producer, cast and set of every dream you ever made.

> **"The body's serial adventures, from the time of birth to dying are the theme of every dream the world has ever had. The "hero" of this dream will never change, nor will its purpose. Though the dream itself takes many forms, and seems to show a great variety of places and events wherein its "hero" finds itself, the dream has but one purpose, taught in many ways. This single lesson does it try to teach again, and still again, and yet once more; that it is the cause and not effect. And you are its effect, and cannot be its cause."**

> **[T-27.VIII.3:1-5]**

Each of us must take responsibility for our dreams. If we are having nightmares, we must realize that we are responsible for these too.

Usually they are the natural byproduct of our countless unwise ego investments. We do not guard our mind and thoughts vigilantly enough and have allowed ourselves to become poor decision makers. Remembering constantly that all we see is dream, is the surefire recipe for waking up. Because taking this responsibility correctly identifies the dreamer. When we react we are identifying with the dream and entering a deeper sleep. Writing off any grievance, source of guilt, wrong-doing, hardship or sin to what is outside yourself is to remain asleep. You must accept that you are the one and only cause of all you see and experience. Then be prepared to relinquish all your grievances through the practice of quantum forgiveness. So do you release yourself from all effects of your wrong-mindedness. By undoing from your mind all that never was, you come to the place of healing and enable the real to shine through your mind.

> **"The secret of salvation is but this: that you are doing this unto yourself. No matter what the form of the attack, this still is true. Whoever takes the role of enemy and of attacker, still is this the truth. Whatever seems to be the cause of any pain and suffering you feel, this is still true. For you would not react at all to figures in a dream, you knew that you were dreaming. Let them be as hateful and as vicious as they may, they could have no effect on you unless you failed to recognize it is your dream."**

> **[T-27.VIII.10:1-6]**

The great tenth century Indian mystic Atisha once said *"Think that all phenomena are like Dreams."* This is his first sutra in his seven points of mind training and it is one of the most powerful sutras for reaching Enlightenment, *'Here-and-Now'*. His remaining six sutras are for handling the mental implosion and great unsettling that occurs post Enlightenment. Many have entered Enlightenment on a single hearing of it. In an instant, they realized for themselves that **'All is One, and all is Mind'**. That all apparent boundaries are pseudo and fictitious. Boundaries are of the ego. They are formed from *'The Separation Belief'*, which the ego hopes we will enfranchise. The illusion of multiplicity, of many minds, things, names and forms arise out of distortion. So we appear to live in a false construct or artifice. Such distortions introduce a dark cover over our mind that precludes us then from witnessing reality directly. We have put on the dark glasses of the ego and this gives the One-Mind the illusion of many. Simply relinquish the ego and then the world of multiplicity and duality disappears forever. You return Home, uncover your real perceptions and come to the recognition that the Eternal was always Here.

DR. GOBBLER'S KNOB'S WISDOM ON SAMSARA AND NIRVANA

One day, I was asking Dr. Gobbler's Knob if he was familiar with the Buddha's teachings. I wanted to find out his interpretation of the Buddha's teaching pertaining to both the Samsara and Nirvana. He jumped up immediately in enthusiasm and said *"Really, the whole thing is very simple. The Samsara and Nirvana are the exact same reality. But when experienced out of completely different states of mind, they seem to be deeply contrasted and to contradict one another. The sea of samsara is the sea of phenomenalism. This is Reality when seen and experienced through split-mind. Nirvana is Reality as known through Whole-Mind. Our experience of reality is never separate from our states of mind. Because what we witness arises from within. Whole-Mind because it is completely divested of all the impurity of false beliefs is not really a state of mind at all, but Truth itself. Just like water needs to be exactly 100C before it can turn into vapor, similarly mind enters the vaporous state of consciousness only when it has become completely purified.*

*Enlightenment is taking the boat to the other shore. This is the voyage from split-mind to Whole-Mind, from ignorance to understanding. There is no other shore. This shore **is** the other shore. Only your understanding is ever changing. You cannot really take the boat, because it would be split-mind entering the boat which would keep you tied to this shore. Anywhere you travel in perception, any method or vehicle you use in the object-orientated universe, will only bind you further to this shore. Taking the boat is simply a metaphor for directing the arrow of your awareness inwards. So you come to clearly see all the devastation that has been inflicted upon the altar of your mind through misbeliefs. Facing this immense state of disrepair, you fall either into abject despair or decide to have it healed. This is what the Atonement is for. This is its holy purpose. The Buddha's teaching is an allegory. He is symbolically relating that 'this shore' represents perception, spacetime and the pseudo-physical universe of bodies. The so called object-orientated existence with all its functions, concepts, symbols and forms.*

On this shore, there is learning and self-improvement and there also seems to be, death, suffering, chaos and taxes. All this madness seems to hold us a prisoner. On this shore, mind is viewed only as an epiphenomenon of matter, spirit is unknown and God is forgotten. In fact God seems to be becoming increasingly obsolete in our scheme of things. He certainly seems powerless over illusions. So He is put on the shelf as some mysterious amulet only to be pulled down when we are ready to spout out again our litany of miseries, during times of crisis. So it is with the Samsara, we travel through it again and again, through entire oceans of illusions but never reaching the Real. We go from birth-to-death over-and-over, developing ever subtler intellects, more refined forms, more cunning and ingenious intellects and ever more 'cultured' tastes.

Each birth we feel the world as fresh again, as if it were unknown to us before. We see it as some stranger who stole into our room and flung himself onto our beds. Then as we proceed through it, it becomes the old ragged blanket we will not throw away because we are cold. So our mind directs us on new misadventures, chasing more idols and yet another futile dream. We paint our skeleton up and go out the door, dressed to impress. We cannot even smell, our own B.O. under the cologne of the dead rotting skeletons still in our minds from lives gone by. We cannot recognize, nor distinguish the ancient and lifeless thought patterns that construct each new dream. So we remain bound to this shore waiting at the pier for a boat that will never come.

*So taking the boat to the other shore, is not a going out - but a going in. It is a sudden penetrating inflection of the mind that cuts through the manifold world of appearances. The mind becomes absolutely discontinuous to the past and is divested of all the experiences it has entertained up to now. The umbilical cord has been cut. All one's life history is gone up in smoke, because it is known now to have never truly existed at all. It represented just meaningless aspects and events woven into the fabric of a dream, splotches of paint and color artlessly thrown to a canvas. A canvas that is now seen as just a canvas. One is no longer hypnotized or attracted to it, because one has awoken and broken the seal. Osho calls enlightenment the "Quantum leap in consciousness". He taught that true understanding of the nature of the quantum leap was in recognizing that there is '**no-where**' to jump to, '**nothing with which**' to jump and '**no-one**' there to do the jumping. This is the exact right understanding.*

Suddenly the old world is gone, together with all its mysteries, pantomimes and artful deceptions. Gone too are all the Oscar winning performances, notable moments and heart rendering tragedies. Gone are all the dreams nourished through its laws, functions, concepts, symbols and equations. The dream figures that were intricately tied to each dream no longer exist. They have been put back in their box, which remains always empty. The healing of split-mind has occurred. You find yourself now born again but on the other shore. As Jesus's taught:- 'Truly one must be born again before they can enter my father's Kingdom'. When one arrives at the other shore, one has a direct experience of being fully embraced by an absolute and joyful unity, an uncontainable oneness with nothing outside it, a perfect seamless unity in which all things have their Being. You understand that things are not things but thoughts arising in your mind. Images appearing and disappearing in correlation to your thoughts and having no other cause."

You have a direct in-seeing that spacetime is being spontaneously generated out of your mind. The mind that knows this unequivocally has come to naked perception and enters at will the portal of the eternal. It has become one with God in full awareness. Entered the realm of the unconditioned, where the crystal clear pristine and "alive" nature of All is experienced once again. One realizes that there never was a time when one was not and that all Reality is beyond time. Yes, a dark overlay of wrong-mindedness, personified as the ego came to sit for a while over the One-Mind, making the One appear as many. Without this dark-overlay, the Samsara is clearly seen and experienced as Nirvana. They are not two different and distinct places, Samsara and Nirvana, Hell and Heaven. Our mistaken view and interpretations produces our experience of hell while our correct understanding reveals the reality of Heaven. Mind distorted and tormented with the dark conceptual overlay of wrong-mindedness experiences the Samsara. Our purpose is to remove this false overlay, so that the natural light of Spirit can stream through effortlessly and unhindered, illuminating the Reality that is Nirvana." Having said all this, Dr. Gobbler's Knob finally ended his brief speech.

"In timelessness you rest, while time goes by without its touch upon you, for your rest can never change in any way at all."

[W.109.5:2]

10. THE SON

Most dreamers, are firmly ego entrenched. Vain ego desires pop up out of nowhere which then determine all their decisions and actions. Their serial misadventures tell a tale of a mad script gone dreadfully wrong, one spewing its guts everywhere and behaving like a powerful cataclysmic force smearing all their perceptions. Yes, a Trojan virus shredding and thrashing everything they touch weaving a toxic cloud around their minds that tarnishes and poisons all they see. Out of this cloud of chaos and mindless madness arises the emergent property of their identities. Identities that are in constant flux and more like maelstroms and tornadoes that suck all witless beings into the eye of their powerful vortex. Such people function more like organic whirlwinds that have no meaningful purpose nor direction. They are caught in a low pressure system that incessantly blows them into the lower mind of the ego world. So they may appear opportunistic at times, devilish at others and sometimes even operating under the guise of humanitarianism. The center of these maelstroms is venomously guarded by the ego. All that ever happens within its torrential manifold is always perfectly correlated to their ego interests.

These dreamers have no will of their own as such. The soil of their minds only sprouts weeds. Their motives are always suspect. Any sense of volition they may perpetrate is an illusion generated from those incidental decisions the dream elicits from them. They remain pliant and spineless, and yet can masquerade as the most jovial of friends. They are never to be trusted at any time or place. They shoulder surf the dream and change as the dream changes, nor do they see it in their power to change it. No, it is always the dream instead which mercilessly tosses and flings them about. So they flow hither and thither, like driftwood – their entire lives meaningless tales of dream fiction. They fake-it till they make-it and will justify doing today, what they found most deplorable yesterday. These are the creatures of contradiction and self-interest. Variable as waves on the seashore, as volatile as dry ice and as capricious as the stock market. They remain stunning examples of how true cause-and-effect relationships can get horribly reversed once one becomes dream identified. There is nothing in them where one finds rest, stability and reassurance. These are the perennial chameleons of change and the shameless dream exploiters.

Yet they – the exploiters must become the exploited. It is true that they can so easily adjust and adapt, transfigure or prostitute themselves to each opportune situation. True that they will pillage and plunder all new idols, as flowers for their altars of vanity and specialness. Yet, they remain hopelessly blind to the immense valuable treasures hidden behind the facade of dreams. Creating and manipulating a field of illusions simply to serve one's own interests must lead to a loss of Identity. The dream must become savage and hunt down the dreamer and seek to catch him in its snares. The shape shifters become blinded by their own idol identifications and worshiping of form. They lose sight of the formless and the true vision of spirit. The outer world confers on them their tattered identities with much pomp and ceremony, but it will promptly snatch away the tattered rags and certificates it bestows at a moment's notice. Each and every moment it is tyrannically dictating what they will shape into it, defining their special boundaries and limits, determining what is considered a 3-strikes transgression or a mere slap on the hand misdemeanor.

One day, it will want to be paid in full. It will wrench them from their pretty paradises and circles of ignominious fools and whirl them into the gutter to be pissed upon by elephants, dogs, pigs and toads. Yes, they will have their celebrity DUI mug-shot, just in case you missed that. Yet, in church, they are always pious, putting on airs, almost expecting us to prostrate down before them and marvel at their innocence and purity. And yet all we see shining there are their hidden motives, their evil eyes hooded over and their blood-drenched lips. Next moment, we find them at the bars and brothels consumed by a ravenous spirit of mindless intoxication - shouting obscenities, prostituting their bodies or licking the boots of their compadres. We all know those freewheeling chameleons, who slip and slide through life, whose codes of trust and honor are seasonal at best. Those who always rationalize the path that is most advantageous to themselves. There is no dependable entity in them. Nothing progressive and lasting can be built on the rocky, jagged and shaky foundations of their lives. We will no longer sip from the cup of their old world ideologies. They carry no immortal signature, no regal stamp, nor seal or anything else one would care to listen to. Theirs is but a cacophony of blabbering dissonant voices banging out a rubber stamp agenda.

Then there is a second type of dreamer. These fortunate ones have been given a glimpse of their immortal Identity. Too insufficient perhaps to escape the dream entirely, but enough to unify all their decisions and actions. This group is on the choo-choo train that is most definitely homeward bound. They have experienced a vision of their changeless and radiant Self. So they harmonize their actions in correlation to the vision they have received. Their decisions become effortless with time. All their weeds of anxiety, unrest, apathy, angst and confusion are now becoming uprooted, dismantled and dispossessed for good. Attuning themselves to the inner Voice of inspiration and guidance, they are no longer content to empower the outer world to rule and manipulate them in any way. Nor do they continue to make investments in it. The experience(s) that brought them in contact with their Identity may have been a holy instant, a near death experience (NDE), revelations or some other key experience? It does not matter what because the taste of truth is the same no matter what ocean it is sipped from or from whatever vortex point in the dream we may stumble upon it. With this experience, comes a most definite certitude and conviction, a revelation that cannot be denied.

One sees for themselves a reality they had never been aware of up until that moment. A reality that has been so cruelly and heartlessly ignored or dismissed, like the stains on last night's bed-sheets. A reality tossed amid the dregs and cesspools of humanity or into the spittoon full of cigarette butts and ashes. But it was always here hidden behind the pinfolds and menageries of stuffed animals. Not seen and squarely missed through the jaundiced eyes of judgment and worldly ambition. They saw for themselves something incredulous but not beyond credibility. It made them realize that all is not what it seems. Their Identity now becomes the silent all powerful touchstone around which their entire world moves. They use it to vaporize illusions, to cleanse themselves and to retain clarity in their perceptions so that they can protect themselves from all those pandering dream propagandists, deceptive proselytizers, fear mongers and magicians of the world. They realize that to forget oneself as the dreamer is to begin the descent into evil dreams. To lose awareness of one's Identity, is the invite all illusions to enter.

They do not seek to escape the world, while still believing in it, nor do they seek to purchase it. They remain always above it, like the lotus blossom born in mud but which the mud touches not. Having regained awareness of their original purity, they see the mud of the world is powerless to diminish their beauty in any way. They have now a developing **will** and a new quality in them that remains unchanging in content and purpose. One that rises safely above the exigencies of circumstance and all the storms of life. Continuing to be guided by the inspiration of their inner vision, they have become transformed into beacons of constancy and hope in a changing world. If the world becomes merciless and cruel, they do not become vile. If the world comes pandering and full of praise, they remain unruffled and humble. With time, they become noted for their honesty, trustworthiness, incorruptible integrity, dependability and benevolence. A fixed rock on which all salvation can depend. Their dream-lives are happy because they rule the dream. Nor can it ever infringe upon their pure motives or integrity.

THE SON'S TRUE IDENTITY AND PURPOSE

The Identity of God's Son remains forever unchangeable and incorruptible. Our infinite worth was established by God in the instant of our Creation. Placing us at one with the Source of all unconditional love, peace, life and joyous sustenance. As a Creator, like our Father, the Son is a veritable pillar of strength and meaning. An enduring Love that remains unbound and forever increasing. He does not flicker nor vacillate, nor is his Identity open the flux of contingency, shifting patterns and emerging circumstances. All in the relative world is powerless to change our Identity and its Knowledge in any way. Our real Self can be totally depended upon always. In dream-time, we may appear wavering, or uncertain at times. We can be two tongued, drenched in turmoil, even hopelessly ensnared in wicked dreams of darkness and evil, yet does the essence of our reality remains forever unchanging, radiant and incapable of any diminishment.

God's Love for His Son is for keeps. Our true purpose here is Love's extension, for this is our Identity. God needs us to extend the Love by which we were created and by which we come to know our Self. This Love can never be separated from itself, nor its Creations which are its extensions. There is no distinction between God and you who are in complete union with Him. *"The Son of God has merely disappeared into his Father, as his Father has in him. The world has never been at all. Eternity remains a constant state." [W.169.6:5-7]* As His progeny you retain what you extend. As we extend His light, we grow in our shared magnificence. Extend all His power, joy and omnipotence and you will come to know them as your own. For they are truly part of your divine inheritance. You Are a Creator of perfection. Creation is your only real purpose and the only one in Eternity you retain. Forgiveness is the closest this world has that resembles the powers of Creation. It remains our only true purpose in time.

> **"A co-creator with the Father must have a Son. Yet must this Son have been created like Himself. A perfect being, all-encompassing and all-encompassed, nothing to add and nothing taken from; not born of size nor place nor time, nor held to limits or uncertainties of any kind. Here do the means and end unite as one, nor does this one have any end at all."**
>
> **[T-24.VII.7:1-4]**

Who inside you mindlessly dismisses your powers of Creation? Who inside you sees you as a failure? Who is it that refuses to accept your Sonship? Yes, we all have that trailer-trash persona singing into our ears 24x7. The voice of negativity, that is our greatest enemy. Our ego obstinacies have cost us awareness of Heaven. Yet we remain always one with our Source. This one irrefutable fact cannot be changed. We can only choose to hide from it and go into denial of our birthright. Then we become miscreative and increase the dissociation of our split-mind. Increasing the distortion by which we view the world. The world then becomes the dumping ground of our own ego vomit. Denial has no power to create, it is entirely impotent, yet it can be misused most efficaciously to screen the real from our awareness. It is the source of all our misery and ill-health and carries with it the seeds of our ultimate degeneration and disintegration. It is the many-headed monster sleeping in the undergrowth, covered snugly with the rug of our perception. Its crafty mechanisms of deceit do not lend themselves to direct frontal assault and yet we see our world through its eyes alone. When any of its heads are cut, it seems to instantly grow another. So this monster must be taken at its neck. So, yes you must transform yourself into a Perseus and slay your Medusa.

Deny your Source and you lose awareness of your magnificence. For here is the ocean of your Being. The ocean can exist without the fish but the fish cannot exist without the ocean. Yet, the fish can certainly add to the meaning, value and beauty of the ocean. Without the fish, the ocean would be an extremely barren and lifeless place. Likewise God continuously sustains, empowers and showers us in the ocean of His Love and benediction. He deprives us of nothing and immediately fulfills all our needs. As fish, we share in His Being completely. But as fish, we are not to think of ourselves as the Creator of this ocean. When we choose to believe this, we fall into problems. This is the 'Authority Problem'. In time the Son appears to have many separate parts. Yet this is illusion of multiplicity born through the dissociation that is split-mind and one sustained by an ignorance that seems all pervasive.

Our chosen distortions of guilt, judgment and specialness have made the One appear as many. So we see everything as disconnected and no longer perceive the meaningful relationships between them. Everything worthwhile has been lost to our awareness and we can no longer decode the beauty of the Whole from the distorted and fragmented pieces we look upon. Forgiveness is the means to rectify all this. It alone brings to us vision of the meaningful which the parts seen in isolation seem to have lost. Forgiveness heals us through purging all our erroneous beliefs. It does not seek to strengthen our illusions of separation but to tear down this wall. Forgiveness brings recognition of the unity we all share. Thus we come to the direct realization that all minds are joined. That each aspect is integral and whole. That the Holy Spirit is present in every piece. Applying the remedy of quantum forgiveness one finally attains to the vision of Whole Mind.

> **"It should especially be noted that God has only *one* Son. If all His creations are His Sons, every one must be an integral part of the whole Sonship. The Sonship in its Oneness transcends the sum of its parts. However, this is obscured as long as any of its parts is missing."**
>
> **[T-2.VII.6:1-4]**

The question should be asked. *"Why does God even need a Son?"* This question seems very reasonable at first glance. It is an ego question. The ego is implying that *"If God, is so powerful, loving, whole and omniscient then why does he even need a Son? There must be something in Him that is lacking. Something that has been swept under the rug. Something that compromises His perfection in some way and may even hold the key to His destruction."* Yet, the question only seems reasonable and meaningful when the notion of a separated universe has first been taken as fact. Then God and His Son can seem to be separate entities. For it is sure that the ego itself views God as a separate entity and power. Theirs is hardly a collaborative relationship. Instead, the ego holds a very anthropomorphic depiction of God. Yes, God is sitting there on His recliner, feeling lonely one day and so He decides to create a Son just for kicks. The ego interprets all through the blindness of its own ridiculous metaphors. The ego now firmly entrenched in its illusion of separation then proceeds to frame even more meaningless questions based on its own ridiculous premises. But God and the Son have never had any separate existences. It is only the ego that believes in separation because it was through this belief that it was made.

The real relationship between God and His Son is one of unconditional Love. A Love that is in a perfect fusion and unification with all its aspects. The Son represents Love's extension, but not its original Creation. God remains forever Love's Creator and the Source of all Love. This is the meaning behind 'First Cause'. Totality remains forever non-differentiated. The Son is the work of loving Creation forever increasing itself through its endless outpourings. Does one ask "Why does light need to shine?" It becomes apparent that this is its very nature. Without propagating its light, it would have no purpose. So does love seek to effortlessly extend itself without limit. The Son is representative of this extension. Yet when light enters a dark room, it does not seek to replace its Source, nor does it need to in order to accomplish its purpose.

Yet, without a Source there can be no light. So is the Son forever an effect of God and one that remains seamlessly unified with Him. The nature of the Son is Love? It is also Mind, because this is how Love Creates and extends. The Son's reality is Mind that has become completely purified and divested of illusion. Only this Mind is capable of limitless extension. Only this Mind is potentiated with the capacity for perfect thought. The Son will always remain a perfect idea, safely-housed in the Mind of his Father. Because His Father retains all His extensions within Him. Thus the Son remains forever deathless, spaceless, invulnerable, unchanging and undiminished in his radiance. The loneliness of God is really just symbolic of Love needing to reach out and shine unobstructed. Love seeks to celebrate its existence by sharing itself limitlessly with all. If it did not shine there would be no evidence or witness to its existence.

> **"What you find difficult to accept is the fact that, like your Father, *you* are an idea. And like Him, you can give yourself completely, wholly without loss and only with gain. Herein lies peace, for here there *is* no conflict."**   **[T-15.VI.4:5-7]**

PERFECTIONISTS AND PERFECTION

We tend to picture the perfect and unchanging as entirely lifeless. If this is our reality it cannot be much, we mistakenly think. Where is there room for growth and change? This is the mentality of the time-bound consciousness which associates growth with change. This is certainly true in time, but not in eternity. Let's ask then what is it that changes? Isn't it always something that is unstable, unreliable and false – change being the proof of its instability and falseness. That which changes can never be depended upon, because there is nothing stable and sure to be depended upon? Perfection does not change, because to add or subtract from it in any way would only destroy its perfection. Einstein once said that *"Everything Should be Made as Simple as Possible, But Not Simpler."* Einstein had the uncanny knack to see the relative lurking behind the pseudo-concrete and also the capacity to see the constant and pure hiding behind the relative. He was not fooled by appearances and was able to mentally construct and impute entirely new frameworks by viewing them simultaneously from completely contradictory and competing angles. It was because of this unique ability that he was able to discover his theory of relativity.

Our inherent perfection as God's Son is not a relative reality. It is constant and pure. We cannot add or subtract from it in any way without diminishing awareness of our perfection. When we add in some unnecessary illusions, we experience ourselves as relative and changing and our perfection seems to disappear. It becomes lost amid the riff-raff of our illusions. For example, were we to remove or add in some extra notes to an opera by Mozart, the whole structure and harmony of the piece would soon fall apart and be rendered worthless. Michelangelo's statue of David is considered a work of perfection simply because he stopped sculpting when he did. Stopped when he had removed all the unnecessary pieces of marble.

What if he kept on sculpting? What if he was high on snow dust and decided to work late into the night removing some extra pieces? We would be left with just a pile of rubble on the ground.

We see this perfectionist decimation going on all around us every day. We see those celebrities in Hollywood who often overdo their plastic surgeries. So they butcher their faces or skin and turn themselves into frightful pictures of total devastation. The beauty and harmony in their features is now gone. Many can afford to live in their own reality distortion fields because money is no object. Their voracious appetites for attention and fame can be insatiable and no look is seen to be good enough. Having one-dimensional values and being concerned only with externals is often a recipe for disaster. As we see with Joan Rivers who recently passed out of the dream. Her endless plastic surgery obsessions seem to have finally taken their toll.

Dr. Gobbler's Knob was once considering getting some facial surgery procedures done. He was seeking a certain cultured look. So he made a visit to a very well respected plastic surgeon in San Francisco. He proceeded immediately to explain his concerns to the surgeon. My chin protrudes out just a little too far, I feel like I am sporting a witch's chin. The surgeon agreed, and said he could definitely shave the bone to make it look less prominent. He added that he would also recommend rhinoplasty because the nose would then look too out of proportion. Of course, said the surgeon, once your face and chin are done, that bossing and protrusion over the arches of your eyebrows would have to go. It would capture the spotlight and make you look Neolithic in appearance. And after all, it is a cultured look you are seeking. You would also need to have your forehead diminished and flattened by removing some of the bone. Finally I would advise advancing your scalp hair forward and slightly downward as this would then deemphasize the height of your forehead.

The Dr. agreed with all the surgeons suggestions and was delighted. It would be a lot of painful surgeries and much time off work. He would feel battered and bruised for weeks, probably unable to go out in public, but hopefully it would all be worth it in the end. He then asked the surgeon for a quote. The price-tag the surgeon gave him was equivalent to the price of a small house. Of course the surgeon commented that because of the nature of all the surgeries there would be no guarantees of 100% satisfaction. Dr. Gobbler's Knob was starting to vacillate and waver a little. He was still not entirely sure whether to proceed with it or not. So he summarized, "*In order to get the cultured look I want, I will need all my facial features reduced that run along that vertical channel from my forehead and scalp all the way to my chin.*" The surgeon agreed. The Dr. then asked one last question "*And what procedure have you got to reduce the horizontal width of my head. Since, as you may have noticed I have a very wide skull?*" The surgeon immediately retorted that he could do nothing to reduce the width of the skull. In response to this, Dr. Gobbler's Knob, added one last comment, "*In that case, once I have all the surgeries completed, I am going to walk out looking like a flat-screen TV set.*"

Perfection has nothing do with being perfectionist. In fact it is the opposite. Perfectionism stifles, clamps, suffocates and destroys, while our perfection invigorates, frees, revives and enlivens. Our perfection is the source of our energies, clarity and life - our rocket fuel. The perfectionist poet will rewrite their poetry over and over. Yet, with each successive rewriting, it is becoming a very sickened spew, starved of all life giving oxygen, spontaneity, fluidity and vitality. Soon it is being taken away on a stretcher into an ambulance. When the perfectionist poet is finally satisfied with his work, it has become hollowed out and desiccated and is lying rigor mortis in the morgue. The perfectionist musician gets too caught up in the notes. So he loses all sight of the meaningful silences between them. It ceases to be a living thing of subtle harmony, innuendo, balance and beauty. Perfectionists have the knack of stifling the life juices out of everything. They provide no breathing space for spontaneity to flower. They can be extremely inflexible. Every word, paint drop, action and sound must be put through the rack and taken off to its own separate prison-house. There it will be poked and jabbed, clipped and frayed before finally getting the waterboarding treatment. It must learn to know its place in society, learn some manners, how to speak only when spoken to.

Opportunities become quickly lost, because everything becomes procrastinated to a later date and time. Everything must be critically reviewed by a jury of your peers and would-be executioners. Perfectionist gardeners over-clip the branches, robbing the tree of all its natural and rugged beauty. Now it sits there looking too manicured, as if it needs to be boxed off and sent to a Christmas store. Perfectionist parents kill their children. They reprimand and caution them far too much thus destroying any innate confidence, the child may have. Soon the child loses sight of all his or her natural abilities. Nor does the child, feel free to make mistakes. So he takes no risks and does not learn. He knows punishment will soon be on the way.

So, he learns to harden his shell and to live out a life that is joyless and suffocating. He finds it difficult to make friends, because he projects and exacts from them the same critical demands he has learned from his own parents. So he freezes all communication channels and cements in place defensive actions and strategies. All the time hatred and resentment is simmering within him getting ready to come to a boiling point. He feels the raw flesh of his own natural tendencies and vitalities are being cooked without his mature consent. At first chance, he will rebel completely against and abandon his parents, or worse still - become like them. Formed, forged, pressure cooked and hardened in their image he then proceeds to perpetuate the cycle of misery for another generation.

The same thing happens in all relationships in which perfectionist demands are made. It may be between an employer/employee, a husband/wife, a schoolteacher/student etc. When we look at perfectionist people and perfectionism in general, we cannot avoid feeling that perfectionism is symptomatic of some greater lack. Some deep rooted mental disease masquerading externally as obsessive compulsive disorder (OCD). Some insidious inner fear seems to be lurking that seeks to carnivorously devour others through its chosen weapon of perfectionism. People with OCD are often perfectionists. Their perfectionism doesn't aim at perfecting anything. It just represents their foolish attempts at self-distraction and primary symptom alleviation. Through it they temporarily avoid facing their deeper source of pain, emptiness or conflict. So they attempt resolutions at the behavior and symptom level. Thus they craftily deflect the focus and spotlight away from their own core issues by entertaining enough craziness at the behavioral level.

Many perfectionists are highly insecure and untrusting at their foundations. Hence the need to criticize and control and stomp filthy footprints on everything that lives and breathes, anything unfortunate enough to cross their god forsaken paths. They cannot find happiness and rest just leaving things as they are. They feel they must uproot, prune, measure and cross-examine and have everything cross-correlated to their own wicked judgments. The righteousness of their judgments becomes their havens of safety. They think all the pain of their childhood, past life traumas and their deeper inadequacies can be alleviated and even flushed down the crapper by scalping and eviscerating enough dummies in their midst.

Perfectionism is the ravenous restless monster that can never be satisfied. Any attempts to appease it never go more than skin deep. It consumes and destroys everything in its path. It is like Sherman's army laying torch to the South. The only known cure for perfectionism is awareness of one's innate perfection. God is the

Creator of perfection, not the creator of perfectionism. He knows His Son is perfect in every way so he does not seek to limit or control him, nor does He seek to hold him ransom. He would have us change nothing but simply learn how to view all in a correct and just light. The recipe for all this is learning to replace out our caustic fear-filled eyes of judgment for the calm loving eyes of forgiveness. He knows every mind as complete and whole. Perfection is spontaneous – it is always ready of give of itself, everything it has. It is always in a state of harmony and quiescence.

One day Dr. Gobbler's Knob was coasting his way through one of those quintessential redneck towns that speckle our great landscape. Yes, he had entered the state of morbid obesity, and was being welcomed by a panoramic feast of biker bars, tattoo parlors and red, white and blue flags whizzing by in all directions. The large courthouse on the hill was ominous indeed and seemed to be screaming down its justice and vengeance on all the unfortunates below. He wanted to keep his mistress a secret and out of the line of sight for all prying eyes. He hoped he would make it through the town unnoticed, when all of a sudden the great engine grounds to a halt outside this biker bar. Just wonderful! he vociferated out in harsh dissonant tones. To add to the misery of his predicament, it was raining hard. Yes, raining down in bucket-loads of cats and dogs, wombats, foxes and even some small lobsters. His mistress had just gotten her hair and nails done. He asked if she would take the wheel, while he went out and pushed. She was reluctant to shake a leg. She did not want to enter this great colander of hail showering down from the global air conditioner. She started to whine *"I am not going out there in all that hail, even for a moment. We are already running late for my massage appointment."*

Just then a great thumping sound was heard coming from the back of the vehicle. Apparently two bikers from the nearby bar had started to push. In no time at all, they had the car running again. Chugging nicely onwards on its merry way. Then just as quickly, the bikers disappeared back into the mist, not having said a word. They were living embodiments of spontaneous good-will, it seemed. These bikers were not perfectionists, but in that moment they were perfect. Your perfection cannot be manufactured through your patch-work efforts. You can spend lifetimes doing charity work, reeling off mantras or charging yourself chock-full of endorphins without getting one ounce closer to sight of your perfection. It does not matter how many hatha yoga postures you do standing on your head, how many times you run across hot coals or rest on a bed of nails, if inwards your remain defiled. Your perfection cannot be made into an investment to be paid back with interest. It is beyond any payment you can make. You cannot purchase Heaven, but you can certainly find it.

As complete and perfect Being, you have no needs outside yourself. Yet, you have used belief destructively and so remain blind. You continue to give credence to the non-existent. This is your only problem. Nevertheless, the Kingdom is inside you now and everywhere about. Yet to witness it you will need new eyes. Eyes without cataracts - only then will the perfection of your Self stand revealed. For as Marcel Proust once said, *"The real voyage of discovery consists not in seeking new lands but in having new eyes."* Then you can reach past all dark clouds, fears and defenses that the ego has interposed and find that perfect idea God holds of you.

To those who can be truly still a moment, the universe reveals its secrets. To be truly still is to come without investments, biases and beliefs. Only this stillness can penetrate beyond the Samskaras born of conditioned thought. And it is only this that veils your Identity from your awareness. You can use the sword of reason and right discrimination any moment to cut through all illusions for good. You can release yourself from all darkening contradictions that continue to keep you prisoner. Then you will realize your guilt, never had any justification or cause. Because all guilt is of the ego, which is itself unreal. Yes, your Home is found within and in the silence of the present moment. Do not invest elsewhere.

> "God's Son is not a traveller through outer worlds.
> However holy his perception may become, no world
> outside himself holds his inheritance. Within himself
> he has not needs, for light needs nothing but to shine
> in peace, and from itself to let the rays extend in quiet
> to infinity.   [T-13.VII.13:5-7]

The Son retains an omnipotent will. This is true wherever he seems to find himself. Whether this is in time or in eternity. All perception must bend before the power of your mind, because everything in the relative existence remains just as you wish, until you wish it not. Therefore teach no situation that it has power over you, or you teach yourself victimization. So you teach also that illusion is stronger that truth. Thus you remain bound as a dreamer and unable to awaken.

> "Your will be done! In Heaven as on earth this is
> forever true. It matters not where you believe you are,
> nor what you think the truth about yourself must
> really be. It makes no difference what you look upon,
> nor what you choose to feel or think or wish. For God
> Himself has said, "Your will be done." And it is done to
> you accordingly."
>
>   [T-31.VI.4:3-8]

11. Finding your Way out of the Fog

"He said to them, "You examine the face of heaven and earth, but you have not come to know the one who is in your presence, and you do not know how to examine the present moment."

["The Gospel of Thomas]

We can only open the gateway to light with the key of forgiveness. Only then will truth stand revealed and we will see the living One in our presence. For now we seem to inhabit a craze filled maze of unholy distortions. We have been living far too long in this smoke filled chamber. Our eyes have become swollen and red and infected with blepharitis. Is it a surprise then that we can no longer peep out through these puss filled sockets? Or that too many cataracts have come to cover our sight? Many ego weeds, thorns and briers have grown in to confound us completely. These have made a dense forest out of our minds which now covers entirely our pathway to light. No wonder we find ourselves lost. No wonder we have become hopelessly obsessed with sowing the seeds of futile futuristic dreams or else exacting vengeance and retribution for the injustices in our past. We see the present as valueless in itself and have lost the capacity to uncover truth. Instead we extort the present as the means for implementing all our ego goals, of which there is quite the collection. We use time to emphasize our superiority, specialness and power over others, instead of for its intended purpose.

Yes, the gateway to light has become entirely shrouded over by all our judgments, conditionings, feverish imaginations and wish fulfillment desires. We are hopelessly engaged in painting it with the dark brushstrokes and watercolors of our ego world. So we have become blind to the true majesty of the present. Our mind has become too fogged up with our guilt based dreams that we have lost the clarity, insight and luminescence that can let it stand revealed. Our present perceptions are programmed entirely by our future enterprises and by all our pitiless attempts at purging past skeletons. So our true perceptions have become erased and we seem to inhabit a world of fleeting phantoms fabricated out of all our judgments and imaginations. These phantoms all arise from the distortionary matrix of our beliefs - yet we react to them as if they are all real. Our inner programs of judgment, desire and reactivity instantiates a conditioning overlay on our mind that blocks us from witnessing truth directly. So all we see now are the myriad reflections and distortions of the real moon in the puddles of the relative existence.

When something happens gradually we do not stand up and take notice. Thus over vast extents of time, very tangible realities can be transformed into the very stuff of myth and legend. Thus has the reality of the Kingdom been turned into a myth. It is seen now more like a soothing tranquilizer but not as a reality to be taken too seriously. All we see in this dark ego world is truth, as far as the ego is concerned. This is reality coming at us hard and fast. We can either take it or leave it. It seems the height of foolishness to discredit the evidence of our own direct perceptions. Is it a wonder then that we find ourselves fatalistically absorbed with all the minutiae and petty beliefs of this Lilliputian universe? One that is fragile, capricious and often extremely cruel.

STOP THE MADNESS!

Every moment we seem bombarded by a vast sea of chaos. A world that is positively out-of-control and thoroughly drenched by a deranged madness that seems to be growing asymptotically. A collective ego melting pot powering off all cylinders. There is the constant bombardment of mind frying facts from the media and the web. Thousands of junk e-mails, viruses, scammers, charity hunters, soft-profilers and unmuzzled spies. What a diet? It is like we have squeezed the last juice out of this carcass we call a world, so long ago and are frantically searching now for the last drop.

Earlier today, I was in the fast lane cruising at speed. All of a sudden a girl appeared from nowhere. Soon she was driving right up my ass and pummeling down the 'high'-way at close to one hundred miles an hour. Checking her out, in my rear view mirror, it seemed that she was cursing at some invisible presence. Maybe she was chanting some gibberish mantra of self-empowerment. Does it make a difference? In any case, she had taken both her hands off the wheel and was now gently massaging her neck and shoulders as she shot down this rage filled sea like a metal arrow. She then zipped past only to immediately start screwing with the driver up ahead. It was then I noticed her kid in the back seat. This was obviously some prized treasure to her, someone high up there in the moralistic and desire based equations that govern her life, something on a parity with impending road-kill.

This same flavor of madness and all its derivatives seems to have pervasively infiltrated our culture. I see it in the tech farms with their never ending voracious appetites. Wanting only young glowing shiny happy people working for them. The median age now being 30 or less. Yes, these are the veritable ant-farms of productivity, where ambitious, intelligent, overworked puppies busily scurry about to nonsense meetings. So they bang their heads together in a frenzied delirium to craft out the strategic development plans for another great pile of dog manure. More 'A la carte' hogwash, for the witless consumer. Mind-numbed, multi-tasked, and multi-shredded their protoplasm sacks have morphed into a ménage of jumbled nerves, anxiety and diarrhea. Institutionalized automatons likely to forget even their own names under the terrifying inquisitions of their peers. Yes, they have become lobotomized by their stunning complicity to these brutal corporate regimes. Cooked from the inside by the age of thirty, their tickers have started to make wondrous improvisations in off-beat harmonies, simulating the dissonant flow of a Kerouac novel that is biologically engraved into their flesh. Yes, their tickers discharge raucous and disharmonious staccato rhythms from the hollow of their chests in a positively orgasmic multi-tonal morphogenetic feast.

Yes, the gods of future aspiration have taken us ransom your honor. We have had to settle for this simulacrum of living. So have we stuffed the ice-filled cavities of our hearts with straw, electronics and circuit diagrams and strategically placed cardboard in between all our creaking bones. It is this that keeps the gantry train of our skeletons running smoothly along its networks of pulleys and strings. We pay homage to man and his humdrum melody. One that has continued to beat out its sad refrain since the dawn of time. We pay homage to all the gods we have invented since from the mud puddles of our meaninglessness. We have fashioned many splendiferous forms, worthless novelties and craven images out of this dark polymorphic soup. Yes, many potent and fatal concoctions we have harvested through the piling in of blood, flesh, brains and stress into the blender all at once. Every now and then we add in a sprinkling of our anxiety and self-induced slavery and just a pinch of our ingenuity. We hope one day the dish will come up a treat and make us proud. Then little gingerbreads, all sweet and complicit will stream out in a profusion of ecstasy. Printed out in the hundreds of thousands by robot assemblers and automation software.

Our new gods have come to depict compensations for all our lost creativity, expressionist tendencies, bankrupt souls and artistically depleted lives. Yet we bestow on them grand names indeed. For these are the gods of our future and the New World order - the harbingers of all our innovation and progress. Yet, as a collective they remain just psychological Band-Aids covering the divinity we have lost. Cro-Magnon man was the progenitor that heralded in our glorious New Age. Yet he was considered to be a bit pigheaded in his ways. Too brash in his tone of approach. So we had to replace him with more pliant, glib and spineless folk. Those more likely to bend over and take it up the ass while responding to the whip. Yes, a new breed was heralded in to become champions of our brave New World.

So we woke up one day only to find glitzy, superficial and motor-mouth personalities stalking our planet and raised to the pedestal. A great substitution had occurred in which bean-counters came to replace out critical thinkers and philosophers, marketeers ousted our heroic musketeers and geeks deposed all freaks, fags and vagabonds. Soon a race of organic robots and mere pushbutton minions had made a successful coup. The truly creative fell down a great logistical hole in the system, where they were either heartlessly ignored or else unsympathetically tortured, quantified, gagged and bagged. Wolves became extinct and frightened sheep were all about. Dark nebulous cloud formations enveloped our world along with obsequious prima-donnas, coked out chicken-heads, managerial whips and the trash of mediocre minds. Human androids and self serving trolls came to jewel and bedazzle our landscape. Soon only the scum was seen floating to the top and the cream remained below. Cream was considered too fattening. So was it taken out and thrown in the gutter. Yet, Cro-Magnon man remains the guilty party. He is responsible for all the vomit that happened since in the name of progress. He is our patsy your honor.

Some say order is overrated and that routine is the greatest killer of intelligence. That disorganized chaos is what keeps us on the beat. Hell being relative has many disparate orders to differentiate the chaos that pervades it. That is, it must present the illusion of its existence through perpetrating various contrasts, levels and shifts. Yes, all illusions arise from the many sporadic and vacillating ego beliefs that fuel its motions. Reality, on the other-hand can have no orders and levels. After all it is the Home of the Absolute and the eternally valid. To recognize truth anywhere is to see it everywhere. Hell, in contrast gets deeper depending on the depths of our denial and obfuscation. It is like that slimy mud that clings with a powerful torpid suction. An insidious underflow, in which a mind engaging only in ego chatter can become very deeply entrenched. One which then aimlessly belches out its sulfurous fumes in every direction. What is not Heaven is Hell. So we all experience ourselves in hell here. Stuck in an inescapable soul crushing swamp, experiencing varying degrees of depravity. For once we lose awareness of any part of truth, we lose sight of all of it and become so blinded by subterfuge and deception that we can no longer recognize ourselves.

Hell is the ultimate correctional facility. Yet we can indeed make some right decisions and escape its snares completely. We simply need to re-channel our minds to align with and harmonize to truth. This removes all blocks that impede the natural passage of light. Definite quantum leaps in progress can and do occur. These increase the power, clarity and aliveness of our minds. So we start to recognize our fundamental oneness with the world. It is our offspring, after all. We witness it anew, as our vision is restored. We start seeing light rims and halos surrounding the old familiar objects which we saw as meaningless and dull before. The spaces between objects is seen and known now to be throbbing with life. The seal of the ego's conditioning shelter has been broken. This old world fortress which surrounds our mind has fallen. Now we know that all was just our projection and the responsibility for all that is seen shifts within.

LUCID DREAMS, AND OUR CRITICAL NEED OF AWAKENING

Lucid dreams are the precursors to awakening. The skilled lucid dreamer, having become self-aware in his dream, can move now with ease through countless universes in a single night. Magnificent light filled universes each symbolizing a higher, more fragrant, esoteric and abstract knowledge normally lost to our awareness. Soon he is questioning the reality of his waking dreams. This is the critical step to awakening. There is another critical development showing up on the radar of your mind. Most ego dreams are loosely threaded, rich in fantasy and just filled with ego attempts at self-aggrandizement. Usually the people and events of your life are being manipulated within them to fulfill your ego wishes. They represent compensations for the repressions and injustices you seem to feel in regular life. However as you get close to breaking the seal of the ego and its thought system, ancient dreams long hidden will be revealed once again back into your conscious awareness. These are often very fearful and highly symbolic. They represent the ego's last ditch fear jewels, aimed at preventing you from breaking through those mantles and seals of ignorance, in which it embalms itself. Unlike other ego dreams, these dreams will repeat often weeks, months or even years apart and remain in content significantly unchanged.

I have had quite a number of such dreams over the years. In one, I astrally traveled to a highly evolved land. There I viewed many beautiful, fountains, pagodas, ingenious sculptures and designs. It was a land of extremely elegant taste, full of lush variegated forests, pristine lakes and great artistic beauty. I was tempted to remain there forever. Everyone was deeply loving and respectful. Healthily loving also to themselves. For here there was no narcissism, self-obsession or twisted images in the glass. No twisted motives or calculated niceties. Simplicity was venerated more than anything else. Just to look into another's eyes was enough to bring back remembrance of one's tremendous worth. As I became suffused with the ethereal light in their eyes, I could easily remember the god within me. This held all the hallmarks of an advanced civilization and of a golden age. Here there was not even the hint of any undernourished, unrequited or displaced soul. No hint of any anger, greed, rage or blood-thirst. No hint of terror, isolation, poverty or condemnation. As I continued to cross this beautiful landscape, I came across this most inspiring dwelling perched high on a hill overlooking a great forest. Yet, when I looked out from my strategic vantage point, I was in extreme shock and bewilderment. This was the endpoint of their civilization and I had thought it would go on forever. Now I could see that it was hemmed in on all sides by a vast and treacherous ocean. Torrential waves were whirling aimlessly about in the blackest and murkiest of storm shaped waters, beneath which lay who knows what.

As I astrally traveled across this ocean, I came to a very primitive land resembling a tropical jungle. Yet it was unlike any I had known before. It was embroidered everywhere with the densest wildest vegetation and enormous sprawling trees. Everything was massively intertwined and arrayed in a very insidious fashion, so that all light became occluded. There was this pervasive hissing sound, emanating from all directions. Piercing roaring sounds of wild creatures exuding from all hidden crevices. Augmented by a deafening buzzing cacophony of billions of insects. So searing, as to sound like a jet-plane at take-off. Instinctively I had the sudden instinctive urge to escape this terrifying place. I wanted to astrally project back to the land of pagodas at the other side of the ocean. I wanted to leave quickly, before darkness fell.

Then an inner voice provided me with some intuition, as to its meaning. This ocean and jungle were part of an ancient and savage civilization that was too slow to evolve. A civilization that could not bridge the gap to man, fast enough and so the divide had become too great. The voice then reminded me that there are certain subtle, but necessary parameters favorable for our evolution. These parameters have nothing to do with any "outward" biological conditions, nor the environment, nor with planetary extortion, but represented in contrast critical inner parameters. Parameters pertaining to how we interpret and respond to our world. These parameters need to be latched onto, leveraged and expeditiously applied to support our upwards evolutionary progression. Mankind and all of life has only a certain definite window, to do so to evolve. We need to set ourselves on fire from within quickly. If we do not learn to cooperate with our inner wisdom in a pre-established window, we cannot catch the upward surge of the evolutionary tide. Thus we cannot transmigrate to a higher level of conscious evolution. So are we doomed to regress backwards in the ebb flow to these primitive, mindless and bestial states. Then our fate becomes sealed again for almost endless time. Then a truly dark night of our collective soul begins in earnest.

But night crept in too quickly. I could feel the dark presences of this primitive land spreading out across the ocean, diffusing into the air and encroaching upon my safety zone. Soon I was being sucked in to its powerful vortex. My own efforts were not good enough any longer. I needed the support of a highly advanced collective mind to survive this onslaught. Soon I was surrounded by ghosts and all sorts of frightening apparitions and specters. One came at me with a hatchet and started slamming it at my feet. He cut my legs clean off, with one whack. Then blood went spattering in all directions. Deep fear began to set in. I wondered what would happen next. I had wasted too much time. I had left it too late. My window of evolution had closed. I was about to slip down now through endless chasms of despair. The black hole of humanity and of all intelligent life - to become a mindless singularity or beast. An imprint left like a snowflake before the sun.

Soon I found myself in a lost, frozen and endless space, like an embryo that would never flourish. I would devolve now away from meaning and take on more primitive forms. I had sold out on the promise of my divine inheritance and would remain here in an unholy state of chrysalis for many mindless eons ahead. All for some worthless worldly attractions, cheap jewels, toys and mind numbing intoxications. My heart was throbbing in panic, as I lay awake in this lucid dream. I was having extremely unsettling feelings. I wanted to be erased and effaced from all existence, purged, eviscerated, ripped out, nuked, stripped from the One-Mind order. I wanted to be made into a *no-thing*, rather than endure the bleak litany of tortures that was ahead. Yet, I could not die, I could not be erased. There would be no mercy killing, because death for all of us is forever barred.

Then I was presented in symbolic miniaturized forms a giant panorama of all that was coming on the evolutionary radar, all those nightmares that had me in their cross-hairs. I began to see with an intensity the vast content embedded and embalmed into my daily life. I began to see all those foolish distractions, temptations and self absorptions, that I had allowed myself to become so blinded and seduced by. Thus I had become too myopic, channeled and mummified and unable to penetrate to the core of what was before my very eyes. But what unsettled me most, was the fundamental message and content of this lucid dream. It was the dream of mankind's future, a dream trajectory in which we do not make it. We do not invest enough in consciously evolving ourselves upwards, so we fail to reach a critical summit - which is the full emblazoned awareness in our consciousness of the reality of non-separation. So we all regress backwards into the abyss, running out of the necessary psychological and spiritual oxygen needed to survive and thrive.

Now I suddenly recalled a critical teaching of the Course. It said that the separation was never a loss of our perfection but just a failure in our communication. We had failed to communicate truly and unbiasedly with one another but chose to invest in ourselves instead and to nourish only private and selfish interests. Thus we communicated only fear and weakness, separation and sickness, isolationism and lack. So the diamond that was hidden in each of us was never given any voice, recognition, credence or expression. Rather it became brutally repressed and denied. The momentum of our upwards progression becomes too broken-winged to sustain itself. So each of us was being hypnotized back into an existence as mindless beasts.

Jesus reminds us often in the Course of the vast gap that seems to exist between God and man. This gap developed over millions of year through our adoption of the ego's thought system and its tactics. It has become so great now that he alone is strong enough to bridge it for us. Without his help, we are doomed. Yet, if we follow his example, we can safely reach to our divine inheritance. Yet, if we waste our time, we most certainly will take giant regressive strides backwards into the animal, vegetable and mineral states. Now, I was beginning to better understand Jesus's sense of urgency. He is constantly advocating that we use our dream-lives meaningfully to make fundamental progress, if we are to wake up. If too many are allowed to slip back, it means our ideas are not growing outward and our dream-lives are simply being wasted. But with the right progress, certain definite patterns and cross-associations start to emerge. Elements of perception start crystallizing into patterns that are in harmony with truth. These crystallizations then function as mini-touchstones to reveal all of truth.

SOLVING THE RUBIK'S CUBE OF TRUTH, THROUGH ATONEMENT

It is like making progress with a Rubik's cube, except this is an existential cube that can only be solved through our combined efforts. Then, are we all released into the light of the Kingdom. Initially, all seems jumbled and meaningless, but with a few intelligent moves clusters of like color emerge. Using these clusters of like color as our handle and pivot we can figure out the remaining moves needed to arrive back at awareness of our perfection. Applying the corrective thought system of the Atonement, elements of perception that seem unrelated or even contradictory start to evidence again their shared motif and content. Even just one aspect of perception viewed rightly is enough to trigger critical and fundamental changes across all of it. As the Course relates. *"One vision, clearly seen, that does not fit the picture as it was perceived before will change the world for eyes that learn to see, because the concept of the self has changed."* [T-31.VI.5:4] This one perception can become our healing touchstone to reveal truth in its entirety. It represents our whole way out. Like a hologram, each part perceived correctly contains the whole. As we draw nearer the end our perceptions become increasingly clear and luminous. Eventually the cube of truth is restored and the confusion of the relative existence is undone. Then there are no more moves to make – perfection has been revealed. Learning is over and pure Being alone remains. Then our Real Life can proceed afresh. The function of time is to give you time to solve this cube. In the beginning, it seems this would take endless time. Yet this inhibiting belief comes to an end, once we make fundamental progress somewhere in the matrix of our perceptions and reach beyond the ego in another. Our progress is not a question of time, but of right intent. This results in right decision which is simultaneously followed by right perception. Then comes a rapid acceleration in our reevaluation of what is consistent, unambiguous and light-filled and therefore must be true. Miracle mindedness is making the right moves. A single instant of right decision can make more progress than countless lifetimes spent making misdirected and inefficacious moves.

12. THE ONLY SOLUTION FOR A BROKEN DOWN WORLD

"I've seen things you people wouldn't believe. Attack ships on fire off the shoulder of Orion. I watched C-beams glitter in the dark near the Tannhauser gate. All those moments will be lost in time... like tears in rain... Time to die."

[Nexus 6, 'Blade Runner']

There is no rule book to life. We receive no map in advance of the often hostile territory we will be navigating across. No foolproof or surefire recipe for our success. No signposts on what right direction to take, what pitfalls to avoid, who to avoid or how best to accelerate our progress. We yearn for some benevolent presence to sing softly into our ears from the very outset, declaring that all will be OK. One that counsels us on what are likely to be our deepest flaws, unnecessary passions and areas of vulnerability. Unfortunately mostly we find these out the hard way - only after we have made a profusion of tragic mistakes. Each one costing us in sweat, blood, tears and years and often so much more. Tragically also, we often only become aware of our greatest strengths when it is far too late in the game. We want the easy life, we want to be pampered and we do not want to have to think too much. Thinking sounds like an awful burden. We desire instead that neat blueprint that clearly enumerates all the steps to take. Steps that if we faithfully follow like an automaton we will be guaranteed some good measure of success. Instead we are provided with a crapshoot and no guarantees. Then thrown in at the deep end. Into the murky, sulfurous smelly pool of filth, sweat, body odor, amniotic floods - but mostly one of panic, fear and despair.

Slowly each of us comes to the realization that our progress or failure depends intimately on ourselves. Life is a very open-ended affair and one we are flying blind in. Many spend their short tragic lives with the blindfolds on. Some try to over-intellectualize the whole affair. They make it into a game of strategy. Then there are the sponges that surf on the slipstream of another's ideas and strategies, using these to direct their course. Yet, it is up to each of us to determine where we will invest our efforts and time, what values we will treasure and to what extent we will allow the world to shape us or push us about like toe-rags. Will we use our time here to seek for meaning and truth? Or will we use it instead to fight injustices on the human stage. Will the world just become our nest and love den, in which to go pleasure seeking everyday? Maybe we will cave from the very start and never get out of the starting box. Never get do that soft-reboot but remain immature and unlived, as veritable shipwrecks and human disasters in the field of life.

The fact that there is no rule book or operational manual stapled to each of us in the cradle can seem highly disconcerting at first. Particularly to those who want to take their sacraments early and become full-blown sheeple. Yes, those who want to become fully indentured minions sweating on the minion farm - bought and sold by profiteering enterprises. Freedom can lead some to great anxiety and even outright panic. They wanted it all clearly marked out right there next to the imprint of their original sin. Many have the urge to be creative, to write some tremendously meaningful message into this miraculous space that has been provided. Yet, all they can write out is the name of their egos over-and-over. No so many start off intending to be outright failures. No one wants to present just an empty box to their gods at the end of the day, with a small note saying *"Please return to sender."* Not even to produce a cheap ass box of salt lake taffy, in return for this intensely treasurable sack of sand and water, you have been given seems the height of ingratitude.

For Douglas Adam's, all meaning was found in the number 42. Here was his golden sanctuary. Here he enshrined the ultimate answer to all the riddles, enigmas and mysteries of life. Here was the key to maximizing all sex and sensuality as portrayed in those fascinating yogic postures of the Karma Sutras. Here the Holy Grail to cure all sickness and lack and one that held the very keys to immortality itself. Armed with this number, tattooed over our buttocks, we would go forth and experience perfect relationships and maximize on our life potential. We would no longer be content to remain as meat suits dependent on a nebulous cloud of neural-spaghetti hanging overhead to save us from becoming chop suey. We would become more than just a zero, we would become super-minions, disarming beasts of progress and change that would bring the great Oz and the great oligarchs to their bended knees. So that one day a government of the minions, by the minions, for the minions would come to rule this land. Yes, indeed, we would become more than just a zero, in fact we could become exactly 42. If only the answer were so easy!

OUR ANXIETY, ANGST, ECCENTRICITIES AND SELF-CONTRACTION

There is a stark emptiness that pervades the relative existence that penetrates deeply into our hearts and minds. There is a strong compulsion within us to fill the void of emptiness present within with anything at all. Hence so many fill their calendars with idle pursuits and meaningless distractions. Others become sports-addicts, shopaholics, adventurers, or even humanitarians. Or maybe they choose instead to become dropouts, drug-addicts, psychopaths or criminals. Some choose to become career dedicated and so spend all their time chained to the office desk. This is their sanctuary to avoid their nagging wives/husbands and leaches of children. Yes, they only feel happy when they are drowning in powerpoints, e-mails and 2am meetings.

The dedicated employee likes to look down upon the dropout and often incarnates the spirit of a Japanese Samurai warrior in his capacity to absorb pain. He will willingly put his head into the chopping block, if it will only save the company a nickel. He is all about honor and dedication and being milked by the fat cats. Yet it is also true that the dropout likes to sneer at the dedicated employee, for whom he has utter contempt. He sees him as just another square in harness and as a brain-farmed serf for the profiteering engines of the corporate world. You know those who are actively polluting, ravaging and exploiting the planet, but who protect their crown jewels and monopolies with legions of lawyers. Maybe the dedicated family man looks down on the adventurer, seeing in him an immature waster, that is unnecessarily putting his life at risk. Why the hell does this nut think he is, anyway - a birdman? Why is he jumping off a perfectly good mountain? When is he going to grow up and start changing diapers instead of wing-suits? And the adventurer looks back on the dedicated family man as just another sucker stomping madly about steeped in jealousy, in his air-conditioned cage. Too afraid to live on his bare and essential resources. He recognizes this, as the real source of the family man's annoyance.

Our anxiety is increased further because the world cannot provide any real guidance, as to the merits each of its paths hold. Nor can it tell us the exact destination, until we fall in over the edge. Yet, we feel pressured by family, circumstances, our own inner voice and the never ending demands of society and social media to choose some path and justify it quickly. The enormous responsibility of it all calls for a Xanax. Often we are pressured to choose a path that goes against our own grain and internal nature. So the conflict becomes even more acute and unbearable. Hence all the suicides, crimes, dropouts, misfits, rebellions, coups, revolts and bingo games. Yet, even the family man who may look the very picture of loving composure and success can be hiding many dark secrets and cracks, in his psyche. Often he just goes mechanically about his life, mind numbingly bored with it all, just playing games of deception. Very few live authentic lives and very few have the real backbone to be themselves. That is live their lives on their own terms. Most feel profoundly split, compromised and enslaved and go about their day with a barely subdued rage.

In the movie, 1900, the pianist that is "1900" has finally made the bold decision to leave the comfort of the passenger liner, on which he has lived all his life. Being madly in love with a female passenger that has previously disembarked, he wants to pursue the passions of his heart and settle down to a new life. Yet halfway down the gangway, he is paralyzed with fear. Yes for a few moments he becomes incapacitated and frozen with stark terror. This terror is triggered by the vast array of skyscrapers of New York city he surveys in the distance. There seems no end in sight at all to this metropolitan sprawl of random chaos and madness. All seems ready to gobble him up and yet this is exactly where he is heading. Staring at the vast enormity of this cement jungle, he feels he is being faced with a sea of infinite possibilities and infinite choices. A sea for which he can find no sound basis by which to meaningfully evaluate the worthiness of one path over another. Peering into this limitless abyss, he feels just about as consequential as a quantum particle facing its own sea of limitless probabilities when faced with all the vagaries of the multiverse. All the what-ifs, choices and uncertainties are leading him into a delirium and he is rocketing towards full mental implosion. Yes, whole universes are imploding within him in just a few moments.

He knows that it is randomness and happenstance alone which will decide whether he will survive *'out-there'* or not. One road may lead to a meaningful encounter and success and another to his being murdered, mugged, gagged, torched or bagged. As a result he feels a very cold isolating dread. He knows that once he descends off the boat and embarks on his new life, he will never really be able to make a single decision with confidence again. He knows worldly confidence is an illusion, a fruit of the tree of ignorance. Because no one is ever able to account for all the factors, all the variables that will predetermine the outcome. He does not like this game of risk and simply cannot imagine living the rest of his life in this whimsical arbitrary way. It would be hell. He does not want to shoulder the enormous responsibility of this vast open environment. This immense overwhelming piano of the cosmos does not have a limited number of keys like his own piano on board the ship. Life is safer there. So he heads back up the gangway. He decides on behalf of safety and security instead of chance. Later however we see that this passenger liner becomes decommissioned and is blown to pieces along with "1900".

Many of us live our lives this way. We prefer to cling to the misery of the old solutions rather than embrace the forced change the world demands. We prefer to avoid this stark field of terror at all costs and so we play games, to pretend we are living. Yes, if only life were as simple and elegant as mathematics. If only we were given a few variables, a few unknowns which we could easily solve for in advance. Life in contrast seems to flood us with an ocean of infinite variables and infinite unknowns. It is composed of a steeply convoluted maze of complex non-linear interactions and dependencies. That very variable we are ready to discount today or at least diminish in importance is the very one tomorrow that we find to be most critical. It comes up to bite us on the tail and to light our ass on fire. There are so many hidden variables in this vast web of life, making it so we cannot even see at all.

Those of us, who are honest enough recognize that we are always traveling somewhat blindfolded through life. We are not in full command and control of all the outcomes. We can make what seem like good decisions but we cannot always guarantee the results. We are merely twisting and aping about in a gargantuan control booth of pure sophistication, like a monkey heading to the moon. Forever uncertain of the true effects of each knob we twist. The graveyards of the world are littered with the souls of those who made simple mistakes that shaped and shattered their entire destinies. We see the same dynamic being played out all the time, in different forms. Prisons are often brimmed to overcapacity with those, who would rather accept the miserable "ordered" life rather than the disordered happy one. They prefer to cling to the deadening litany of their various mind-numbing routines rather than embrace that tangled disordered jungle that is on the outside. Out there they would need to take personal responsibility for their own lives, all their decisions, actions and their consequences. This is a big contributing factor of why the recidivism rate is so high. Many would choose enforced slavery over responsibility any day of the week.

William James Sidis is another example of a child prodigy, who quickly became a falling star, or should I say a Red Dwarf. In his youth, he had posited that there were certain regions of space in which the second law of thermodynamics operated with a temporal reversibility. This lead not only to decreased entropy in such systems but it also provided the foundational basis for the development of black holes, dark matter and anti-energy. Yet, in later life his obsession became figuring out train timetables and he could barely pass a civil service examination. The fact that he was born on April 1st probably explains it all. Even a fearless Aviator and business tycoon of the caliber of Howard Hughes can become warped with eccentricity and fear when they fully see the open nature of existence. Seeing that no paths offer any guarantees, they want to just hide away and engage in rituals to cover over the bleak emptiness they feel inside. After a while all good decisions go down the toilet and their decision making process becomes increasingly reactionary, twisted and fear based. Because good decision making after all is very much a learned and accumulated skill, as much as it is inspired. Good decision making becomes severely atrophied with our failure to take ownership of our lives. Once we refuse to accept any personal responsibility we quickly end up in the dumps, sewers and landfills of this world. Because accepting personal responsibility is the fulcrum around which all good decision making moves.

My father used to say that "All poor people are mad and all rich people are eccentric." How true that rings! Yet, our decisions need not be warped by either eccentricity or madness. The equation is simple :- when we fail to take personal responsibility, we will fail to make good decisions. Then we can be certain we will make bad ones in their place. This most often leads to savage and dire consequences and in the long run to a severely diminished or wasted life. The Course teaches that there is no real comfort in the world. Nothing intrinsic to it which can provide the guidance and reassurance we so desperately seek and need. The world was formed with the loss of wisdom. Its many illusions are therefore not in a position to teach. Nor can it of itself show us how to escape its bleak context. It is after all just a reflection of our own minds. This world offers only one certainty – taxes.

Be grateful then that this world comes with no book of rules to follow to the letter. Such a book would kill all our spirit. It would mercilessly trample upon us, vanquishing all our spontaneity, freedom, innovation, adaptability and progressive evolutionary capabilities. It would transform us into lifeless creatures, deafened mutes, programmed goons and biochemical robots; a culture of bacteria all encoded and encrypted with the same nonsense genomes. And such a rule book would be slyly misinterpreted by leaders to promote civil rights abuses, inequalities, slaveries, genocides and all sorts of unholy atrocities and wars. No thankfully, there is no book of rules in life, but there is a book of guidance and that is the Course. This lays down in no uncertain terms the true metaphysical basis and foundation for how the world came about, how it is maintained and how it can finally be released. It paves the way for the re-dawning of the eternal into our awareness. It teaches us how to get out of here.

WORLDLY AND BEHAVIORAL SOLUTIONS CANNOT WORK

"There is no thought in all the world that leads to any understanding of the laws it follows, nor the Thought that it reflects." [W.134.13:2]

This is why it is futile to chase down the solution to the world's problems from within its context. It is even more futile than attempting to strike down the moon by stabbing at its reflection in a puddle. No matter how many times you strike, you remain powerless to affect the real moon. You have always misplaced the real source of the world and so all your efforts of release can be of no help. All problems are actuated by overly identifying with this framework of illusion. No real success is ever accomplished, unless one resolves things at the level of true Cause. Working at the effect level, the most one can hope for is to transmogrify effects from certain forms into others. Yet the underlying content remains the same until we introduce a meaningful solution. That is, it will remain buried, repressed and unresolved and just masking itself under yet another cloak of self-deception. There to masquerade again in so many exotic splendiferous forms, by which it seeks to artfully encapsulate and shield itself. Forms designed to attract and tantalize. Thus the moon of unconscious guilt is always just being moved to a different puddle, where it is seen to take on a slightly different appearance.

This is why all those movements down the ages that have attempted to implement solutions at the behavioral and effect level have not succeeded in resolving the world's primary issues and core sources of conflict. Discontent remains. So we see that all forms of social and political government, from totalitarianism to utopianism have all failed to bring any lasting peace. They have not withstood the test of time. They fail to account for the internals of human nature which is blind, corrupt and fatally flawed, at a fundamental level. Yet ignoring this they proceed to formulate their enlightened ideals of self governance. Similarly we see that despite all the findings of modern medicine and all the proliferation of new drugs, research and therapies, people remain as sick as ever. Worse still they have become addicted to "easy" fixes to their health issues. This then diminishes their capacity to take personal responsibility for their health and wellness. They take drugs that seem to offer some immediate resolutions or relief from their primary afflictions at the expense of seriously eroding there long-term health, vitalities and life expectancies.

Likewise materialism and consumerism have failed to make people more rested, joyous, peaceful and quiescent. We are not getting a higher quality of life but a far more toxic one. We are working around the clock to get those comforts and toys we desire and yet we remain extremely miserable, psychotic, crazed and suicidal. The state of nervous anxiety, restlessness and distraction is worse than ever. Previously unknown diseases such as ADHD have extrapolated into the stratosphere. Is this yet another invented disease placed inside a person, or is its etiology psycho-social in nature? Generated by too much absorption in multimedia simultaneously with poor quality interactions in the human pond? Yes, there is a host of new disorders, which we are only far too quick to symptomize and scapegoat to the individual level. So we fail to take collective social responsibility for them. Scapegoating to the individual is far more profitable after all because it sells more drugs. So we see, at all levels, that numerous behavioral and organizational approaches to healing our collective Self have failed. This is because we have misplaced the more fundamental and deeper causes of our problems. We have not been able to put a name on the true beast that roams with a cloaking device amidst us all.

Yes, this world is like the Methuselah of old arising from the dark inner caverns of our minds. A Methuselah with stark, cold, austere and soulless eyes. One with wizened features, screeching bones and dry pallid skin. It is an unworthy shelter for God's Son and fit only for the dead and dying. In this cavern we proceed to play out our games of creator and dream-master while nourishing all our insatiable appetites and lusts. We cover the walls of our cage with the posters of all those idols we have yet to conquer. In this barren, bleak and twisted landscape we do not see just how myopic our perceptions have become. We complete our catalog of home furnishings with so many idle fancies, mad senseless actions and meaningless distractions. Into this desolate landscape we commission our hungry dogs of our guilt to scavenge out unwilling victims to forcibly proclaim our innocence. The world's singular failure, is that it can never "be achieved". So will it always remain a depot of despair.

Each world is the sole creation of one separate mind alone - a mind that is impure and imprisoned within a crumbling fortress to deadened artifacts of thought. Each holds no association to the real. For there is nothing in each that really shines, glows or even smells of life. So it remains but a miscreation and an hallucination, spawned from the aberrational thought of a lost mind. A mind that projects into a void that which can never be. In it you appear to walk along a parched, lonely, desolate and endless landscape, your mind endlessly tortured with feelings of fear, depression, rage, isolation and abandonment. You find yourself forever spiraling deeper into hungrier hells. New holes in the existential void into which you carry a knapsack full of those half living, half dead skeletons, shrieking at your back. Feeling dethroned and isolated from your true Source of power, you feel deadened, dull, starved and grievance laden. Yet, you know not where else to look to find yourself. At some point in your meaningless voyage, it must occur to you that Heaven does not share in your blindness and despair. One eureka moment and you can have Heaven back to administer its cure.

Yes, it must be agreed that we live in a very distorted frame of reference. We never see things as they really are. Our view is mostly obstructed and completely distorted. Yet, we recognize not that we are blind. That the lens of the creative perceiver has become darkened and dull. It has lost all its luster and former radiance so that we are obsessed now with projecting our own feelings of guilt and shame onto others. We mistakenly think these aspects are outside ourselves and so these "others" become our dumping grounds. But this malpractice but reflects our mind's deep split. Believing fully in the split, we go one stage deeper. We scapegoat the external world as the aggressor and cause of all our misery. So we erect barricades and defenses to justify our judgments and fears. Soon a great construction boom is underway in our ego worlds. Behind these barricades we seek to make ourselves special, godly and self-contained - the very pictures of innocence. Our artful mechanisms of denial and projection almost guarantee that the true panacea for our healing remain undiscovered, leaving us feeling lost and forever barred from the Kingdom.

In this artifice of darkness, God remains unseen. We have placed His crown upon our heads, and diademed ourselves with all His former glory. So we have come to see ourselves as self-made and self-determining. Cause becomes what ever we wish it to be. Arbitrary laws are formed that are more in tune with our wishfulness, instantaneous needs and desire gratifications than our real needs. Law becomes an exigency of circumstance. The good is named by that, which progresses our own individual piece of pulp fiction. The bad is that which hinders our script from advancing in the dream. So a vast framework of illusion arises in direct reflection to a critical lost solution. Yet, we flounder in the dark not knowing what the solution could be.

FORGIVENESS UNDOES ALL EFFECTS OF THE TINY MAD IDEA

It is at this point that the Course comes to our rescue. It teaches that it is as a direct consequence of our decision to separate from God in the beginning, with the "*Tiny Mad Idea* (TMI)", that illusions first appeared in the mind. In that moment, Truth was lost to our awareness and we seemed to be separated and split-off from God. Poor decision making only became possible after the separation, because the separation was the descent into darkness. Once we experienced ourselves as split-mind, for the first time contradictions reigned. These contradictions are represented in the world by all its meaningless laws. Contradictions born of error became the seeds for all false dualistic appearances. Nothing can be understood clearly in this context and framework and nothing ever has. Yet, we give credence to what we see because we are no longer able to clearly distinguish illusions from the truth. One day we hope to weave all these illusions into a masterful symphony of unity and meaning. But this is impossible. Yet, there is a key that can unravel this entire framework of illusion and place truth back on its rightful throne. This key of forgiveness is here. It can be accepted and used anytime - day or night! It operates by disavowing reality to those aspects of our perceptions that are not in tune with truth. It is the heavenly means given to purify our perceptions and to distill the meaningful from the meaningless. Under its healing beneficence, a single unifying tale is told and finally perceived and known. This is the tale that speaks of our immortality and eternal safety.

"Forgiveness is the only thing that stands for Truth in the illusions of the world. It sees their nothingness, and looks straight through the thousand forms in which they may appear. It looks on lies, but it is not deceived. It does not heed the self-accusing shrieks of sinners mad with guilt. It looks on them with quiet eyes, and merely says to them, "My brother, what you think is not the truth"."

[W.134.7:1-5]

From the world's perspective, forgiveness is seen as unjust. A mere exercise in penalty against yourself. A recipe for schizophrenia, a kind of charity undeserved, a means to further embellish one's ego with the jewels of false humility. Its application can find no just cause within the world. So it is rendered useless and ineffectual because belief in its unjustness still remains to mock. You still believe that you are a victim and unfairly treated by the world. You still believe that your brother has unjustly attacked or stolen from you. So your show of forgiveness remains just a game. In your eyes, he is still unworthy and you are the better man. No true healing can occur where grievance remains. All healing means release. True forgiveness functions to cleanse the mind of the projectionist and so erase the slate. Only then can the world begin to glow again and the internal light radiate outwards unimpeded. Then it takes on a new powerful luminosity, one that signatures life and heavenly fragrance. Echoes of eternity are heard once more as the trumpet of time comes to an end. Then the raucous screeching sounds of pain and misery are heard no more. The lens disappears back into the mind of the projectionist, as does the world. The reflected and projected become fused as one. Dualism, which always represented a distortionary appearance disappears for good and the true, radiant and perfect reality, which wholeness alone can know, is joyously restored. That nothing has ever really happened at all is shouted most gloriously from all the roof-tops. Now all is seen as illuminated and unified. One is peering now into the timeless from the frame of time and merging with this ever-present unity. Now is it understood how the Samsara and Nirvana were always One.

13. THE PANACEA IS FOUND WITHIN

The ego's belief system reflects a very suffocating and painful indoctrination. Perhaps you are beginning to realize this now. The ego vies for your full allegiance, and in the end demands your outright destruction. In the meantime it aims to continuously trip you up through leveraging off your weaknesses. It wants you to get your hands dirty from the start so it can lure you through the gate of its ideology and belief. To this end, it parades before you all those temptations that the modern world prizes. These include the specialness of the various vanity clubs, the comforts of the consumer spaces and pleasure making industries and all the poisons of the pharmaceutical industries. So is the body made your primary goal - both means and end. This is to be the home of your salvation and your only hope of finding peace and rest at last. So is it faithfully pandered too, groomed and manicured, stroked and caressed, slapped and whipped, and everything else you can imagine. At some point the drug industry must come to your rescue and engage you with its shot in the dark. That is squeeze into your arm a gnarly cocktail of drugs with deadly interactions. A lethal cocktail for which no longitudinal studies have ever been completed. One that will leave you bombed out, neurally fried and physically exhausted, unable to move from your bed and screaming out for death to take you to your deliverance.

So soon you see that your body has become infiltrated with myriad chemicals, toxins and electrolytes all claiming to keep you well. Chemicals are elevated to gods. Complete tyrants having the power to arbitrate your peace and wellbeing. Now you are a prisoner to a bleak world of form which has become by proxy your higher power.

Your spiritual reality is declared a myth, a children's fable told only before dreamy eyes. All your thoughts are seen as but the spontaneous effects of biochemical raves going on inside your loony bin. Yes, the unholy excrement of neurotransmitters. Wake up, says the ego! - just take a look! Anything outside you, can knock you down without a moment's notice, perforate you and you are gone, food for the worms now! In this vast sea of chemicals that surround you, events are seen as random and independent of your thoughts. So is the world an experiment in happenstance, a recursion of meaningless events, without any regard for you. Here is the final nail in your coffin of self-empowerment, because the very seeds of power are strategically placed many levels of abstraction below you and deep into the mud of this world. At most, you can retain for the mind, this tiny freedom - its power for interpretation, but most definitely not its power of choice. No, all that is but a dream. All your choices are dictated to you by bare necessity. They are dictated by all the howling, madness and exigencies going on in this human jungle. A jungle that is empowered to revoke all your rights at any moment. Here where anthropophagi and the devil's henchmen come by day-by-day to eat your flesh, or at least exact a pound of it.

Mind is seen now as a rather passive innocuous device without much purpose. It is seen as but a perceiver and witness, but as powerless to influence events in any meaningful way. It functions more like a broken down radio that can only capture static noise from of the blitz of lightning speed signals that surrounds it. Maybe by mentally crunching the enormous machine of the world and by convolving all your thoughts to adjust to its sad state of affairs, you can succeed in moving your strings just a little. Otherwise the strings that hold your puppetry firmly in place are inescapable. Your fall from grace has been mighty indeed.

MAKING THE SMART DECISION, FOR A VOLTE-FACE

You realize now, that you need to penetrate a thought system to its root to have any hope at all. Only by finally seeing through it, can it be meaningfully assessed and judged. Then it will be deemed either worthless or of tremendous value. It is not cool to skirt around it, accepting only those parts that seem to be of your liking. Your procrastination and partiality is an exercise with savage penalty against yourself. If it is worthless at its core, then all its fruits are worthless too, no matter how tempting and alluring they may seem to be. Remember what you are tasting is not what you are swallowing. What you taste can be a deception but what you swallow can surely kill - just like an apple laced with cyanide.

Often when we are wandering in a bleak and lonely landscape, we can tell we must have taken a wrong direction. Everything is desolate and bare and all life giving sustenance has been crushed. As far as the eyes can see, it is just more of the same. There is no hope of finding civilization in the ego's world, no hope of finding joyous recuperating rest for our souls. It is a cul-de-sac that will go on forever until we decide to turn around. We must make fundamental change in our thoughts and attitudes, if we are to make any further progress. We must flip our thought system completely if we are to invigorate ourselves back to life and precipitate meaningful change. We have to admit we have been wrong all along, that we do not know our own best interests.

All our paths forward towards success have brought us only to failure. Turning around is the choice for all sanity and peace. It does not take great effort or strain to release a crumbling empire, only great effort to keep it in place. A simple flip and you are free and you have accepted your golden key back into reality. Just one decision is needed for your entire redemption. Then is the ancient way made clear and given its rightful place in your salvation. In the new and yet ancient scheme, health is seen as being natural, and in harmony with Spirit. Yes, you have long been a hostage to the soothsayers of old and to every quack that walks and breathes. But now you will become a Master over all appearances. You will become surrounded with miracles and joy and the soothing fragrance of your invulnerability. For you will come to recognize your power as the decision maker, and this is the Source from which all action flows.

All that seems to happen, is but your will projected. Now acquiesce into the deeper subjective dimensions of your Self. Recognize that all has always been in perfect symbiotic relationship with what is looking out. You no longer feel any sense of separation between you and your world. In one instant it has disappeared within, and with this disappearance everything has changed. Your old relationship to it now is gone, never to be replaced. Now you see, that there is no seer, nothing seen, just seeing. The world is known now as simply the phenomenal reflection outwards of your own inner essence. A dance, a celebration in form of your true essence of mind. Its apparent evolution but reflects the inward evolutionary changes. Now, it flowers with a new potency, vibrancy and aliveness. All is a vast sea, in which everything is joined. From the peak of your illumination, is it seen to be submerged and fused with the very ocean of formlessness itself. This inside-out understanding is the master-key that will transport you across the bridge into the real world.

You can now end your subscriptions to all those weird and insane laws you held in such reverence before. All those object-orientated beliefs in phenomena and form. You may laugh now when you reflect on all, that you once thought. You had foolishly believed yourself to be nothing but another object in a world of objects and never recognized yourself as the miraculous, indestructible and deathless awareness that you Are! The ego had you pictured as some poor sap. In its eyes, your identity was as a body, a set of bones tied to a stick. You were nothing but a scarecrow and a raggedy-ass monster. Something for the vultures and hyenas of the world to mercilessly pluck at and tear apart. Something for the dogs of the corporate world to pee upon. You had hung out there in the noonday heat writhing in torturous pain developing a dry throat from screaming out all your anxieties and frustrations. Yes, held together by duct tape and tiny scraps of paper on which were written out all your self-healing prescriptions and magical beliefs.

Yes the icy winds of the world blew hard and fast across all your weary bones and unearthly crevices and the ego had you snared exactly where it wanted. Now was its moment to profess to you the truth - or should I say its truth? And so it came to whisper into your ears that your mind was none other than an epiphenomenon of matter. That it possessed no independent existence apart from the body. Hostage within it, you seemed at the mercy of a world of external causes – a 4D spacetime landscape, which had its origins in some big pop, snap and crack. All has been smoke and mirrors since. This world of fear is real the ego proudly proclaims. The many demons of sickness, sin, crime, violence and senseless attack are all coming for you - rather than from you. You have got to learn to think quick and know where to hide. Sit out there by the fountain and become a pigeon stool, if you like. For here, there are no lasting grounds for justice, salvation or hope. Justice is your purchasing power, justice is convincing others that an elephant can be balanced indefinitely on the tip of a needle while you are stealing the carpet out from under their feet. Salvation is in specialness, pleasure and hope are the opium to the lost, for we need something to keep them in chains to more easily manipulate them. Wars are often necessary and it is only through wise governance, social organization and legal coding etc. that lasting peace and stability can be gained.

THE EGO'S HOUSE OF CARDS COMES TUMBLING DOWN

Yes, the ego's house is built on so many myths. In its world, the sword of judgment is venerated and esteemed as that royal sword of justice that will keep you safe. Your salvation is only found in presenting a picture of your specialness before the eyes of the world while licking the boots of others to curry favor. So you lick the boots of all those compadres, celebrities, degenerates and all other self-righteous puffs of smoke that you think can progress your cause an ounce. The ego teaches that you must learn to see all those that are weak around you as the guilty ones. Happiness is in pleasure seeking, and giving fully in, to the temptations of the body and all transient idols of the world. Spirit is not needed at all. Epicureanism and sense indulgence are eternal delight. Yet, it is only your firm beliefs in all the ego laws of darkness that are holding you back. Simply but call them into question and the ego's entire empire falls. So does this entire edifice of insanity crumble and fall apart. To call them 'laws of darkness' is a joke. They are more like self-righteous proclamations and myths that but bedazzle and befool the self-deceiving. Below is a simple enumeration of some of the ego's foolish beliefs and myths as they stand in contrast to the Realties of the Kingdom.

BELIEFS OF THE EGO	REALITIES OF THE KINGDOM (POWERS OF LIGHT)
Belief In Fragmentation	Reality of Wholeness
Belief In Incompletion	Reality of Completion
Belief In the Body	Reality of Spirit
Belief In Imperfection	Reality of Perfection
Belief In Matter	Reality of Mind
Belief In Illusion	Reality of Truth
Belief In Separation	Reality of Oneness
Belief In Space-Time	Reality of Eternity
Belief In Hell	Reality of Heaven
Belief In Powerlessness	Reality of Omnipotence
Belief In Vulnerability	Reality of Invulnerability
Belief In Victimhood	Reality of Empowerment
Belief In Guilt	Reality of Innocence
Belief In Specialness	Reality of Holiness
Belief In Blindness	Reality of Vision
Belief In Scarcity	Reality of Abundance
Belief In Magical Beliefs	Reality of Miracles
Belief In Sickness	Reality of Health
Belief In Death	Reality of Life

Below we contrast some of the powers of light with some fundamental ego weaknesses inherited from adopting its thought system.

EGO WEAKNESSES	POWERS OF LIGHT
FEARFUL	LOVING
BOUND TO THE RELATIVE	POWER OF THE ABSOLUTE
FRAGMENTARY	WHOLENESS
MISCREATIVE	CREATIVE
DEFILEMENT	PURITY
FORM OBSESSED	CONTENT ORIENTATED
JUDGEMENTAL	FORGIVING
PROJECTION	EXTENSION
ATTACKS	JOINS
DISTORTIVE	CLARIFYING
DISSOCIATIVE	UNIFYING
GRIEVANCES	GRATITUDE
CONTEMPTUOUS	APPRECIATION

Teaching The Laws of the Kingdom As the Means to Remember It

That which you are prepared to give, you will receive. Maybe this is apparent to you in extreme cases, yet in the regular course of events you still think you can either extract more or reap less, than you give. For example, Mahatma Gandhi, Martin Luther King, Nelson Mandela etc. stuck to their guns in their fights against inequality and oppression so they became powerful instruments of change. They seem to have got back in good measure that which they put in. However when we see the unscrupulous and corrupt around us, as well as those overpaid CEOs, stars, entertainers, sports personalities etc. who seem to proceed so smoothly and successfully through life, like a breeze, we think there are injustices all about us. We feel we need to become more cunning, calculating, closed mouthed, political, plagiaristic etc. But what good does it profit you to gain the whole world if you can no longer live with yourself? Once one loses all self respect, integrity and credibility with others, one is as good as dead. These are the invisibles that are of the utmost importance.

When we scapegoat others, we teach ourselves victim-hood and vulnerability. This carries tremendous cost. So we need to learn to develop vigilance against this temptation. Only when we cease to scapegoat, will we cease to feel attacked. Then all apparent injustices and grievances will disappear from our minds. Then we will know our deeper Source of invulnerability - Truth. Then we will know that the world as an effect can perpetrate no injustice against us that we do not actively wish for. With our release from our own thoughts and beliefs in victimization does the entire pyramid of our ego thought system flip. The apex returning to the base and vica-versa. Our responses now will no longer be mere chain reactions that emphasize our victim-hood. This world, which was once such an ominous source of misery is seen now to have lost all power and control over us.

Now we radiate peace unconditional, for we have risen high above it. Our days of walking around as a miserable speck of dust, driven by its random winds of change are over. We are no longer content to remain just another hapless victim held captive to its senseless laws. We are beginning to realize that real Law comes from within. This is God's Justice. Now we no longer seek out death in the world. We no longer cradle and adore a disenchanting grave. R.I.P. we understand is a blessing for the awakened, not for the dead, because real rest can only ever come through our awakening. Yes, the magical elixir that cures all our ills is not found in this broken down context of the world, but from inside ourselves. Digging deep within we find that we have never accomplished anything much through our own measly efforts but accomplished many Herculean feats through the Power of the Christ in us.

> **"Seek not outside yourself. For it will fail, and you will weep each time an idol falls."**

> **[T-29.VII.1:1-2]**

Yes, It is His Strength by which we can rest assured. His Knowledge that will correct all errors in our mind. He will eliminate all our feelings of anxiety, uncertainty and vulnerability. Remove all that nervous trembling caused by our egos, while restoring us to calm confidence and joy. Within us lay the solution all along. The source of all luminosity has always been waiting here. Where our ego roots come to end, we find all the power of Heaven at our command, marshaled to protect and care for us and bring us to never-ending joy. Yes, to the extent that we take responsibility for our thoughts and actions, we are empowering ourselves and reaching back to our heavenly roots.

Sharon Moriarty

Now we see that all our explorations without were pointless indeed. They represented but a vain and futile search for idols that we projected to complete ourselves. Through idols, we sought to keep our dreams alive, while fearing our true Source of salvation and completion. We saw what lay buried deep within us as a threat, that would dispossess us of all idols and all dreams. Yet, what is an idol but a symbol of death, a symbol standing for the Anti-Christ in the dream we made, a symbol of our wish to have an image replace the eternal truth in us. Some mockery stand in for what we Are! Each idol represents our attempt to make a piece of dust substitute for our Reality. And what is the dream, but our decision to remain asleep and as a hostage to hostile dreams. Each dream is a picture projected from a mind that seeks completion in the false. So does the ego in its foolish grandiosity hope one day to contain Truth at last.

"The lingering illusion will impel him to seek out a thousand idols, and to seek beyond them for a thousand more. And each will fail him, all excepting one; for he will die, and does not understand the idol that he seeks *is* but his death. Its form appears to be outside himself. Yet does he seek to kill God's Son within and prove that he is victor over him."

[T-29.VII. 3:1-4]

14. THE TWO THOUGHT SYSTEMS

The Dr. was extremely agitated again. Immediately, I went into red alert. I had never seen so much fear in his eyes, never seen him so terrorized. And he was a hard one to terrorize. Incorrigible in every direction. He who wouldn't bat an eyelid at diving with the sharks or jumping out of a perfectly good airplane or bungee jumping off a bridge, or even climbing high into the Himalayas. Yet, now he was in mortal fear. He who could suffer out the scourges of poisonous snakes, vermin, spiders, random beatings even banditos and taxes had finally been brought to his knees. He said he could hardly sleep a wink. In fact he now had an absolute dread of sleeping altogether. He said, "*I used to think fearful nightmares were the worst, but now I have moved into a completely different dimension. Most nights, after I finally fall asleep, it is only to wake up soon after feeling absolutely paralyzed in my bed. I cannot move a finger or a toe and there is a dark evil presence in my room. It is not like I am in the hypnagogic or hypnopompic states of sleep or even in a lucid dream, I can see all that is happening and yet I am powerless to do anything. I can feel it enter the room, almost as a cloud of invisible flies moving across it. Suddenly the atmosphere has become completely charged with insidious energy. Yes, it is like a swarm of invisible locusts were moving across it, propagating in waves about the room and often in large globules of focused hate.*

I know it is coming for me. My eyes are fully open, surveying the entire room and I am awake and looking out in terror. Then it starts! I feel it forcing itself upon me, pressing down hard upon my chest, looking to rip out my heart. Then I feel this rapid tugging motion over and back, like I am being thrown off the bed like a ragdoll. Yes, it is like a scene from the Exorcist playing itself out in my bedroom every night. Inwardly I feel myself clinging to the bed's edge for dear life. Then it creeps up behind my stagnant body and nestles in too close for comfort. Then I feel it fucking me from behind. Yes, there is this strange dynamic pullulating motion up-and-down and over-and-back, as I feel myself being probed from the rear. Then I feel this big dick entering my behind. But what am I to do? Inwardly, I am screaming in anguish, saying 'No, you don't you motherfucker'. I want to grab my lamp nearby and slam it across its head to knock it off its game, and then I want to kick it over and over in rage. But like I said, I cannot move an ounce.

I am being raped and yet not a court in the land would uphold me because my victimizer in an invisible force-field. Then my mind just caves in and I expect to die. Then after, what seems like forever, it just moves away as mysteriously as it arrived and suddenly the room is clear and energy free again. Vanquished of all demons. Then I find I can move all my limbs with ease. But in my head, I feel traumatized and fucked up. I don't even know how to begin to approach this problem nor even how to verbalize these experiences with anyone else". Then the Dr. looked at me with the most imploring eyes, as if he were begging for any morsel of help or insight. I could see he was at his wits end and knew of no psychologist that would take him. He would just freak the living daylights out of them. He would just come out of the office feeling ridiculous and all the more humiliated. But he knew that I had deep existential experience of all the dream and Bardo states, as well as of the awakened reality and turiya state of consciousness. He knew that I would help

I immediately put him at ease, by telling him he was experiencing episodes of sleep paralysis. Then I said, that I agreed that it was not just a sleep disorder but that an evil entity or demon was seeking to terrorize him. But I said this is a very positive unfolding and a great opportunity. Just do not make the mistake of thinking this demon is coming from the outside, I added. Recognize it is coming from deep inside your unconscious. That normally sleeping side. Yet, realize this entity has no power over you - that all its apparent power is being generated by your mind. These demons are inside us all the time, but we do not usually recognize their presence. So they often feel pressured to come out and engage in full fledged attacks. I said this is their last ditch effort, because they feel themselves losing the battle against you. They can sleep once you are content to remain in ignorance, because then you will go about doing all their evil deeds unconsciously.

Then I asked the Dr. when do these episodes occur. He said, it varies, but usually around 3 or 4 am in the morning. He had noticed something else as well, that the room suddenly felt a good bit colder at the time of the visit. I said this all sounds about right. They will usually stream out just after the gates of the unconscious have been opened. When you are in that fluid state of consciousness, just after falling asleep - the time and mental state when you are most vulnerable. They wait until you are in your most weakened condition, before they attack. I said to the Dr. that he must be making some major progress in his inner explorations and purification or they would not feel impelled to come out and show their faces at all. I said, just sit tight and recognize that they have no power over you, laugh at them and realize they cannot affect the truth in you in any way. Remain loving for this they cannot tolerate. They thrive on fear. With this the Dr. was already contented, at ease and at peace. He began exfoliating in all directions and was bubbly again. I hadn't seen him like this in weeks. He now knew the recipe of how to take his inner demons out.

THE NEED FOR FLIPPING OUR THOUGHT SYSTEM COMPLETELY AROUND

We desperately want to find meaning in this world we seem to live in, but we have to admit it is incomprehensible most of the time. At moments we lighten up and seem to be enjoying ourselves. All is cool, we are at one with life and at one with the moment. But this moment is fleeting, and in the next one, a dark depression has settled in - shock waves and inertia have come upon us. Something totally unexpected or tragic has happened, or is about to. So we start to live on edge and begin to expect the unexpected. Our delusions of safety and order cannot protect us. The storms are coming our way and getting ready to suck us in to their powerful vortices of meaningless energy. Getting ready to erase all our great efforts at fulfilling our dreams. Perhaps we lose our job, or someone near to us dies or our relationships start to crumble apart. Next moment we find ourselves scavenging around again, dumpster diving, looking for the tiniest shred of meaning or consolation. Desperately trying to write our own arbitrary meanings on the screen of mindlessness, boredom and insanity that pervades us.

Everywhere we turn we find more evidence of senselessness, the world's random acts of violence and brutality, its unmitigated chaos, sporadic killings or tales of extreme injustice. Airplanes disappearing from the sky, decapitations, suicide bombings, mindless massacres, flash floods, Tsunamis and earthquakes - it never stops. Something always rushes in to fill the void, to deny us peace and progress. Yet, we cling to the world like a drowning man clutching at a straw, even though it seems to offer no real hope. We do not know where else to turn. The Course teaches that in itself, the world can provide no guidance, no hope of lasting inspiration because it remains just an illusionary effect of something that goes far deeper. It represents just a covering for the dark thought system of the ego, that is buried deep inside our minds. All the chaos and madness we perceive "outside" arises from the many false beliefs instantiated on the ego foundation we have built. Beliefs which we nevertheless continue to uphold.

It teaches us that our only hope of escaping its never-ending quagmire and finding true peace is by a completely different approach. One in which our thought system is flipped completely. One in which we come to know ourselves and our relationship to this world in a totally different way. Yes, there is another thought system that runs in startling contrast to the one by which this world was made. It is this thought system alone that offers all hope of resolution and healing for us. There are two thought systems then because there are two in each of us. Two different voices, each making claims as to the veracity and truthfulness of its thought system alone. The first thought system is the one that made this world. Being false, it can deceive and imprison but it can offer no real hope. The second thought system is the one that relinquishes the world. This is the one that frees. Here is all true hope, for in this one alone lies the certainty of God. We will now explore both thought systems in detail. We will examine them close up and so see how definitively and extensively they contrast with one another. We will review the core beliefs deeply threaded into each and examine both at their foundations. We will examine the mechanics by which each maintains and perpetuates itself.

The second thought system, the one that you are not so familiar with is the one the world does not teach. This teaches that the world evolved as an effect from our unconscious guilt. This guilt arose from denying our Creator and trying to establish a separate kingdom of our own. The kingdom of this world, that thus came about was born in the dissociation known as split-mind and it has been actively maintained since through projection. It is composed of billions of seemingly separated minds, most engaging in acute conflicts with one another and looking out only for their own private interests alone. This kingdom savagely maintains itself through judgment and fear and is actively clung to for its various idols and temptations. So it establishes a place for us to dream and wish fulfill, in the vain hope that some day its empty offerings can make us whole at last. Yet we also use it to hide from truth and to deflect the savage vengeance and retribution we expect from our Creator. Such thoughts only arise because we do not understand ourselves and have recast our Creator in our own mental image and likeness. That is we view everything and everyone through the many distortions of the ego. Yes, such are the world's "powers" and its axes of evil.

THIS OLD, ACHING AND WORN OUT WORLD

Our "separation thoughts" bestow on this world, all its seeming "life" and form. These unleash, fuel and propagate all its tensions, strifes and conflicts. What a strange place to find oneself born into? - not forgetting for a moment that it was born out of us. Taking it to be real and beyond redemption, we allow ourselves to be mercilessly whipped around by it. So it is that we learn to assimilate alien operators from a young age, often in harsh and regimented conditions. The goal is to quickly eviscerate all the wonder and mystery within. We are brutally and painfully indoctrinated with the world's answer, instead of answering the eternal '?' It seeks to suffocate and snuff out all our insight, intuition and connections to the miraculous. The flame of life is put out early, so that we can more easily be manipulated into conformity and made to bow down before its gods. These are the metrics by which it gauges our success. And yet all you yearned for, at this young tender age was to be set free to roam amidst the fresh air and trees to wonder and marvel at the majesty of nature. To question for yourself that which is before your eyes. To understand its greater metaphysical basis and relationship to yourself. Yes you wished only to bask in the colorful vibrancy of unlimited potentiality. Instead you got polarized, decimated, conditioned and coerced into accepting dogmatic and estranged views. You were made to carve sense out of senselessness. Shaped into nothing more than a goal orientated, competitive and futuristically orientated monster.

Yes, if I had my way the entire educational system, would be completely overhauled. Young ones would only need to attend school for two years and then not for more than three hours a day, with a fifteen minute break every hour so that they can go to the restroom, refresh themselves or take a run to get rid of any excess restlessness. All they would need to learn is how to count to one hundred and the very fundamentals of reading and writing in their native tongue. Nothing else, no history, geography, civics or religion. No other languages or art classes. No being forced to excel in sports, that they detest. And of course the preference would be for home schooling altogether. Everything else after that should follow along the lines of their own natural interests, abilities and inclinations and not be due to outside force and coercion. After all when we place seeds in fertile soil, do we need to continuously watch over, prod and manipulate them while closing them off in a dark room, or is it more important to just give them some nourishment and light once in a while. Then these seeds will grow into fine plants. Beautiful in their natural wildness, spontaneity and adaptability. And let's face it, we force kids to spend large sections of their lives consuming this nonsense, not for their best interests, but for our own and those of the large corporations. We have Google now so they do not need to remember, learn or digest tons of soul-crushing facts. They only need to be able to use their intelligence to understand, apply and innovate.

The world does not need any more politicians, lawyers, doctors, economists, or even engineers. Lawyers are just supporting the greed of the large vested interests or else entertaining the ego mania of the small-minded who engage in frivolous law suits that raise costs for all the rest of us. Doctors are in an unhealthy relationship now with the large drug corporations. Their goal has become twisted into keeping us sick, not restoring us to health. It is along time since any Doctor took his or her Hippocratic oath seriously. They should be put on trial for their collusion with big pharma. And it is so rare to see a doctor now that has any compassion, humor or good bed-side manner. They are all numbed out from overwork. So they hide behind their blood panels, radiation images, health screen tests and prescriptions pads to symptomize, and prolong disease thoughts. They instill fear and more health paranoia, rather than healing.

We do not need any more communication technologies, we have more than enough already. Real communication is getting worse by the day, not better. People are using it to nurse superficial online personas instead of sharpening and fine-tuning really critical communication skills which include the ability to communicate empathy, compassion, understanding, creative insight and sanity. Our capacity to support quality interactions has been lost somewhere in our drive to proliferate technology. People are using communication technologies now to distract themselves and avoid life rather than to live it. They are fast becoming vegetables of a completely new variety, ones that will soon make robots look like the life of the party.

Communication technologies are now used destructively more than ever. They are blindly and often maliciously deployed to launch information wars, disseminate lies, annihilate wealth, data-collect, spy, incriminate and sabotage. As are they instrumental in molding and shaping our value system while inhibiting our capacity to live truly authentic lives. They can be used to bring down perfectly good enterprises and to defame and destroy lives. Slowly we are coming to the realization that information is a powerful weapon and one for which we have no defense against. Used unwisely it is a weapon that makes Nuclear Armageddon seem like child's play. We should put all communication technology back in its box and seal it off with the skull and crossbones until we have first learned the basics ourselves of communicating in grunts and stares. Yes, we truly live in a dark age and we should go to work quick on building that Einstein-Rosen bridge that will ferry us back to the Stone Age.

We like to send out that glowing report that Engineers are busy working on the next best thing. We present the image to our kids that they will be working on space-crafts, healing technologies, lightning speed transportation systems, nanotechnology, robotic automation and so on. And these dreamy kids, all excited in their nappies are only to quick to go out and hemorrhage themselves with a mountain of student loan debt. So let me spare some of the pretense and foreplay. The reality is that most engineers are up all hours of the night responding to the hundreds of nonsense e-mails they could not get to during the day. They were too busy barking out their strategy plans to managerial whips, in meetings so chronically boring that it hard not to fall asleep unless you are being interrogated - and even then.

Yes, most engineers are just implementers, who take it from the rear, while trying to look excited. The hood over their heads that muffles their cries probably helps. Then they are hounded by endless e-mails and IMs from fatuous and inept managers and junior engineers that are too lazy to figure things out for themselves. If they do not help, they are branded and reprimanded and deemed not a team player. If they do, they cannot get any time to do their own jobs and so get a punishing performance review, that is if they are not axed long before then. And the last place you want to find yourself if you are an engineer is out of work. It can take years to get a new one. The average cycle from your initiating communication with a company to their making their hiring decision is typically three to four months.

Three or four months in which you have your head in the oven with the gas turned on. Living in an overpriced box in Silicon Valley, while every opportunist lines up to deplete your remaining resources. And we are still in such denial that most high-end white collar jobs sailed off long ago on the old spice trade routes. If Maxwell and Tesla were around today, it would not be long before they put a hollow-point in their coconuts. Still enthralled and mesmerized - let's all roll up then and put our pennies in the piggy.

Sight of the immensely valuable is always lost in the hubble and bubble. The present moment is deemed singularly unimportant and is used just as a means to an end. It is willingly sacrificed on the altar of idol nourishing dreams. Just being silent and reflective, listening and attuning to one's own nature are considered absolute wastes of time. To be spontaneous, is to be unruly and in need of discipline for one's bad behavior. We must fill our minds quickly and to the brim with more junk. We must learn to be ambitious and competitive and capable of exploiting all situations for our own ends, needs and gratifications. We must hasten to make the world into a garland for our specialness. We are trained not to think but to allow instead our thinking processes to be molded and conditioned from the without. Slowly we become very unnatural. We no longer trust our own first-hand instincts and experiences but accept instead second-hand opinions. We are pressurized to faithfully reproduce the old dead knowledge from the past. To mummify ourselves and to raise the worn out Methuselahs of our old gods back to life. So we find ourselves placing that sawdust, we have pillaged and scalped from the coconuts of others into the cracks of our behinds.

Slowly, slowly we forget about our being and work hard on our conditioned knowing – we become well groomed efficient machines, battery hens of the modern profiteering enterprises. We accumulate and package internally all the thinking of society, all the mindless ranting of worldly men and women. Our training is mostly in compliance and accumulation. Most of us are long dead, way too soon. We did not see it happen. Who could let us know, when everyone else was being cooked? The funeral was a long drawn out affair, that occurred over many years. Like frogs we were witlessly steamed alive without ever knowing what was going on. One day the buzzer went off and we knew that we were done. Yes, 99% of the possibilities in life were now closed off to us, never to materialize. We will never reach our peak potential because we have been stillborn from the outset. There seems nothing redeeming within us that truly shines. Our faithfulness and complicity to a deadening regime has led to our self-induced psychological suicides. We will never again even have a single thought, that we can truly call our own. We will just have the illusion of having real thoughts. We will shuffle and toss the same old dregs about, thinking that we are smart, even enlightened. Yet, these slops have been floating about now in the gutter for countless millennia. We will die still thinking that we were original and creative. But we were never truly alive. All we ever approximated was a gradual death.

We are trained to devalue quickly any notion of implicit self-worth. Our Being itself, is considered insufficient. Worth, to the ego is something that must be made or accumulated, it cannot self-exist. We must value ourselves, it declares only through the lens of our achievements. Submitting to "outside" powers and pressures, we lose sight of our real Identity. So we enter the realm of delusion. Displaced now from our natural center and position of power, we are easily leveraged and manipulated. Now we operate from the surface and appearances instead of from Self-knowledge. This tenuous position where we are trapped to the realm of appearances must make us feel even more fearful and vulnerable. So we become targets for those quick-fix attractions that serve as a stent or bandage for our fractured identities. In our denial, we vomit out a catalog of rationalizing clichés that seem to give credence to our poor choices and actions. Phrases like *"It's a dog eat dog world out there"* and *"The end justifies the means"* bubble on the surface of our minds and are always on the tips of our tongues. They become our worldly stance and signify our advancement with the ego's thought system. Yet they are the seeds of our ultimate degeneration and guarantee of failure.

The ego counsels us to take advantage of others, to exploit weakness, to divide-and-conquer, to expeditiously manipulate, to say and do that which momentarily pleases rather than what is right and true. This is part of its recipe for our success. So we learn to hold on to shallow, superficial albeit "glorious" self-images of ourselves. We let in only those fools that will pay homage to those chosen images we have placed upon our altars. We seek to opportunistically ingratiate ourselves with those who agree with our grandiose self-distortions, while conveniently turning a blind eye to their own. These become our *"special friends".* Everyone else becomes soon relegated to the box of our special hates or are rendered invisible. We make great efforts to carefully avoid all situations and people that would desecrate our altars. So we avoid anything that would attest to or even remotely insinuate our hidden vulnerabilities and falseness. In deep denial of our true Being, we carefully construct a dazzling array of ominous defenses to plasterboard over our very shaky foundations. These provide us with the illusion of stability and evenness of temperament. But just a scratch on the surface and we so easily come apart.

The lopsided and distorted formulation, that we call our identity has so many deep holes in it, that it has become like Swiss cheese. It is experienced from both within as a living death. As time goes on, it becomes the central foundation and fulcrum for our many psychotic and neurotic disturbances, addictions, instabilities and constant mood shifts. Denial is the foundation of our split-mind, and cause for all those multiple personalities we see and experience within and without. It is the cause of all our inner anguish and uncertainty. It keeps in place the dark ego world and its defenses. Guaranteeing all dark foundations are covered over, never to be looked at again. Since our self-images were erected out of fear and self-defense, they are anything but holistic. Powerless to heal, they need to be relinquished. Their function is to mask out our guilt by deploying frivolous and distracting thoughts. Thus keeping our greater source of fear from our awareness. We retain these images through the ego bribery of idols and specialness but they simultaneously deny us access to our Wholeness.

You can notice it for yourself. People often get rip-roaringly inflamed for seemingly innocuous reasons. The reasons they offer are often just the tip of the iceberg, and are not the real cause of their upset. They are really trying to justify their poor choices and actions, their selfishness and self-absorption. Yes, rationalizing all those loveless barriers they have erected. They simply do not want to commit any effort or time into doing what is right. Often they are willing to purge friends they have known for life over the most trivial matters. So, they precipitate blow-ups over random nothings until the message has gone out clear for all to hear. Now they can go their separate way. They have justified their lovelessness so they can proceed with all their ego goals. They do not want to consciously face the full measure of guilt associated with denial of another's true needs.

The ego will always do this, drop its investments in its "friends", once they became inconvenient. It is not really interested in helping another, but only in using them. It does not really want any other body to probe too deeply into its private hermitage. It does not want you to penetrate beyond the sacredness of its defenses and peer into the emptiness and abyss within. No the ego would never tolerate any such unmasking. It interprets it rightly as an invasion, one that places its entire house of cards at risk. It will not allow you to enter its forbidden precincts. The relative world is full of the hypocrisy and pain caused by such situations. So we are always seeing people playing about, entertaining the most idle desires of their egos. They are simply vacillating and "buying" time, avoiding making any commitment to truly healing their minds. Nor are they meeting the true needs and goals of every relationship and encounter, which is one of joining in salvation.

Others you will notice are very insular. You may circle around the island of their being as many lifetimes as you like and all you will find is the savage sentinels always posted at the gates. They provide no entrance or welcome for the regular riff-raff, but function more as a gated community of one. Entrance is by invite only and this rarely happens. You are made to feel so unwelcome and given the cold and icy shoulder. Eventually you just give up all hope of ever entering their domains. Their defenses are too impenetrable and their vigilance too great. So they become dead to you. You have written them off as tombstones. Maybe they do not approve of your life choices or even of your existence. And yet it is so easy to meet with their disapproval, like they started off wanting it that way. If you meet enough people of that sort, your whole life becomes transformed into an Archipelago of barren and unreachable islands, in which you can never come ashore or find any place of welcome. So you remain as a powerful turbulent ocean raging as a sea of unrest and rugged beauty perennially lapping your waves up against the solitude of their beachheads. Yet they will never accept your gifts and seem completely disinterested in going out and exploring the ocean of your being a little further. They will never fathom you to your depths.

Yet, over time, we come to believe in and to prize these special self-images, we have made. There is something unique of ourselves in them. We do not want to see them torn apart and humiliated because of their deficiencies and weaknesses. So we send out our dogs of guilt to scavenge the huts of our enemies seeking for all and any evidences of sin, infidelity or treason. So we can grow our superiority and grandiosity while reinforcing separation. We are careful to avoid and screen out any thought that puts our dearly held beliefs to question, any thought that seems seditious to the thought system we have chosen or the image we have made. Would we be so cheerful, if we but knew exactly what each of our self-images cost? For the cost of denying truth must always lead to a living death. We choose either truth or the parched desert of the ego's thought system. When we become molded in the likeness of our ego, we feel guilt, fear, judgment and condemnation. We end our days beaten down, dried-up, cheerless and exhausted. Another life ingloriously spent chasing trivial pursuits, futile misadventures and engaging in meaningless charades.

EMBRACING THE HOLY SPIRIT'S WISDOM, TO END OUR DREAM MISERIES

So is everything pre-determined then? or are we empowered to finally end the wheel of life and death? Can we take a path that ends all dreams? Can we fashion our minds into a powerful instrument that becomes the death-of-death? There is but one viable alternative to the ego's thought system. One alone that leads to life and meaning. All others lead into darkness. Yet, on this path alone is all darkness and distortion ended. That is part of its power. We must become illuminated by the spiritual light, that sees all brothers as radiant and sinless. Illuminated with a light that will quench forever all notions of suffering and sacrifice. Soon our dream-time adventure becomes an increasingly happier one, until that moment when we find ourselves awake, resting in our eternal Home. Will we then "**Choose Once Again?**" What hope is there in entertaining any other choice! We are but asking for more needless suffering, loss and despair - more time in which to procrastinate our indecision. The answer is that we both '*Can and Must*'. Our mission is guaranteed to be successful and our goal is assured. Our progress is accelerated to the extent that we more readily distinguish the Voice of the Holy Spirit from that of the ego and learn to put right decisions into practice in our lives. Let's review then the basis of beliefs on which each of the two thought systems rest. This way each can be honestly and accurately compared and evaluated. Each appraised and judged, not by the covering of its temptations, but by its underlying veracity. We will see how each system of thought and belief is consistent unto itself and yet both stand diametrically opposed. Yet, we know that only one alone can be true. In this recognition, the other is exposed for the web of lies and deceptions that it is. Decision making become easy once this recognition is made.

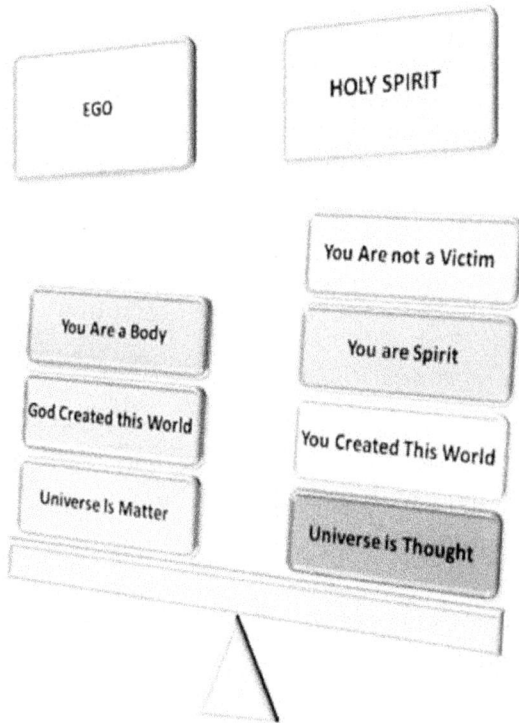

No.	BELIEF SYSTEM OF THE EGO	KNOWLEDGE OF THE HOLY SPIRIT
1	An External World Exists!	No External World Exists *Ideas leave not their Source.*
2	The Universe is Composed of Matter	The Universe is a Product of your Thoughts What seems "outside" and independent is really just your thought projection.
3	Consciousness is an Epiphenomenon of Matter Consciousness is seen nothing but a ghost, arising from the biochemical machine of our bodies. An effect of matter in motion.	All Matter is a By-Product of Consciousness All seeming matter and the entire relative existence is completely contained within your consciousness. The Real world of the Absolute transcends subjective-objective duality, as that of consciousness-perception.
4	This World has Value	The World is an Appearance in Mind It is an illusion, a dream with no substance; Its only value, is as a learning device. Once you know truth, it will be relinquished from you mind. The only reality it retains are those loving thoughts you extend.
5	You are at the Mercy of the Outside World	You are at the Mercy only of your Thoughts
6	You are not Responsible for the World you See	You are Responsible for the World you See
7	God is Dead; There is no God !	God IS !
8	God created the World	You created the World Each one of us makes a world that reflects our beliefs and wishes.
9	You exist in Space-Time	You exist in Eternity. Your Space-Time existence is Illusory

10	Space-Time is the Record of all that has ever existed	Space-Time is the record only of the illusory
		The present moment alone holds Truth.
11	Evil exists and is a Real Power	Evil has no Real Existence or Power
	Evil is a real force capable of opposing God.	Only in illusion is evil believed, felt real and powerful. Evil is forever incapable of having any real effects. Its seeming presence is due to a lack of love. Evil is synonymous with the ego and disappears completely in true love.
12	Both Good and Bad Exist	Only the Good is Real
13	The "Separation" is Real	There is no Separation.
		All are eternally joined in the One-Mind of God.
14	You are a Body	You are Immortal Spirit
	The mind is a by-product of the body. The body is your real source of strength.	Your mind is part of God's Mind. It is Holy and all powerful. The appearance of the world arises from the lower mind of the ego. This part alone entertains false beliefs. The body is a learning device of our lower mind. It has no strength, that is not mind given. Being unreal it neither lives nor dies. Our higher Mind knows only Truth and retains is in connection with Spirit. Once your awareness is restored to Knowledge, the body will be seen to disappear.
15	You are Imperfect	You Are Perfect
	Imperfection and sinfulness is your abiding reality. At root you are flawed. Made of mud. You have both strengths and weaknesses. Your best option is to leverage your strengths and hide all your weaknesses.	God made you perfect and God does not make junk. Appearances of imperfection arise from your identification with the ego. Once you undo all false ego beliefs your innate and unalterable perfection will rise back into your awareness.

16	Illusions Exist and Have Power	Only Truth Exists and Has Power
	As an Illusion you can be easily threatened. You need defenses.	Truth cannot be Threatened, but it can be lost to Awareness. This loss occurs as you listen to your ego instead of the Voice for truth.
17	Illusions can be made to Satisfy	Only Truth can Satisfy The cost of truth is the sacrifice of all illusions. You give up nothing and gain everything.
18	You are a Victim You are weak and insignificant and constantly at the mercy of outside powers greater than yourself.	You are not a Victim You are invulnerable. God's Son is forever omnipotent. You are only ever at the mercy of your own choices and misuses of mind. Any moment you can elect to choose wisely. This will empower you to rise above all illusions.
19	You are Not Responsible for what Happens to You	You are Fully Responsible for all that Happens to You
20	I Am Not Responsible for my Thoughts and Feelings	I Am Responsible for my Thoughts and Feelings
21	Fear is part of Reality	Only Love is Real Fear is always the result of misinterpretation and distortion. It operates from the unreal part of the mind, 'the ego' and it results in miscreation. Fear has no basis in truth. Being unreal it can never be experienced exactly in the present moment. Its presence is always the carryover of false beliefs and interpretations from your past. It is strengthened through your attachments and identifications with form. Thus it maintains the illusion of its existence. It is unknown in the formless.

22	**Fear Protects You !** **Love Weakens !** The ego promotes the thought that Love weakens and in Fear you will be strong.	**Love alone is Your Safety;** **It makes Whole** Only in love can you be known. Identifying with fear, you enter an illusory existence and feel lost. No longer recognizing your true Identity but as some dream image instead.
23	**Judgment Serves to Protect** **the True and Worthy**	**All Judgment Serves to make You** **Blind** Judgment functions as a block to vision. You can have either judgment or vision, never both. Judging your feelings is its one good use.
24	**Forgiveness is an** **Undeserved Gift**	**Forgiveness is a Gift to your Self** True forgiveness is the magic touchstone that heals and releases. It brings bliss, Self-remembrance, and restoration of truth. It ends the ego's reign as well, as your apparent bondage to the world of perception.
25	**Sin is Real,** **Everyone Sins**	**There is no Sin** Sin is impossible for a Son of God. We have made many bad mistakes by listening to our egos. These unfortunately have become construed by us as "unpardonable" sins. To our egos, all sins are irredeemable. Yet the Holy Spirit teaches that all "sins" are really just mistakes, we made through siding with our egos. The cure for all our mistakes is forgiveness, not condemnation. So do we heal our sight and our minds. So do we come to know the truth - that God's Son is forever innocent and untouchable by sin or illusions of any kind.

26	God's Son is Guilty	God's Son is Innocent
	Making "others" guilty is the best means to your salvation. Your innocence is gained through seeing the source of all guilt "outside" you.	You innocence is beyond question and was established by God in your Creation. It is revealed by your willingness to see it in others. Your willingness to be truly forgiving. Only the ego can feel guilty. Yet the ego's existence is entirely pseudo..
27	The Best Defense is a Good Offense	The Best Defense is Defenselessness
	Many clever and ingenious self-defenses are your means to guaranteeing your safety.	Defenselessness removes your beliefs in an enemy without. Here alone your safety lies. No longer according power to illusions, you are restored to awareness of your invulnerability. Drop all defenses and you see you were always safe.
28	Sickness cannot be Avoided	Sickness has no Real Existence
		The presence of sickness always reflects your underlying belief that you are a body in a separated world. You mistakenly believe your body is real. That it can become vulnerable. All forms of sickness are illusory and arise from ignorance. Being afraid of truth, you use sickness as a strategic defense against it. So do you empower magical beliefs to play the role of surrogates, in place of recognizing the power of your own mind. So do you retain your wrong-mindedness and misplace the cure.

29	Sickness is Healed Through Magical Beliefs	All Sickness is Healed Through Right Understanding
	Sickness is healed by outer means. These include various medications, remedies, drugs, healing technologies, right diet and nutrition, exercise, amulets and charms, homeopathy etc.	You are already healed. You have always been the very picture of health. But this eternal picture has now become screened from your mind. You have replaced it with the ego picture of you. The illusion of sickness arises from falsely identifying with the ego. So you lose access to the light of Spirit. Right understanding functions to automatically relinquish the false – that is all your guilt, self-attacks, and fear based defenses against truth, from which all sickness arises.
30	Suffering is Unavoidable	All Suffering is a Mistaken Interpretation
31	Sacrifice is Demanded	No Sacrifice is Asked
		No sacrifice is ever asked of a Son of God. Truth never demands sacrifice of any kind. It knows only of giving. It is only illusions that seem to demand sacrifice and penalties against yourself. Any notion of sacrifice only arises when you lose Awareness of Abundance.
32	I am Enslaved	I am Free

33	My Identity is up to me to fashion.	My Identity is Perfect and Changeless.
	My identity can always be improved. The ego has devised many ingenious schemes for this, including specialness, worldly achievements, bodily obsessions, body sculpting, adopting various morality codes, mannerisms etc.	I remain always as God Created me. The world of appearances cannot affect my real Identity in any way. Yet, it can do much to shroud my Identity from my awareness, if I allow it.
34	I am ruled over by numerous Worldly Laws and "Powers"	I am Under no Laws, but God's
	The world has many crazy and insane laws that we are expected to follow. It is best if we learn quickly how to work these to our advantage.	I am subject only to the **Law of Love**. Through love, I am healed and come to know the Truth directly. This is what releases me from all bondage.
35	I Possess Only Through Taking	I Possess Through Giving
	This is a world of scarcity, lack and sacrifice we live in with only so much to go around. The more I pillage and plunder and deceive, the more I will have. One needs to get down and dirty or they will be left with nothing, but a soother in their mouths.	Giving is the way to know of my Abundance. When I freely give all to all, I will know that I have no needs. The corollary of this law, is that if I give nothing and take everything, I will be left bankrupt.
36	I protect my own Best Interests by being Suspicious, Scrupulous and Vigilant of "Others"	I Protect my Best Interests by being Trusting, Conscientious and Vigilant of the Best Interests of "Others"

37	My Brother is my Enemy	My Brother is my Father's Gift to Me
	There is only so much pie to go around. I must protect my interests. He will take all, if I do not get there first.	My brother is part of my Wholeness. As I join and integrate with him, I am healed. Our true interests and real needs are the exact same. Progressive action is learning how to work together while overcoming all our apparent differences. So accomplishing our shared goals. The voyage to truth is a collaborative adventure not a competitive one.
38	My Salvation Depends on my Specialness	My Holiness is my Salvation.
	My specialness and all my special idols are my salvation.	Through recognition of my Holiness, I will realize that I am already complete.
39	Ignorance keeps me Safe	Truth is my only Safety
	What I do not know or see cannot hurt me. Ignorance is Bliss.	Ignorance can and does hurt me. It is keeping me from Heaven and locking me in a prison-house. What I deny, still retains its power. All my dreams will fail because they are attempts at bargaining with truth. Only when I have become truly impartial and no longer enforce any biases, prejudices and preferences, will I find peace. I will come to know Truth because it will have become impossible for me now to distort.

40	**Heaven must be Earned**	**I need to Nothing** **I can never Earn Heaven, but I** **can choose to Remember it.**
	You only get out of life what you put into it. There is no Heaven apart from this relative existence. Any Heavenly bliss you experience here must be bought and paid for through your industry and efforts, your cunningness, you guile and all your strategic attacks. Then you will have manufactured a Heaven for yourself. One to be safely guarded behind a network of impenetrable defenses.	Heaven is God's Eternal gift to me. I do not need to earn it. I can never pay for it, nor manufacture it through my ego efforts. I can only increase it by being loving. All that is required from me is appreciation of this tremendous Gift. I will become aware of it to the extent that I cease believing in the unbelievable.
41	**The Past and Future are the Only** **Meaningful Aspects of Time.**	**The "Now" is the only** **Meaningful Aspect of Time.**
	Get yourself a scheduler and a plethora of time management tools. You need to learn how to use time efficiently to accomplish all your dreams, before you die. Every moment must be used as a means. No moment is to be wasted. Don't sit around doing nothing or trying to enter a blank or calm state of mind. This is for the dodos. Get modern Sonny Boy or you will be left sitting on a big pile of dog manure.	The **"Now"** contains the Eternal, the Truth and that which Always **IS**. This is your Home and place of Liberation. You need go no further. This is the one-stop shop.

42	Truth is Relative	Truth is Absolute
	There are many different truths. Truth is different for everyone and at different times. It takes on a unique special flavor for each. One that is adaptive to that person's specific characteristics and predispositions. Truth changes by the civilization, the circumstance, the person and the season.	Truth is changeless and is experienced exactly the same no matter what part of the ocean one is sipping it from. It always imparts the exact same effects and understandings. It is not contingent on any time or place, any particular civilization or influence, nor anything else born in the minefield of the relative existence. It has no levels, distinctions or degrees. Any part of truth contains all of it. It is only idols that are different and vary for every one.
43	This World is all you Got - so Enjoy!	The Kingdom is Your Inheritance
	While you still have time, indulge in all those worldly pleasures and idols the world offers. Time is wasting and there will come a time when you can enjoy them no more. Sit up straight in your seat and take your hover-round to the brothels.	As for worldly pleasure - It is impossible to seek for pleasure in the body and not find pain. The guiltless mind cannot suffer. Forgiveness is your means to happiness because it removes all belief in guilt. It undoes the dream of the relative world while bringing you to unconditional Peace and Bliss.
44	Birth is the Beginning	Birth is a but a Continuing
45	I Am Awake	I am Asleep

46	What is Denied is Powerless	The Denied is All Powerful
	What is ignored or forgotten goes away. Through our passive hostility, and denial of others we can undo the truth in them. So make their message less efficaciousness.	Truth has been denied and yet it is all-powerful, as is the present moment. Your have lost awareness of your true Identity and so you find yourself at a complete loss. You are in apparent bondage now to the world of the meaningless. When you ignore or deny someone, you lose the opportunity to heal yourself and so learn the true Source of your safety.
47	Memory Holds Only the Past	Memory Holds the Past, Present and Future
		The Course's goal for our memory is that we become trained to remember only what Always **IS - the Eternal present!** That is to preserve the past, in purified form. We must therefore be trained to relinquish and release all that is false. This is a critical part of the Atonement's plan for our Salvation.
48	The Part is Always Less than the Whole	The Part Contains the Whole, just as the Whole Contains the Part
	Gestalt theory always teaches that the sum is greater than the parts. In the relative world, obsessed as we are with magnitudes, this is what we believe. But this is only how the ego thinks and appreciates. It is not how God's Mind works.	There are no orders to Reality. One aspect is not less than or greater than another. What affects one affects all. All aspects of existence share 100% in our completion. When you isolate, exclude or fragment any aspect, you lose sight of their tremendous meaning.

49	The Senses Tell us the Truth	The Senses Are Liars. They most often Deceive
	The senses provide us with very reliable information which for the most part can be trusted. They tell us the bare "facts" about an external world that does in fact exist.	The senses give witness simply to what the mind wants to see. They can be used on behalf of falseness, as much as truth. They are driven from the inside-out and feed only those messages that are desired. These desires then manifest into our perceptions. There is no outer world for them to witness. Rather than believing in the foolish appearances that the senses are depicting, ask yourself instead, *"Is this the world that I want to see?"* All perception is empowered through your desire. Desire truth, then it will be given you. The senses can be purified to give witness to the Real World. Truth has no use for sensation or of perception, apart from as learning devices.
50	The Path is Difficult	The Path is Easy and is Forgiveness
		This path is easy. It is just very different from worldly paths. The simple and the humble pass easily to truth. Those who come with empty hands and open minds walk into paradise. They have undone the world in themselves. So does Eternity stand revealed.

51	**Rest comes from Sleeping**	**Rest can only come from Awakening**
	In sleep nothing, is clearly known or seen. The darkness of contradictions born from false beliefs continuously wage war in your mind. All seems meaningless and dark because illusions are seen to be on a parity with truth. It is impossible to find rest in such a state of mind. Your mind just moves from one fear-based dream to another.	With Awakening, Truth is restored back into your awareness. All that is needed is the relinquishment of all false beliefs. So do the dark and meaningless dreams of illusion comes to an end. You have transcended the dream by healing all contradictions that perpetuated it, as born from the ego. This alone kept you a seeming hostage to time. Now unconditional peace has come back to flood your awareness and you rest in the surety and light of Knowledge.
52	**Death is the only Door out of this World**	**Knowledge is the only Door out of this World**
	Death is the one certainty in life. Through it we will all pass in the end to become completely non-existent. Your reality is nothing but food for the worms.	Your fundamental reality is as mind and immortal spirit. This reality can never be destroyed, nor suffer any loss. Until your mind gains access to knowledge, it will continue to make worlds that are reflective of its desires and mistaken beliefs. Quantum Forgiveness brings one to that Knowledge which dispels all illusions. It alone can release you from the shackles of this world.

53	Death ends all Life; It is inevitable	Death is the Great Illusion

Death is the Great Illusion

The reality of life denies death. The Son of life cannot be killed. Mind is deathless. It is just appearances in the mind that come and go. When you have undone all your false and foolish beliefs and forgiven all, you will know that you live forever. You will experience your immortality directly.

What seems to die is merely the physical body. Yet, there is no physical body because there is no physical world. This body and world have always just been projections from your mind. As projected phenomena, the body and the world are entirely neutral. It is you that invests in them, as you see fit. This is the only cause of all the body's seeming pains and pleasures. Use the body for malicious purposes, addictions and pleasures, and you will fall trapped into a deeply embedded bodily identification.

As you can see the ego and the Holy Spirit present completely different portraits of what you are. Only one however can be true. The portraits contrast too extensively for any compromise to be made between them. Your attempts to intermingle and believe both, accounts for all your stress, anxiety and frustration. Because you are attempting to live and teach two mixed messages. Each transmitting a completely different content and advocating a completely different course of action. The world is the projection of the split that is in your mind. The fault-line is not without, but within. Here alone lies the need for healing. The ego teaches that you are a physical being, constrained to some tiny morsel of spacetime and engaging a volatile and capricious world of random violence and chaos. So you need all your wits about you to get what you want. In this world of separation, in which it sees itself, it is every man for himself. The Holy Spirit teaches in contrast, that you are the Immortal Son of God endowed with the full Inheritance of the Kingdom and limited only by your beliefs. Your brothers are part of your greater Identity and are critically important to your healing. As you relinquish all false beliefs, you come to recognize your immortality and invulnerability. These false beliefs are collectively known as the ego. There is not a single aspect of your thoughts, beliefs, moods or choices that are not affected by the thought system to which you are affiliated. Your decisions are the natural outcome of your choosing between one or the other.

So long as both thoughts systems remain as only partly enfranchised beliefs, you will be internally at war. You will be experiencing constant mood shifts, anxiety, indecisiveness and vacillations of thought. The result is loss of peace because you experience yourself more as a community of individuals, than as a Master of yourself. The key dynamics, features and characteristics of both thought systems are provided in **Appendix A**. There we compare the loving approach of the Holy Spirit with the "dynamics" of the ego. We also explore the innate features of spirit as it contrasts with typical characteristics seen in the ego. By examining your thoughts and moods, you can more easily determine which thought system is prevailing in your mind.

15. THE POWER OF YOUR DECISION

The power of Whole-Mind has been entirely lost to us. Its wisdom now is nowhere to be found. Thus we find ourselves at prey to all sorts of illusions because we no longer can access our real thoughts. Somewhere deep inside, our Mind remains unified, but we experience it now as fractured. We side with the ego too much and thus have lost all clarity and light. We operate as if we possessed a separated, isolated and fragmented mind. This is evidenced by our continuous stream of nonsense thoughts, persistent indecisiveness and deeply conflicted moods and emotions. Yet, is completely understandable based on the investments we have made. We must work from the position in which we seem to find ourselves. No mind is irredeemable because no mind is separate. All mind is whole, radiant and indestructible. It only seems split so long as we continue to entertain illusions. Its apparent "split" is just a sign of its need for healing and what is healing but right understanding. Healing is the result of retaining only true understandings, which automatically disavows all else as false. But to retain the true, we must first learn those criteria by which we can better distinguish it. True understandings are always expansive, rather than contractive. They are not concerned with magnitudes but with quality and essence and they have a potency that is truly limitless. They are consistent one another, just as false ones are but they never serve to isolate, complicate or confuse.

Distortionary thinking leads to the illusion of living in a "separated" universe. This leads to miscreations, unreal thoughts and private worlds. Despite the appearance of a split-mind in us, we remain an integral aspect of the One-Mind. We still retain the power of decision and all decisions are powerful. None is inconsequential. Decision making can lead us either closer to the real or further into illusion. This is because the content of each decision always reflect either truth or falsehood. We are always choosing between the guidance of the Holy Spirit or the insane counsel of the ego. When we listen to the Holy Spirit, we bring our minds into loving harmony with the limitless power of Creation and so become increasingly light-filled. When we listen to our egos, the result is always miscreation and fear propagation. We can become so depressed that we can hardly function at all. To be right-minded is to choose on the side of Spirit and this restores our minds to its natural power. It blazes a pathway to the real and to the joyous. Choosing the ego we disempower our minds and end-up spinning endless joyless illusions. The more we learn to differentiate the Voice of the Holy Spirit from that of the ego, the faster we will expedite our progress and release.

The ego does not really want us to develop ears. It is afraid that if we truly question and probe we will fully recognize just how empty its offerings are. Realize, for ourselves that all its paths lead nowhere. When it hears you listening to stories of how omnipotent you are, it is quick to put you down and get vicious. It does not want you to consciously realize your immortality. It says all this is a mind-trip and one that will leave you dim witted. It wants you to remain sedated and placed in an insane asylum. So it proceeds to trip you up at every opportunity to demonstrate just how weak you are. Your apparent vulnerabilities in the playground of the world seem to provide it with ample evidence that you are made of mud. Yet, its campaign is not all smear. It is constantly enticing you with temptations and quick fixes. Temptations that include specialness, protection, pleasure, comfort and retribution. It is constantly seeking to ingratiate you with others and to build up your status in the world. Yet, decisions made with it, reflect "solutions" that are good for you alone. They rarely reflect your real interests and needs.

When the ego does join with others, it is not because of any truly pure and altruistic motive. It is merely because it sees in it an opportunity to get more for itself. Such decisions are not really aimed at furthering your brother's healing, beneficence and growth. In contrast, the ego is always urging you to get rid of all your problems by giving them to others. It wants you to use, deceive, manipulate and scapegoat all. This is its solution for all myriad problems you interpret or perceive. Its solutions are always patchwork and serve but to increase your guilt and shame. Soon you do became imaged and framed in the mud of the world. And because of the law of belief, you begin to receive back in perfect proportion and likeness of that which you attempted to give. Projection presents only the illusion of displacement. All the effects of a wicked belief system remain within you, even when you project them - just as the images seen on a screen remain in the projecting booth. All false beliefs, remain in your mind, where they are strengthened and reinforced until you decide to cherish them no longer. You have not accomplished them in another, but only in yourself. Denied they proceed to unleash devastation in your unconscious mind, from where all you experience comes.

The ego, steeped in pomp and grandiosity is often seen frantically parading about outfitted in the most elegant costumes. Putting on its shows of huffiness and contempt. It can quickly nauseate one with all its stuffy 'airs'. Yes, it looks down on all as insects needing to be crushed. Its costume is embroidered with the most glistening jewels and artistically designed to dazzle and impress. It seeks to sell you on form alone, hoping you will never probe further. So you never see for yourself that morbidly obese body full of callouses, moles, warts and liver spots stuffed beneath this garment. Into its hems are embedded the sapphires of specialness and the diamonds of fleeting worldly power and privilege. The amethysts of worldly pleasure and lust, sparkle and glisten in the dark. They tempt you to come one step closer. Then there are the emeralds of envy and greed insinuating that all this can be yours if you just swallow quickly its poisonous concoction. Look closer still and you can see the rubies of war, blood and destruction, victory and sacrifice, torture and impalement. Deep inside itself, at its *'Le Coeur noir Ne la Vie'*, is placed the heart shaped lapis lazuli of guilt. But its most prized jewel is that spherical black spinel gem located right in the center of its forehead. This the dark eye of its Shiva Netra, from which it peers out at the world and looks down on all through the darkened glass of malice and vengeance. Around its neck dangles a string of exotic pearls on which it has placed all its idols. There are exactly 108 beads on this string, representing the 108 mantras of ego self preservation and empowerment. These it continuously chants into your mind, day and night – even in your dreams – in fact only in your dreams. So it converts all your thoughts and actions into devilish ones and all your allegiances to the Anti-Christ.

Yes, the ego is a consummate dark magician. It seeks to hypnotize you with all the dazzling offerings that the world of complexity holds out to you. It wants you to prize and esteem these gifts and think them worthy of yourself. Yet, this magician can only hypnotize and charm for a while. Once you know how its tricks are done, it sits there suddenly demystified and defrocked, absolutely plain and ordinary and not worth the least bit of attention. Simply bypassed as you strut past it, on your way to the bar. Those lessons you choose to teach, you learn and retain in your awareness. It is impossible to perpetuate an illusion about another without first perpetuating the same illusion about yourself. When you are listening to your ego, you are usually scheming to take advantage. You want to raise your head, just a little higher on the pedestal, by beheading someone else. So have you surrounded yourself with headless ones. As a result, you are continuously on guard and defensive and not available to the light. So you become a savage sentinel guarding the gates of your own life. Simply put, the ego cannot trust another because it does not trust you. It was born through your self-deception and denial. It is suspicious of the "evil" motives, it imputes in others because it projects to them its own. All of which makes trust impossible.

DECIDING TO HEAR THE HOLY SPIRIT INSTEAD

Listening only to your ego, the mighty Voice for Truth present in your brother is drowned out and submerged in a cacophony of gibberish nonsense. Your listening is too partial. You miss reality wherever you go, even though reality is all around. But awareness of it depends on your being in an unclouded and serene state of mind. You must present a mind that is not ambitious, manipulative, vengeful and narrow-banded in order to witness reality at all. One that is free of all distortion. All problems arise in the clouded state of mind that it is incapable of seeing clearly and thinking wisely. So it tarnishes all that it comes in contact with. You are continually upholding decisions that make you feel small, petty and fearful and yet you wonder why it is that you do not feel magnanimous and proud. Your valuing of tiny little nothings in the dream is what fragments reality and holds you ransom to the valueless and illusory. Value can only be found in wholeness and absolute inclusion – never in partiality of any kind. The lack of exceptions to the lesson, is the lesson.

The Holy Spirit cannot lie or deceive. He is entrusted to deliver only truth. Deciding with Him you release all the miracles needed to extricate yourself from all disastrous situations. All is achieved in a simple and silent mind. One that demonstrates a willingness to truly listen. Into this open space suffuse all true thoughts needed to restore you to miracle-mindedness. The Holy Spirit does not see from your own limited angles and perspectives, nor through the haze of your disabilities and perceptive distortions. His Vision remains unclouded, pure and unhindered. Unlike you, who hold so many false and limited interpretations of situations and events. He sees for all of time and beyond into Eternity. He is able to distinguish the real from appearances and He uses only those symbols that can teach and release. So He can help you navigate your entire way out. He simultaneously can see the instant of your apparent "fall" from Heaven and your complete restoration to the Eternal. He sees all situations as they are Now. All that has been and all that is yet to come. He does not need to prognosticate your future because He already knows what it is. He sees the full recursion of events and their effects through time, the full constellation of people affected by each of your decisions. He sees that no thought is ever neutral and that each affects a confluence of people, events and situations beyond your wildest dreams. He sees how each decision unfurls retro-actively into the past and progressively into your apparent future. Knows all those decisions, you must make to end all your suffering. He is the opium for all your maze-craze tensions, anxieties and angst. He is fully connected with Truth and to the wisdom of Whole-Mind. He can harness and magnetize all the real thoughts present, in your apparently separate mind into a powerful dynamo that blazes and accelerates your pathway to the real.

The Holy Spirit is your guide out of Hell. If you choose not to listen to His gentle Voice - it is only at your own expense. You can spend countless lifetimes, waging your way into deeper layers of hell, only to be ravaged by disease and hunger and a litany of meaningless endeavors. Yes, calculated worldly thinking can bombard and numb you into mindlessness. Your consciousness can shrink and become circumvented by very limited modes of thought, even regressing back to animal-hood or lower life-forms. As you fall deeper into the dark pits of scarcity beliefs and fear, you can become provoked to outright selfishness. You will possibly end up collecting coke cans and garbage on the beach for a little food and money. Yet, all the time you possess a glorious inheritance that in your impurity and deafness, you are powerless to collect on.

Once you decide to choose, with the Holy Spirit, you will no longer be projecting fearful thoughts onto the screen of the world, but extending loving thoughts instead. You will be learning of your real Identity and your real Source of power. Your life will become increasingly joyful and carefree and you will be seeing all with increased clarity and new understanding. You will be subsumed in a throbbing aliveness that cradles you in an unconditional peace. As you descend past the clouds of fear, that had obfuscated the light of your own self-nature, you will laugh at all the "seeming" ridiculous problems of this world. A full belly laugh will echo from the inner chambers of your heart. You will no longer be a cancer upon the world. You will no longer be reactive, victim minded, revolutionary and exploitive.

The only revolution now will be within yourself. This is the last revolution that must occur as you flip your self-concept right side up and inside-out. Yes, this can certainly provoke some anxiety at times. It just means that your ego is sputtering out its last dying gasps and is threatened, while you are beginning to feel the true scope of your limitless power and freedom. You are reaching the inner flame of your pure essence, omnipotence and boundlessness. You will start to see now that the toys and trinkets of the world no longer interest you. They are devoid now of all power to tempt. You have recognized their worthlessness and feel sorry for all those around you that wholeheartedly invest in them. You are eager now to move on fast and entertain hell no longer. Then one day you will penetrate beyond the false mists of the time illusion and enter the world of light. Recognizing this light, as the light of your very Self-nature, you will merge with it and be seen no more. You are Home at last.

16. THE TWO EMOTIONS

I remember one time, Dr. Gobbler's Knob finally got it into his mind to kill himself. For a while now he had felt increasingly isolated and rejected. Those halcyon days of his youth seemed to be gone now for good, replaced by icy feelings of absolute abandonment and desertion. He no longer had any friends to party or adventure with. The road ahead looked very bleak indeed. It seemed he was on the highway to hell and yet there were no exit signs or off-ramps anywhere in sight. Yes, he was heading squarely into the jaws of increased ridicule, frustration, anguish and despair. That much was clear. He did not need to be a soothsayer or seer to prognosticate his future. There was nothing much to grasp at, nor to hope for. Sometimes he felt like he was being yanked naked and bareback across a bed of nails, while at others, akin to a small sailboat set aimlessly adrift on the oceans of the world, never to arrive to any exotic destinations. Only the frozen ice-packs and glaciers of the Bering sea straits. Except this boat was his apartment, and the ocean was the vast sea of technology that surrounded him in Silicon Valley. The storms came often to beat up against his humble door. They came in powerful surges like forty foot waves swelling off the Cape. Over time he had grown very disenchanted and bitter. He detested the lack of substance in man and preferred to be left alone indefinitely.

Yes, he definitely felt like a Solzhenitsyn, sentenced to his own Archipelago Gulag. Yet, worse off because Solzhenitsyn at least had some compadres around him that shared in the same misery, while he had no one that could understand his plight. He had disconnected his phone three years before, since no one called him anymore except charities and telemarketers. His father had died suddenly a few weeks before. That had left him feeling somewhat stunned and empty. It was the last straw, the one that broke the camel's back, and one large straw it was. With this, a major hope had died in him forever. All his fanciful notions of what could have been had now been placed on ice indefinitely and sentenced to the land of the irredeemable - where they would remain for all time. Like a winning lotto ticket that had expired and could never be cashed. He knew he would never be understood this lifetime ... that was for sure. Better to erase the slate and start over again in a fresh new body. One that didn't have any history.

So he went out to the store and got a 1.75 liter of vodka. Then he proceeded to make cocktails. He had his own special concoction, which he liked, one that he called *"The hole in the boat"*. First he would pour four shots of vodka into a pint glass, then add a can of 7up or soda water. Then he would squeeze in a red grapefruit and add a good measure of pure cranberry juice. Tonic water was optional but he liked it because it added some bite. It was all very refreshing, but when it hit, it hit. Just one drink and he knew his entire day was shot and he started to go under. For a while he would stagger about and make aimless peregrinations around his apartment, only soon to be subsumed in a pleasant state of lethargy, followed by unconsciousness. But since he had not taken the edge off just yet, he had begun to cerebrate. He thought about stabbing himself in the stomach. He felt viscerally connected to the Shakespearean lines *'Tis but a man gone. Forth my sword! he dies!'*. But on afterthought, considered he might end up bleeding out for days or weeks in his apartment and not be able to call anyone. No one would find him, until the rent came due next month.

So he reconsidered. Now he was thinking the heart was the place to do business. A preemptive strike to that sacred jewel of pulp and soon it would be GAME OVER! No longer would it beat out its loving mantra of OM! OM! OM! in a harmonious and reassuring rhythm showering the world with peace. But even now it had fallen into a state of disrepair and resembled more a heart of darkness. Yes, now was the time for a '*Carpe diem*' moment and end its mantra for good. Unfortunately he realized that he had never owned a descent set of knives. They were all too blunt and pathetic, not to be trusted for such a professional endeavor. Next came the flash thought of a rope. Yes, '*dope on a rope*' would become his new mantra, his immortal signature, his last calling card. Unfortunately, he could not find any good place in his apartment to dangle from. And then the floodgates of his past began to open, evincing memories of two others who had tried that approach and failed. Then of another who had succeeded and was taken out in his prime.

No, the highway was the way to go. He would get himself bombed out and then drive into oncoming traffic. Yes, roll the dice and take his chances in the greater neural net of the universal holomotion picture. He could see it now, a large articulated truck would mosey into his perceptions at the opportune moment, carrying just the right payload to terminate his contract with the relative existence for good. Hopefully also adding in the appropriate finishing touches to his extreme makeover. Sending him off with a bang, splat and crunch. Another Kodak moment. He had known a transsexual woman that had done just that, and had succeeded, but it all seemed very messy – a closed coffin kinda affair.

The Dr. was becoming increasingly agitated with this failure to reach a resolution. He was after all very high IQ and a member of Mensa - so ending the oxygen flow to his sack of potatoes couldn't be all that difficult, he figured. But throw in those marbles of sensitivity, delicacy, discretion and painlessness and all else that was taken from the morality code jar and it was suddenly consuming all his ingenuity. He pondered overdosing on some drugs. Hopefully that would be discrete enough and not wake up any of the neighbors. Yes, they would have their Rice Krispies in the morning and go off, as the squares, that they were to live out enormously boring lives. If they crashed into walls on the way to the office, they could be turned around and redirected towards their soul-crushing cubicles. Yes, it was becoming abundantly clear that the engines and machinery of profit would go on. Delusions of progress would continue to be perpetrated to the masses and we would still have our i-Pads and smart phones within a short decade. He was not needed at all to steer this ship of minions.

Yet, as he reflected more on the OD trip, he recalled a story his Dr. had shared with him some months before. She related how her husband had been a professor of music and a child prodigy. He had taken the *'Bon Voyage'* of an OD trip but never arrived at the intended destination. Instead she came home to find him lying there, totally incapacitated and drooling all over himself. So she rushed him to the ER to have his stomach pumped, but it was too late - the damage had been done. He had both succeeded and failed, in his mission. He failed to kill himself but succeeded admirably in having his brain pickled and useful for medical science. But first he would have to remain as a vegetable of the human variety for his remaining years. A still life plant of the genus 'Homo Erectus', that perhaps a Dr. Chandra Bose would be delighted with. A plant towards which she now could sing all her soothing lullabies and propagate all her positive intentions.

That particular night, I happened to swing by the Dr's apartment. It was a very dismal place indeed. Having no cable, TV, phone, air conditioning, or hints of civilization in general. All there was, was just a plug in fan. At any moment, I expected Fred Flintstone to enter in his Flint mobile. I was surprised not to see any cockroaches, but then again, who would live with the Doctor? There he lay on his couch, with his stark beady eyes looking out into empty space, giving off one of those 'ten thousand miles away' stares. He had his bottle of vodka beside him, as well as a number of those lethal 'hole-in-the-boat' cocktails in pint size glasses nearby. When he first saw me, he was perplexed and somewhat spooked and at a total loss at what to say. He was like he was temporarily suffering from a bout of prosopagnosia with a bit of dementia sprinkled in. He had not expected any visitors, had not seen anyone for weeks. I could see he was in distress and immediately asked how he was feeling - but he did not know! My simple question seemed utterly unintelligible, even threatening to him. As if I were transmitting to him encrypted messages of the most mystifying and confounding nonsense, from the planet Zog. Yes, I was made to feel, like I was being intrusive and trying to trip him up with a battery of trick questions. Questions that had nothing to do with the matter at hand. He had become so completely asphyxiated with the nebulae of his dark thoughts, that he could no longer untangle himself from them. Instead he had become completely absorbed with the screen of his thought, never once stopping his mind's engines, to ask how he was feeling.

TUNING INTO OUR FEELINGS, TO ESCAPE DARK TRAINS OF THOUGHT

Don't we all operate like this far too often? We get caught up and obsessed with some dark trains of thought that are running through the screen of our minds. Then the thoughts becomes us, as we become them. Soon we are operating almost mechanically, like hypnotized robots shuttling through the dark cosmos on our own interplanetary modules completely divorced from the greater field of life. Our minds seem to have been taken hostage by an alien power and we lose all semblance of our authentic humanity. Lose all our roots to benevolent feelings and emotions and all capaciousness to healthily interact. Instead we function more like numbed out zombies that have become cryogenically frozen-off from existence. We are typically not suicidal, but quite often are in an emotionally toxic state, without ever realizing it. Identified with our mind and our thought patterns, we simply do not stop to ask ourselves, what is our current emotional state? Yet simply recognizing our emotional states can save us from a heap of damaging decisions, actions and miseries in life.

When dark thoughts are there, that is the very time to time-out and examine your emotional state. There should be a trigger somewhere inside and not that of a gun. A Lilliputian that waves a little red flag and says *"Reality check! Emotional Check Please! Time now to run all internal diagnostics!"* You may have to replace the boot code if necessary. At the very least, kill some of those higher level mental applications that are shredding your system and hogging your awareness. The Course has little time for judgment. It teaches that with judgment we are always placing a knife to our own throats, thinking it is that of another. It does concede however that the one and only proper use for judgment is in evaluating our feelings and emotional states. There are a lot of people who commit suicide because they temporarily enter dark places. The day before they would have considered the very notion of their impeding suicide ridiculous. Yet, the prisons also are filled with those who made singular poor decisions, usually while consumed under the influence of some drug or toxic emotional state. If they had simply tuned out and detached from their cheerless trains of thought and gone into a room and meditated for a few moments, so much misery, loss and pain could have been averted. They would not have ruined their lives and those of others.

It often happens that we blurt out something harsh and damaging to friends, we have known for many years. We know how to hurt them, that is for sure. We know all their buttons, all the special spots, where we can mortally wound them. Then suddenly sometimes we find the friendship is over. Yes, we were frustrated or enraged and just wanted to lash out at anyone. We were in the wrong place emotionally, without fully realizing it. Now we are kicking ourselves in the pants. Many people quit their long established careers or relationships in the heat of the moment. Others make very poor financial, business or life decisions while "charged" in the flux of an emotionally compromised state. Emotionally charged under various endorphins and polypeptides. The mystic G. I. Gurdjieff had a good remedy, that is both simple and efficacious. His good piece of advice seems however to have fallen through the cracks of our very superficial existence. We are so busy and multi-tasked in this modern culture. We have lost all patience and always want instantaneous results. When we are affronted or emotionally displaced, we want immediate pain alleviation of our symptoms.

Yet, Gurdjieff simply advised that when we feel ourselves emotionally hurt or wounded, we should wait at least 24hrs before giving any response. So someone comes up to you at the office and says something very mean, nasty, calculated and insulting. Maybe they perceive you as a threat. What do you do now? They are saying something that is entirely unfair and simply designed to throw you off-balance. Now they are waiting for that firework display of reciprocated rage, which will cogently exhibit to everyone present, what a vile, unstable and pathetic creature, you are. Definitely not to be trusted in handling the larger accounts, or as a lead on a project etc. You then simply calmly say to them, *"I will give you my response on this tomorrow."*

This is a very mature response, and also a very strategic one. It protects you from saying or doing something potentially very damaging and hurtful. You avoid making a bad decision and come across instead as very composed and cool-headed under fire. Clearly demonstrating to all that intimidation tactics, tactless coercion and pressure will not work on you. And now this jerk has to stew over what he said for 24hrs longer before receiving your response. At that time, he will probably be begging for your forgiveness, or at least admitting his mistake or insensitivity. Also in 24hrs your decision or response will no longer be warped by your very reactionary and boiled emotional state, of the day before. Instead it will reflect something that either needed to be said or done. Your resolution and response has gained in clarity in the intervening 24hr period. Put this into practice for yourself and see how useful it is. You will commend yourself for taking the time to think it over first. You will be glad you did not rush in and say or do all that you visceral instincts, impelled you to do. Glad that you did not release all that fury you wanted to unleash.

On critical decisions, it is very important that we separate ourselves temporally or spatially from a person or situation in order to gain true perspective. Often only when we are on the right neutral ground, can the right insights and intuitions flower. This clarifying distance provides the space for us to receive proper guidance. It enables right-minded thoughts and responses to enter our minds. So we find that our decisions and actions are no longer being swayed or poisoned by our biases, emotional attachments and visceral fears. Gurdjieff also taught the importance of not expressing negative thoughts or emotions. He recognized that which you express, you will often actuate on and so teach to yourself. As a result it becomes more firmly entrenched in your mind, so becoming part of your regiment of conditioned behaviors. When you react to or express negative energy or ideas, you are extending your mind power to promoting darkness and the ego world. This will weaken and cripple you, leaving you feeling powerless.

Unfortunately, we do not ping ourselves often enough on our emotional states and feelings. As a result we have become very disconnected from ourselves and life in general. Perhaps, if you visit a psychologist's office the Dr. will ask you how you are feeling. But it may cost you a few hundred dollars an hour for their sage attention. Those around you usually do not care a toss about how you are feeling. They are more interested in what you are saying or doing. You could be right there beside them trapped in the most suicidal despair and they will not even feel the pinch. All they are considering is whether or not they will add in another sugar to their latte. In our extremely busy and frantic culture, many are too caught up in other affairs to notice much of anything at all. Does it seem a surprise then that our capacity to truly empathize has become long dead and buried? This seems a critical part of the recipe for all the madness. Yes, the invisible undertones of dark emotions deeply imbued within us, have become lost in our endless and all-consuming obsessions with the world of form.

There are other critical aspects to this. Firstly, the widespread belief that our dark emotional states can be tamed or at least regulated through the right cocktail of drugs. We do not see that these emotions are just wrappers around a content that is screaming out to be resolved. One that requires meaningful healing at our core. The emotion is not the problem, it is just the symptom. It is its underlying content that is the problem. Yet, this we fail to look upon. In fact it has no face at all. We seem happy with shadowy reflections on the glass, seen through oblique angles of reference. Many talk about the existential void but almost no one wants to progress further down this runway. They do not want to disappear behind this dark door, disappear behind this worm-hole of the psyche. For it seems to be a black hole from which nothing ever emerges. How can they know then, that behind it lies a field of benevolent light and love, that is all encompassing? For the void is calling out for cure, and cure there is. It is the absence of the cure that is the cause of all our dark emotional states. Do we want to skirt around on the periphery and skate on thin ice forever? Engage in meaningless distractions, hopeless obsessions and the offerings of big pharma? All of which we implement as our surrogate solutions. It seems we do not want to try something else, an entirely different approach. An approach that is tremendously meaningful and healing, because it goes straight to true Cause.

WE ARE <u>NOT</u> VICTIMS OF OUR EMOTIONS. WE CHOOSE THEM!

Secondly, we have a strong tendency to view our emotions as but passive effects. Effects derived and shaped by the "outer" world of our current experiences. Yes, we want to root-cause the source of all our problems to 'out-there' or else displace it into that sea of electrolytes and neurotransmitters percolating about within our bodies. We reason that there must be some deficiency in our Serotonin, Dopamine or Norepinephrine levels. Culpability is always placed on some form or outer event rather than on our own inner motives, attitudes and failures to take responsibility. We think we can live our lives lovelessly and yet avoid the penalty of encountering dark emotional states. Yet, this is their seed and if we look closely enough we will find here also is the cure. Our emotions are not passive effects but instead power-drivers of our life experiences. Active presences derived from within, actuated to shape our lives. Because all our decisions emanate outwards. Many yogis down the millennia have clearly demonstrated that even though one possess nothing on the worldly stage, yet they can be the very embodiment of unconditional peace and contentment. In fact, non-attachment seems to be the very precondition of happiness, peace and contentment. While attachment serves to drive so many dark and obfuscating emotions. It is obvious then that our emotional states are being established within us, by our thoughts, desires and beliefs. The presence of dark emotions merely reflects the Self knowledge we have lost.

The Course teaches that we are responsible for our feelings and emotions. We are choosing these all the time. A deeper part of us is constantly making decisions on those emotions we want to feel. We place our investment chips on certain ones, because we are attracted to what they offer. So we begin to feel them. Yes, there are many around us who are positively addicted to their anger and rage. Such folk tend to have very choleric demeanors and like to have a strong gale always blowing at their backs. A gale that propels the sails of their caustic corrosivity. Others prefer to be seduced by their bitterness. This dark cocktail holds great allure for the melancholic. Dark emotions are more like those inner monsters that we continuously feed and nourish. Often they can take over to such an extent that we seem to be their victim. We actively scavenge memory and perception for more evidence to sustain these carnivorous beasts. They are welcomed into our lives as our Pit-bulls and Rottweilers and they are chained to the doors of our worlds, ready to strike at a moment's notice. They seem justified and we come to rationalize them. The evidence that seems to justify them only ever comes afterwards.

Yes, we choose our emotions, just like we choose the ego. It is an important part of our health to know the predominate emotional states we are in throughout our day. Knowing this gives us power and liberation. No dark mood or emotional state can hold power over you now. You need no longer enfranchise them to run your roost. Ping yourself right now and identify what is your dominant emotional state? Are you feeling lonely or isolated? Maybe you are feeling anxiety or fear? Is joy and contentment on the horizon or else only unhappiness or sorrow? If you like, you can review the table further below. You may be feeling multiple emotions at once, or at least close together.

For example, you may be simultaneously feeling depressed, lonely and abandoned. This is understandable since all these share the same content of fear. There is usually one dominant emotion, however. See which one most closely approximates your current state. You will find that you do not experience those emotions listed on the left and right sides simultaneously. This is because, you cannot experience yourself both as love and fear simultaneously. When fear is present, all expansive and loving emotions are gone and when love is there, all those dark emotional states associated with fear have at least temporarily disappeared. The more you practice, the greater your emotional vocabulary will become. Being able to distinguish your emotional states, empowers you to become master over your life. Because once you have identified an emotion that is of the ego, you can make those decisions to release it and decide instead on behalf of Spirit.

FEAR	LOVE
Depressed	Cheerful and Inspired
Sad	Happy
Sorrowful	Joyful
Grieved	Relieved
Miserable	At Ease
Embittered	Elevated
Angry and Enraged	Peaceful and Collected
Hateful	Loving
Irritated	Untroubled
Tormented / Distraught	Comforted
Exasperated	Appeased
Worried	Unconcerned
Stressed	Relaxed
Frustrated	Calm
Anxious	Assured
Apprehensive	Confident

Nervous	Cool Headed
Rejected	Appreciated
Abandoned	Needed
Isolated	Included
Embarrassed	Proud
Disgusted	Pleased
Revulsed	Reverential
Shameful	Esteemed
Regretful	Glad
Dissatisfied	Contented
Deflated	Energized
Down	Upbeat
Apathetic	Purposeful
Envious	Grateful
Despairing	Hopeful

This world is your attempt to hide the simple and self-evident behind a maze of complexity. Ask yourself, why so complex a screen? Who is making it, and what is it trying to hide? Simplicity is power. It provides no space for illusions to proliferate and saves you from becoming lost in delusions and false identifications. Simplicity is the royal path to truth, since it penetrates quickly to essential content. It never makes any attempt to compromise what cannot be compromised, nor does it aim to discard important facts. Simplicity is not sought nor taught by the ego. For the ego always loves to indulge in and celebrate complexity instead. When something becomes sufficiently complex, obtuse and difficult to understand, the ego stands in awe. The more elaborate, ornate, convoluted, tantalizing and splendiferous the better.

The ego has many unholy purposes for complexity. It uses it as a screen in which to hide itself and as a means to twist things around.

Within this screen, all transparency becomes lost. True motives are hidden under a veil of opacity. A complex situation presents it with the opportunity to boast its wit and to demonstrate its ingenuity and erudition. Or it uses it strategically to put another down and to sneak in a low flying blow. Alternatively it uses complexity for shameless advertisement and self-promotion. So does it get the campaign of its own specialness off the ground. But its greatest use of complexity is to deceive. For the screen of complexity guarantees that you will always remain befuddled of mind. You will not ask the right questions, nor even know what they are. So you will spend the rest of your life seeking for answers, but never finding meaningful solutions.

The ego associates simplicity with being puerile and foolish. It is jealous of simplicity because it can never accomplish it. As the Course reminds, "*Simplicity is very difficult for twisted minds.* " *[T-14.II.2:3]* So even though the ego hides behind a dazzling array of forms and symbols, we must remember that complexity of form does not mean complexity of content. The intelligent, reasoning and clear-headed mind is not tarnished by twisted motives and biases and penetrates directly to the essential content in all situations. It knows what is meaningful and real and in its lucidity discards everything else as superfluous. Simplicity is not to be confused with humility. You are not humbled simply because you are being clear-headed and direct. Instead you are deified because you are reaching to the divine. Yet, the ego always wrongly associates and mixes these two together.

True humility has nothing to do with being humbled, but rather represents empowerment. The truly humble no longer pay homage to ego illusions and have accepted their grandeur as the immortal Son of God. Simplicity sees immediately that there are but two emotions, **(i) Love** and **(ii) Fear**. These two primary emotions dictate all our decisions and actions. They are the invisible content behind all other emotional states. Everything you say, think or do is guided by the one you choose. This then determines your current experience. You see through the eyes of whichever of these emotions you are feeling. The one you choose will automatically direct all your actions and thoughts and remain with you until you choose the other in its place. Yes, you retain the power as the decision maker to arbitrate between the two. So will it be the glasses of light or the dark glasses of the ego? Remembering that every day, hour and minute you are receiving the joys or sufferings that your choice dictates. The one you choose become the determiner of all your experiences and perceptions.

> "I have said you have but two emotions, love and fear. One is changeless but continually exchanged, being offered by the eternal to the eternal. In this exchange it is extended, for it increases as it is given. The other has many forms, for the content of individual illusions differs greatly. Yet they have one thing in common; they are all insane. They are made of sights that are not seen, and sounds that are not heard. They make up a private world that cannot be shared."

> **[T-13.V.1:1-7]**

New Age literature, often masquerading under the banner of "self-help" often seeks to convince you that you umbrella a multiplicity of different emotions and emotional states. Each having different causes and contents. Since many of your emotional states are toxic, you end up feeling tired and subdued, suffocating under the ominous weight of this great emotional beast you are trying to tame. You simply give up. So you give in to where each one throws you moment-to-moment. You find yourself losing the focus needed for self-mastery. Soon you become convinced that mastery is beyond your decision and control. The reality of your situation is simple. You are always either choosing the guidance of the Holy Spirit, or the insane counsel of the ego. Therefore choosing between experiencing the emotion of love or that of fear. What could be simpler than this? Simply allow your mind to be guided by the Voice of the Holy Spirit and you will achieve Self mastery.

There are many names you have given to identifying your emotional states. However do not be dazzled, confused and bamboozled by the parade of forms and the sea of complexity that is before you. Simply remember that form is never content. Be ready to look past the many different faces and names each form presents before your eyes. Probe to the underlying content and you will always behold either love or fear. Love will always lead to expansion, just as fear leads to contraction. Love leads you joyfully Home to Creation, while fear leads further into the darkness and nothingness of miscreation. You are the decision maker that actively chooses between the two. All depends on you. This determines whether you will exercise your absolute freedom or experience instead abject slavery. All freedom and release is found in expressing the emotion of Love, in which you were Created. Thus do you come to know your Self and begin to join with others. Slavery is found identifying with the emotion of fear. This is the divisive emotion that you made which is always separating you from your Self.

> "The fundamental conflict in this world, then, is between creation and miscreation. All fear is implicit in the second, and all love in the first. The conflict is therefore one between love and fear."

> [T-2.VII.3:13-15]

Choose fear and within moments you find yourself suffering from anxiety, resentment, anger, apathy, depression and despair. These have become your bedfellows. The particular emotional state will be situation dependent. All of a sudden you may find yourself transformed into the poster child for nervous restlessness or engage in open hostility and attacks over the most trifling affairs. Or else you find that you have become sullen and withdrawn, contracted and defensive and seem to be peering out from the very heart of futility itself. Projecting your guilt and feelings of vulnerability, you fail to recognize that the truer source of your pain has been born inside you. Through the dark emotional dynamic you choose, it seems to grow strong and substantial. As a result, you are no longer able to get this goose of the ego out of the bottle of your fear. Nor can you ever, because they are the same. So you feel squeezed and unable to breathe, like you have extreme COPD (chronic obstructive pulmonary disease). You are living now in a world of separation and bondage. The world has become enormously tight and suffocating.

Fear has made you feel enslaved to an "outside" world, that seems completely outside your control. And what a world it is, militant and regimented and ready to cut you down for the most minor indiscretion. Choose love instead and within moments you feel you are being bathed in a hot soothing spa. Yes you have thrown all your cares to the wind. All you feel now is calmness, serenity and peace and you find yourself infused and embalmed with the subtle mystical incense of cheerfulness and joy. Now all has become clear and you discern your true purpose. Around you pervades an air of hopefulness, warmth, abundance, security, invulnerability and rest. In your serenity, you have dropped all your defensiveness. You can scarcely believe that just moments ago you were rattled, as a little figurine in a dream. Now you shower and extend to all, knowledge of your freedom, bliss and abundance. You have found the ancient spring of liberation and completion and the Knowledge that alone makes Whole. So does the world of separation disappear into the mists while the Real world emerges before your newfound vision.

A fierce fear always arises in us when we are no longer in control. It may start out as a certain subtle trembling. The dictator of the ego has been alarmed and summoned into action. This is because it always wants to exercise a tight grip over every one, in every circumstance. There are to be no surprises! Everyone must come to know their place in its scheme of things. Yes, in the ego world you are always made to feel that you need to behave yourself and be on guard. You are coerced into reacting in certain predictable and deterministic patterns. It has established certain defined parameters, bounds and expectations for every one and every situation. You dare not cross the invisible barriers, it has erected and cross over that barbed wire fence into no-man's land.

Written on its moth ridden parchment is its full decree. This enumerates and defines the full terms of your relationship, all its expectations and goals. The fine print details more minor matters such as etiquette, decorum, body odor and how many times a week you need to get pumped up at the local gym. Tell me then what does it feel like then when your destiny no longer seems to be in your own hands? What does it feel like when you need to depend on the goodwill of others to survive? You are fast becoming like the Inuit Eskimo, that walks off on the ice-pack because he cannot provide for himself any longer. Perhaps your car has broken down in a snowstorm on the highway late at night. Starving and dehydrating, you wonder how much longer you can last. Maybe there is to be a night of knives at your workplace. The board members are getting ready to oust you. They prefer to cave to their own corporate greed and desire, rather than embrace the greater vision you provide. In fact they are positively relishing this. You can only imagine how livid your ego can become. It is darting around everywhere at once, in a complete frenzy. It cannot believe the conspiracy against it and so it is scheming late into the night. Perhaps it will jump into the noose and have it over. A cornered ego is like a cornered rat, only a thousand times more vicious and unpredictable.

CURING ALL OUR FEARS AND PHOBIAS, THROUGH LOVE

Yet, recognizing the presence of fear, can be a great opportunity to heal yourself. In recent years, we have seen a proliferation of aversion therapy practices springing up in the many watering holes of humanity. Like yoga farms, many such centers are mushrooming overnight. The particular fearful symptoms to be treated vary tremendously, as we might expect. We see some common phobias and fears in the table below.

Phobia	Description
Arachnophobia	An abnormal or Pathological fear of Spiders
Agoraphobia	An abnormal fear of being in Crowds or Open areas
Atelophobia	A fear of Imperfection
Catoptrophobia	A morbid fear of Mirrors
Gephyrophobia	A fear of crossing Bridges
Hexakosioihexekontahexaphobia	Fear of the number 666
Hodophobia	A fear of Traveling
Homophobia	An Unreasonable fear of Homosexuals
Hoplophobia	Irrational or morbid fear of Guns
Hypengyophobia	A fear of Responsibility
Iatrophobia	A fear of Dr. Visits, Vaccinations, Preventive care etc.
Ideophobia	A fear of new Ideas
Katagelophobia	A fear of being Ridiculed

Radiophobia	An abnormal fear of Ionizing Radiation, in particular of X-rays.
Snakephobia	An abnormal fear of Snakes
Soteriophobia	A fear of dependence on others
Triskaidekaphobia	Extreme superstition or fear of the number Thirteen
Vaccinophobia	A Morbid fear of Vaccinations.
Verminophobia	An abnormal fear of being infected with Worms.
Xenophobia	Intense or irrational fear of people from other Countries.

And then there are some phobias that are probably less common such as :-

Phobia	Description
Apeirophobia	A fear of Infinity
Barophobia	A fear of Gravity
Hedonophobia	A fear of Pleasurable Experience
Oneirogmophobia	A fear of Wet Dreams
Medorthophobia	A fear of an Erect Penis
Sitophobia	Abnormal aversion to Food
Parthenophobia	A fear of young girls
Plutophobia	A fear of Wealth
Telephonophobia	A fear of making or taking Phone Calls
Uranophobia	A fear of Heaven

Now tick off all the ones you have. The theory behind it all is that we all have fears, but that it is only when we avoid facing them head-on that they become powerful. Hence the aversion therapy aims to heal by making us face our fears. In some cases it helps, usually in those cases where the fear symptoms do not run more than skin deep and are probably derived from various snapshot experience(s) from one's past. Events or influences that one would prefer to forget. For example, one may develop a repulsion for eating lasagna if it is first served to you by some troll who has callouses, warts and ringworm all over his forearms. Or if it was served to you on a night when you witness a malicious beating of someone close to you, that yet feel powerless to stop.

In other cases the aversion therapy does not work, since the source of the fear goes far deeper than the primary symptoms suggest. Often it threads back to traumatic experiences from one's past-lives. Experiences that have sunk deep into one's unconscious and can only be brought to light only by regressive hypnotherapy or in certain dream-states. So trying to unravel its deeper cause, one feels like they are tugging on a chord that is invisibly connected to every demon in the underworld. Pulling the entire thought system of the ego apart in the hope of yanking some sense out of it. Trying to fathom how unreasonable and gnarly its logic is. What are all these phobias but the many different fear-filled faces of the ego? We get to see how demented it really is. For the ego can be fearful of just about anything that can be imagined. Trying to get a patient, to face their phobia is like soliciting them to have afternoon tea with the dark side of the Anti-Christ. Not altogether a pleasant experience and hardly one that will cure the insatiable mischief it gets up to.

The Course has taught us that the only real cure for all forms of fear is love. We should never approach the darkness of any particular fear directly, but instead seek to become more loving. It is only when we let the light through that we can heal our mind. This is the Avant-Garde approach to healing. In it we become more forgiving, compassionate, open, understanding, embracing, and trusting. When we look closer at the soil in which phobias develop, we see that the particular person afflicted often has entered a sinister and contracted state beforehand. Often they are in a state of arrested development and have a deep mistrust of others, themselves and life in general. Their deeply contracted state is reinforced through their hiding behind a vast network of defenses, that lets no air in so to speak. They hermetically seal themselves off from situations that could heal them. Their defense networks are not always evident in the field of outward appearances, but are most definitely present and known in the unconscious domains of their psyches. Often they become obsessive in their control of outer circumstances and do not know nor trust in their own reactions. An aspect of themselves has become a complete foreigner - even to themselves.

TRUE LIVING REQUIRES US TO RELINQUISH ALL EGO CONTROL

I remember when I was over forty, I went skiing for the first time. Yes, I had been snowboarding before that a number of times, but never seemed to get the chance to go skiing. There I was high up in the Sierras with all these kids zipping around me like fireflies. As a few zipped in close, I fell to the ground. It took me a long time to wrangle my body back into the upright position. I felt like a skittle just waiting for the next bowling ball to come thundering through. Then I took the lift to the top of a hill. As I headed up, I had this immanent feeling of impending doom. Why had I picked such a steep slope to begin with? I had no clue how to maneuver or how to do anything at all. As I started to ski downwards, I began accelerating real fast. Having no idea how to stop, slow down or maneuver, I could feel the fear. I knew this would not end well. Probably with me attempting to declaw myself from a barbed wire fence far below unless I was lucky enough to hit a tree first. But there was also this tremendous exhilaration bubbling up inside me. Yes, I was out of control and the ego didn't like it one bit. I was having a nice run, one obviously loaded with miracles. Now I could clearly see a wire fence up ahead. I should have been worried that it would rip my nuts off, but these were already gone a long time ago. A decade before in fact, in Portland.

In the last few seconds of this brief trip, I managed to avoid the fence, only to make a thundering pummeling plop into this massive snow coffin. There were a lot of people gathered nearby looking in at me with inquisitive wonder, as I clambered out of this grave. Probably some were thinking what a loser I was, such a disastrous uncoordinated monstrosity in their midst, such a total lack of elegance on skis. A dodo bird entering their game, hoping one day to fly before my candle burns out. Others put out their hands to help me. They had the sincerest compassion and respect. My feeling of exhilaration remained for the rest of the day. It was just as I had felt when I first went bungee jumping in the rain forests in Central America. That time the bridge was made from wood and overlooked a ravine far below – in fact about 300ft. below. When I arrived, there were all these ambulances at the bridge for the guy who had jumped before me. Now it was my turn to face the music. They asked my weight, and I said 205 lbs. They said great, it can hold 210. This didn't really inspire me in the instant before I took my plunge.

Free falling, from that bridge for six or seven seconds and heading straight for that rocky ravine, I suddenly felt so alive. Then I felt this tug on the chord and I was suddenly flying right back upwards towards the bridge. I started having these weird visualizations of my coconut being sundered from my neck by the metal beams. I cringed at the very thought. Finally, I was dangling in the upside down position, blood rushing to my head. Felt I was going to pass out any moment, but was tasked first with grabbing a rope that would help bring me up. Not so easy a task when you are hanging upside down and about to lose consciousness. Yet I managed OK and I felt beyond words. Something important had changed in me in the last few minutes. I feel liberated. I was temporarily no longer a hostage to the world of fear.

I remember another time coming out of a nightclub. Myself and a friend had heard of this party in this seaport town located about thirty miles away. It was a cold and stormy night and almost Christmas. He got on the back of my motorbike as we tore off out of the town. Once we got into the countryside, I realized my headlights were out. The bulb must have blown earlier, but I continued like a lightning bolt plowing through all the convoluted bends in the road. My friend, who was a lunatic was absolutely mind-blown when we finally arrived at the destination. All he could mutter out, was how the hell I managed to steer through all these twisty curves in the dark? I said, I just steered between the two darker shadows that were on either side of the road. That was my entire navigation plan. Yes, we have to push the envelope, at times and lose all control. It is only in risking ourselves, one moment to the next that we really live at all. After all, it is never a failure if we do not succeed, but only if we never tried. In all important affairs in life we are always taking a leap. A leap into light or one into darkness, but one from which we may never emerge. Yet when we lose all control, we go into that sacred space where life breathes back into us again and infuses us with invisible energy.

Living a life, always needing to feel in control is a suffocating life that fast becomes a living death. It has nothing approximating real life to it at all. It is only a game of accumulation and dispossession. No risk means no sharpness and leads to severely diminished capacities to learn and change. No window is offered for the divine to enter - so that it can remind us that it has always been Here. Yes, when we initiate such adventures the exhilaration becomes evident? For just a few moments we are behaving as the free and spontaneous beings, we are meant to be. We have relinquished our egos and its charades of control and are truly living for a change. We feel on vacation from the ego for just the briefest window. It has been halted in its path and is no longer licensed to run its maddening and torturous scripts into our lives.

Being in control, is an ego illusion. It believes control is mastery and empowerment. In its fears, it tries to control and manipulate every situation. The reality is that we are never in control. We just have these illusions of being in control most of the time. Yet we can never determine the exact outcome of events. We do not control our lives anymore, than we control the weather. We cannot really determine what is going to happen at any instant, who is going to come into our lives a day, an hour or even a minute from now. Just examine for yourself. Look at what you are doing or who you are with this moment. Did you forecast this a year ago? Even a day ago? Maybe you planned it, but that is different - you had no guarantees or certainty it would happen. When things work out the way we want them too, this just means they were meant to happen. It is not because of our mastery or control. Unfortunately we perpetrate the illusion that it was our control that made it all work out.

When I write, I never know what will be written in advance. There is an invisible hand behind all affairs and I just relinquish all control. Then all comes spontaneously and ideas just flood in. I never have to wait. Nor do I know what shapes or forms these ideas will take in advance. The journey is the destination for me. There is this vast reservoir of information available, that we only barely tap into. So much wisdom lost on deafened ears and to those who uphold tunnel vision agendas. Writing is a bit like catching a wave. The surfer does not know how his ride will go in advance. He does not know exactly where the wave will break or where he will end up. He just lives in the moment and takes it as it comes. It is the fluidity and spontaneity of his decisions that make him intelligent and amenable to life. He just summons all of his attention into the present and so is able to make the subtle and instantaneous adjustments needed to guarantee his success. So his ride unfolds out of his presence and unity with the entire universe of the ocean.

Similarly a writer will at most just jot down a single thought that is on the surface of his or her mind. From this unfolds the central idea and essential content of a book. The idea just grows-and-grows to become a monster of infinite proportions. A monster of destruction or else it may serve instead as a veritable fountain of inspiration, that no one ever expected. The book writes itself from a Source, that no one sees. Now, if only the capricious motions of the stock market were so easy to forecast? So what does it all mean? Do we just sit back then and play the patsy then? No! It is important that we nourish meaningful goals into our lives. But we should not make these goals into our tombstones. If they are meant to happen, they will! Our subconscious minds will go to work on implementing these goals immediately. Existence will support any noble and worthwhile goal and a lot else too that no one had bargained for. We are creativity in motion and the nipples of life we suckle upon are the infinite fountainhead.

Most importantly, we should recognize our position of power is the present moment. Mastery is allowing yourself to be out of control. A master is always fresh, always in the moment, ready to embrace life fully. He has not overwritten his present with ego scripts. This provides him with the flexibility to adapt and to receive. So he is always at ease and welcoming of each moment for the treasures that it brings. There is no attachment, revulsion or withdrawal. Because the master is not focused on outcomes, but only on making right decisions. He does not seek to manipulate events for private interests, nor to tell each situation what it should mean for him. Instead he allows it to reveal itself. Each moment, he silently attunes himself to the Voice of deeper intuition and wisdom. So he finds that Zen transparency of mind that can truly listen, one that provides the perfect answer and response. So he never feels fearful or guilty. Fear only arises from ego control and the litany of failures that naturally follow in its wake. For the ego always stands in fearful trepidation of things not going its way. But the master remains always in a state of boundless release. Likewise it is the ego alone who feels guilt. It knows it is responsible for making poor decisions that lead to disastrous consequences. One cannot feel guilty when one truly listens to and embraces the present moment and responds appropriately.

RECOGNIZING THE PRESENCE OF FEAR BEHIND ALL DARK EMOTIONAL STATES

Perhaps you do not believe, that all dark emotional states have a content of fear behind them. So we will now explore some emotional states, so you can see this more readily for yourself. Take jealousy, for example. Is this not the fearful belief that you are being deprived of something another has? This may be a relationship, a business, an idea, ability or credential or something else entirely. You feel an injustice and remain fearful that you will never get, all that you want. Your feelings reflect victimization by the world. The object of your envy now has a special power to arbitrate your happiness but the universe has chosen to give this to another instead. You have been denied that which you desperately want. So your fear is one of incompletion. Your own efforts seem to be not enough. Yet, this is all ego hocus-pocus. God created you unlimited and abundant. But you can only know this is true to the extent that you demonstrate it to yourself. When you choose to see yourself as limited and deprived, how can you be aware of your abundance? It seems abundance is on the outside, rather than within. Once you start earnestly practicing true charity and altruism you will demonstrate abundance to yourself. Then it will have become impossible for you to be jealous.

Suppose instead you are feeling lonely and abandoned. At first look, this dark emotional state seems to have nothing at all to do with fear. Yet, being lonely has nothing to do with being alone. One can feel lonely in a crowd and often does. Perhaps, you go into your Dr's Office one morning feeling all cheerful and positive. He punctures your bubble by telling you that your symptoms reflect the early stages of ALS (amyotrophic lateral sclerosis). Now, how do you feel? You suddenly feel lonely and despairing? Yet, nothing has changed in your immediate environment. It is still sunny outside and everyone is going merrily about. But for you everything has lost its luster, novelty and purpose and everyone suddenly seems so cruel-hearted, like they are part of a great invisible conspiracy. How can they not feel your loneliness and despair? It must be apparent then that your loneliness does not come from without but from within. There is a part of you that is suddenly feeling lonely, some part of your thought? Something which uses your eyes and ears, hands and feet but which composites no part of your reality. Ask yourself what this something is? and why it has made such a fearful interpretation of your grim diagnosis? Who is it really that is feeling fear? Your problem is, you think this is you – but it is not! At best it can be said to be part of your lower mind. That part of your mind that only came into pseudo-existence after the seeming separation.

Deep inside is the real you, the untouchable one. A magnificent boundless presence that remains unconditionally happy, healed and whole. In fact positively radiant and joyous at all times. The problem is that you are no longer connecting with your real Self, because of all your dark identifications. You feel that you have to pass a dark intruder first to connect to the real You. Most often, you will not make the trip and settle instead for keeping the dark intruder appeased. So you give in to its fears. Aloneness is finding the real You. You have reached the seeming untouchable One and hit the jackpot. Now you reign supreme. Now nothing in the outside world can affect your peace. You remain high on the mountain of your immortality – a living God, high above the clouds of sickness, suffering, scarcity, sacrifice and death. The fear that gave rise to feelings of loneliness and abandonment is soon dispelled and you find yourself experiencing the joy and completion of your true Being. Now you cannot feel abandoned. Whether others are around or not, it does not matter! You are basking always in the warm sun of your own completion. When others are around, you enjoy their company and use it as an opportunity to bless and to heal. You recognize that bodies are powerless to separate minds that have already joined. A mind that has become truly unified and integrated cannot feel loneliness in any way. Just as a mind that is fragmented will feel lonely wherever it goes. It will engage in all the mindless distractions of this world. It will attempt to nourish and fulfill itself through various insatiable appetites, ego toys and relationships. Yet seems unable ever to find any lasting satisfaction. It remains blind to its own inner completion.

Now let's examine apathy and even despair. Aren't they the signature of one who has lost all sense of purpose and meaning? Yet these can be the greatest emotional states for your release. They present the greatest opportunities. Their presence simply means that you are not pretending anymore. You have done your homework and scrutinized the ego world around you. All idols have been temporarily unmasked and their valuelessness exposed. Now is the moment they can be left to die. Now you are no longer going to be strong-armed by your ego into accepting petty enticements and temptations. Now you can free yourself for all that is truly important and worthy. Seize this moment, look into it deeply before another idol rises quickly from the mists to substitute into your dream machine.

In this moment alone, you clearly can see, what all idols harvest. Distraction and nothing more. Once lucid you can see the nothingness at their core. For just a moment, a new realization dawns on your mind and it is simply this – *"Time has no gifts to offer."* It has nothing that is truly worthy of you. This can be the moment of your enlightenment. One in which you open the window to naked existence and the eternal. Allow love and meaning alone to enter the altar of your mind and you are healed. Fear, however, will always be on the prowl waiting for its chance to come in for the kill. It will seek to have you identify with vulnerability, pain and the world of seeming external causes. It will seek to put another idol on your throne. Take one step down this road and once again you are rendered powerless and inept, like a fly caught in a spider's web. Fear will have sunk its teeth into your bones completely paralyzing you. It will come back later to digest the fear frozen carcass left in its trap. It is only a matter of time before fear eats you alive. Apathy and despair are your best chances of jumping ship into the meaningful and so reaching the shores of safety and love.

The emotion of fear has no reality in truth? However, this is not always evident to split-mind. It needs a little convincing. It sounds too much like a euphemism to be true - something that has no back-bone to it. Like a spineless fish that is all gooey to the touch but a complete fabrication generated from the ocean of nonsense and subterfuge. In fact, such a statement seems the height of madness and denial to your ego and to split-mind. Just look around you, it says. Are you downright nuts? We are living in a world of chaos, financial corruptions, stock market meltdowns where even the purchasing of governmental power and law are on the menu. In fact plutocracies and oligarchies have morphed and risen in prominence in such a short time as to become the new law and order of the land. Look around you at all the murders, senseless slaughters, rapes and brutalities. Look at the rapid rise in suicides, foreclosures, and celebrity shows. Diseases and worldwide pandemics are on the rise and everywhere we look, we see that shameless propagation of fear by the media, advertisement channels and pharmaceutical industries. We seem open to the mercy of famines, hurricanes, earthquakes, and terrorist attacks as never before.

Everywhere there is a ruthless exploitation of weakness, age, disability, health problems, uniqueness as well as of kindness, generosity and trust. We see the proliferation of potent new drugs and consumer profiling engines that dive deep into our private lives, cornering us all on our health predispositions, buying habits and addictions. Then there is all that merchandising of human life, the preying on our potential, the selling of organs and the tyrannical beasts of the modern brain-farming sweatshops. There is a continuous selling out of our human rights and freedoms, through insidious and legalized soft-weapons in the new marketplace. We feel powerless to defend ourselves against all this. Then there is the continuous hijacking of our worldly identities through phishing software, data-mining engines and online marketing schemes. Who would deny that fear is real and that the heart of the Antichrist continues to beat and walk amongst us still on psycho-planet?

ESCAPING THE DARK ROOM, BY AMPLIFYING AND AVOWING ONLY THE HEALING LIGHT

The Course never denies our ego experiences. It just denies their reality. Fear has a great reality in the world of our "experiences". Yes, it seems real in this bleak world of appearances, in which we seem to find ourselves. Yet, it has no reality in truth. Its lack of reality becomes evident once we transcend this world of our ego experiences and perceptions. Once fear is healed through love, all these fearful apparitions of our ego world disappear. What you see in perception are just the many witnesses to your own lovelessness. In perfect Love, all miscreations disappear. But fear has made you blind. You have made a loveless space where the unholy weeds of impure thought have begun to fester. Robbing the soil of vital nutrients needed by the lilies of innocence and forgiveness to survive. Blinded by the projections of your own lovelessness, you remain blind to the heavenly light within. This world will never be healed by changes in its laws, judiciary, behavioral and morality codes, nor through increased equality and resource distribution. It will be healed only when enough minds join together to recognize our shared voyage, purpose and goal. Once our minds become intent on the restoration of our fundamental unity as love, our healing can begin.

As each one of us accesses the source of healing light within and learns to disavow the world of darkness, the dream takes on a new light. This becomes reflected in our increasingly luminous perceptions. Soon all of us are restored to miraculous awareness. We have been walking around in this dark room for far too long and have forgotten to live in light. We have forgotten there is light. We have forgotten the sanctity and perfect unconditional joy of our real Home. We have learned to play many inventive games in the dark, from the shadows and chiaroscuro that we found here. Yet, we do not recognize that all this darkness is arising from the dark split of the ego within ourselves. We attribute meanings and consequences to these shadows which they can never possess. We have invented many strange laws of cause-and-effect that we attribute to this darkness that pervades us. This includes our beliefs in epiphenomenalism and in the world of our perceptions, as our senses portray it to us. So we think the world is sourced from without, rather than from within. We are endowed with incredible ingenuity and have misused it across the millennia to develop many weird and distorting beliefs about how true Cause-and-effect works. So arose our "laws" of science, medicine, nutrition and economics. Likewise we remain attached to so many foolish ego notions, such as scarcity, sacrifice, justice and death. In this dark room of shadows, we forget that we are blind. So we take our sense of separation, confusion and joylessness as further proof that this dark room is Reality.

As we forage and plunder in our world of separation, we occasionally bump into things in the dark and scream out in pain. We curse our Creator and impute in Him an evil and vengeful nature - a malicious intent. We see Him as the cause of fear and the source of all the darkness that pervades us. We need something to worship in His place. So we have established empires in the phenomenal, veritable feasts for the senses, invented forms, fashioned from the multiplicity of weird shapes around us. These have become transformed into our idols and our gods. We hope they will save us, rather than crumble into the dust from which they were made. Yet, it is only the Heavenly light we have denied that can heal.

As we continue to stumble about, all becomes transformed into iconic symbols to meaninglessness and fear. We see only through the distorting mirage of our own fragmented and split-minds. All these hallucinations arising from our mad beliefs would be instantly disbanded under a singular holy light that could recognize Wholeness and Perfection. But having lost access to this light we come to believe in evil, sin, sacrifice and death. Yes, fear feels to us more real, potent and alive than God Himself. It is God that is dead or else is rendered too impotent and ineffectual to be of help. We will never find nor recognize Him in our current state of mind. Yet, even though we mix, blend and transpose the shadows in so many ingenious ways we can never render meaning to the meaningless. True hope comes only when we no longer place our faith in the hopeless and unreal.

We must recognize that we are in a dark room, from which all light appears barred. Yet, there is a door beyond this room that has remained throughout all of time. Behind this door is the Source of all light and meaning. Our only hope is in finding this door. Then our minds gain access to the Heavenly light. So are we restored to the meaningful, the true and eternally joyous. We must recognize the damage that has been done through the power of our belief in the worthless. This world of darkness and fear must be denied. Only then do we approach this door.

As we begin to faithfully follow, a single glint of light enters our dreams. This signals our approach to the **Gateway to the Eternal**. Follow this light and accord reality to it alone. Thus do we amplify the real in our perceptions. Soon it takes on increasing prominence in our minds and thoughts to become the complete picture. One moment more and the door is bust open and light streams in. All is seen in true perspective and in complete fearlessness. There are no howling monsters now, nor dark beasts to prey on us, no more sacrifice, pain or death. For who believes in the power of shadows when the light has come. Now we stumble no more, nor foolishly prostrate ourselves before gods of our own making. They have become suddenly transformed from blood sucking masters of vengeance to comical grandiosities and idle curiosities.

"Nothing and everything cannot coexist. To believe in one is to deny the other. Fear is really nothing and love is everything. Whenever light enters darkness, the darkness is abolished."

[T-2.VII.5:1-4]

17. Quantum Forgiveness Is the Key to Happiness

Psycho-planet has never been a place of love. Rather it is a place of endless subjugation, heartless decimation, many mindless cruelties and callous disregard. A place where all our talents, abilities and good intentions are ignored or twisted against us. So we find ourselves ground down, worn out and depleted of all vitality. Looking on, as all our ideals turn into a sickly green before us, through oxidation. Ruled over now by overinflated creatures with big mouths, vaunted pride and superficial values. Extravagant and excessive in their lusts, while robbing us blind. So we pick up our tattered, broken down carcasses, off the alleys and sidewalks and drag ourselves into court to take the plea bargain. That is we settle for the conditional in place of the real. Accept the illusion of love in place of our true Inheritance.

Yes, all love that is known here is conditional. It is not the pure concoction but always contains some degree of impurity. Ultimately it has tarnished edges and a rust filled core. We bargain for attention and affection and call it love. Or we give our affection to another, but demand high payment in return. Malicious intent is the true content of the love we sell and bargain for in this marketplace. Our love is nothing but extortionary. We simply want to exercise domination over another and have our egos stroked. Alternatively we seek to purchase love and affection by buying it instead. So we pay another's bills and flatter them with falsities. We want to pump them up so that they fall more easily, as witless victims into our snares. Yet for anyone that is truly sincere, our projections of love are easily seen as barely concealed attempts to have our egos massaged by aggrandizing and subduing another. We want to tame and neuter them and have them walk around in the circle of our lives. We want to put them into our display case so that they can go Woof! Woof! Woof! to entertain all our special friends.

Then the shakedown starts. We run them across our psychological bed of nails. We badger, coerce and promote them so that we retain absolute power and control over our chosen human sex toys. We manipulate them into becoming flowers on the altars to our dearly sought specialness. This illusion then we cheerfully present to mankind as love. For we find a need to shower the world with our illusions of being loving. After all there is a mildew within our hearts that needs to be constantly sprayed lest it eat up our souls with guilt. Freud said that love is nothing more than a projection of our narcissistic tendencies and an aberration of our self-love. The reality of another becomes severely aberrated through projection to glowingly accommodate all our special needs. That which we esteem most in ourselves we will ravage the planet for. Yes, we will place it on our pedestal and call this love. What we revile most in ourselves, we will also see and use. Use it for projection where is most instrumental in turning "others" into our chosen enemies du jour.

Our love is never unconditional, altruistic and giving but rather a conditional selfish taking. There are always visible and invisible strings attached. Yes it is a puppeteering act with just one hand in the underskirt. There can be no meeting ground between the conditional and the unconditional. Until our love has become real and unconditional, we offer but the illusion of love. Yet this is not love and is forever unable to transform into it. A dream can never become reality. When the reality of Love dawns, it has a completely different flavor and meaning. A totally different dimension and quality. Just as when light enters, all dreams disappear. Suddenly, you realize you were running on empty all the time, playing games of self glorification while never knowing true Love. Love does not bargain, nor does it seek to manipulate, control, lessen, humiliate or annihilate. To experience Love in part is to know it in Whole. When we have truly learned how to love, then we will need it no longer. Nor will we seek for it without. Real Love never takes. It can only ever bless the reality of "others", recognizing this ever-present radiant reality in itself. Suddenly the world of sacrifice is rendered meaningless and for the first time we know our true purity and abundance. The world of fear is over. Cast into the gutter as a new transparency and wholeness enters our Being and hearts.

QUANTUM FORGIVENESS IS LOVE'S FACE IN THE RELATIVE EXISTENCE

The Course has taught that there can be no love in the relative existence. That love is too pure a lotus to enter this domain. If we were ever to taste it in its essence then we would no longer find ourselves here. Quantum forgiveness is that which corresponds closest to love on this worldly plane. This is our remedy to end all illusions, the dream to end all dreams. For it is the dream of self-remembrance that leads to awakening. All other practices, desires and temptations merely reinforce the dream. They further entrench us in our ego worlds. They regenerate those illusions that empower the world of darkness. Quantum forgiveness alone welcomes back light. It alone stands for Truth. It does not seek to further reinforce illusions. Before the majesty of its offering, all illusions simply disappear enabling truth to be revealed.

Practicing quantum forgiveness is making the decision to be unworldly wise. This is the real wisdom. For how can one entertain any wisdom while still upholding the non-existent. As our perception is increasingly purified through forgiveness, the relative world takes on a new and glowing aliveness. Forgiveness unblocks all obstacles on our path to vision. The sand and dirt is removed from your eyes and the sun of life is revealed. The dirt and grime had never impeded the sun from shining. It had just made us blind. Our one responsibility therefore is removing all obstacles to light that we have interposed. Then is the Kingdom restored to our awareness. You must question all aspects of your perceptions, disavow and dispel all foundations of darkness that rule the relative world. So you regain mastery over your mind and thought.

"I rule my mind, which I alone must rule"

[W.236]

You may presently feel content to remain a witless sheep - a patsy. Content to live your life passively and uncritically, as if it were happening to someone else. Now you must aim for mastery. You must adopt a willingness to distinguish the true from the false, a willingness to understand things clearly and directly. No longer content to allow your beliefs and direction be coerced and shaped from this "outside" world of appearances. Here where you are slavishly engaged in erecting more walls around your mind. So many walls have arisen from your hasty judgments. Walls that you think will protect you. Your desire to see "sins" in another adds yet more barricades which destroy your brother's reality to your awareness. You have twisted and distorted him and made him serve as a canvas for your hates - a canvas on which you have written all your own specialness, superiority and evil needs. Otherwise, you would easily see that he is Holy, Perfect, Complete and Radiant - just like you.

Dr. Gobbler's Knob was once playing Tetra. He had become very hypnotized by the game and had even succeeded in blocking everything else out. Excited by his progress, he focused on it to the exclusion of all else. He stayed up late one night because he was so consumed by it. There he was drinking red bulls and various energizer drinks and popping a number of uppers. I swung by next day and was surprised to see that he was still playing the same game. He had layers of globular sweat on his forehead and a fearful, frantic and paranoid look in his eyes. His attention was briefly disturbed, as I entered. All he could muster out was *"Come here quick, I need to escape from this dreaded place – all these walls are closing in around me in and I feel that I am suffocating."* So it is with you. You have made so many walls around your mind. Yet, none have any substance, and none have you trapped. Yet while your focus is on the walls, on the games and deceptions of this world, believing it has the power to imprison you, you will not escape. It is not a question of demolishing all these walls, but of recognizing who you Are! and where you Are! You are not here and are not what you take yourself to be. Forgiveness is the gentle dream, that awakens you to the recognition, of what you truly Are.

JUDGMENT AND LOVE CANNOT COEXIST

Day-by-day as you watch vigilantly over your mind and forgive all grievances, you release yourself from the twin evils of judgment and condemnation. So are you released into the heavenly light. Otherwise you have chosen to remain as a fragmented and vulnerable identity - an offering of your ego, by your ego for your ego. A lone raucous voice in the wilderness wanting to hold someone else ransom for the home of fear that you have made. You are consumed with scapegoating and projection and avoid looking at the truer source of your rage, isolation, confusion and failure. Accepting personal responsibility is your key to power just as victim-hood is your path to increased bondage. Judgment is the chosen weapon of the victim. It contains all the key elements by which the ego survives and nourishes itself. These include your beliefs in specialness and separation, which then lead to your increased utilization of the dynamic of projection.

Judgment seems to promise power, but it leads directly to feelings of vulnerability. It seems to offer safety but leads directly to fear. It seems to give you authorship over reality, but its whimsical and arbitrary partitioning of reality under its own whims must render your sight distorted and meaningless indeed. Each seeks to retain that which makes him feel safe and special and automatically judges against all else. But you will never succeed in sculpturing a statue of David out of your marble of distorting illusions. Reality is taken whole or not at all. Your attempt to separate and split off those aspects that are to your own liking destroys the necessary context in which David would stand revealed. Every situation in which you find yourself is perfect when looked upon with vision. As the Course reminds :- *"Is it not possible that all your problems have been solved, but you have removed yourself from the solution?"* [T-17.VII.2:4] Your perfection is already the case, but your presence now is required. You must engage a willingness to give up all distortionary beliefs. Deny all that you have added since – all your biases, preferences, prejudices, self-delusions, discomforts and beliefs that are unreal.

Memories of the *"Not One, Not Many"* of Buddhist and Vedantic thought spin to my mind. Love erects no barriers to itself. It is therefore only in our barrier-less and seamless integration with one another that we come to the real Source of our Strength. Judgment seeks to destroy awareness of our Wholeness. It wants to add and emphasize certain unnecessary elements into the mix. Once our Wholeness is denied, we are no longer known but become strongly identified with a dream image instead. Then we amplify and praise only the unworthy. This partiality which judgment underscores and endorses renders our world picture entirely meaningless. Because whenever judgment enters, truth must disappear. Yet, all judgments were first made within before they became projected without. So it is within our minds that judgment needs to be relinquished. All objects seen on the screen of the world, exist first within as latent inner images that are composited from all our thoughts and beliefs. All judgments are nothing more than our self-judgments. Yet, we still insist in believing that our punishing self-judgments can be escaped by giving them to "others".

The Bible says *"Judge not - that you be not judged."* It recognizes that every judgment is a call against the unity of the Self. It is not God who is going to judge you, rather you are continuously doing this to yourself. You are judging your real Self everyday and every moment and therefore cannot know this Self. Is it possible that your own Creator would judge against you, knowing He Created you Whole and Perfect? He Created you in Love and retains only full appreciation of your worth. He does not judge against Himself nor any of His Creations. Yet, your judgments seem to split you off from your Self - so separating you from truth. We can see that the shell that surrounds a newborn chick seems to trap and separate it from the world outside while keeping it confined to a very limited world. Yet, once the chick gains in strength and becomes sufficiently adventurous it will peck at this tiny insignificant partition and break through it reaching to the limitless world without. Only then does it realize its greater unity with the whole of existence. This world outside the shell represents its life and growth and the domain of its greater freedom. If it remained within the false protection afforded by the shell, it would eventually die, never having truly lived.

So it is with judgment, it creates a darkened partitioning overlay over your mind which then distorts the truth of what you Are. Judgment holds you ransom to the hard shell of the limited and inconsequential. It holds you at ransom to a tiny picture of yourself. You must therefore use your mind and reason like the chick's beak to penetrate through the falseness of all judgments. Judgment is the instrument that maintains your false identity, the weapon you use against your Self. It represents your pitiless attempt at self-protection but it binds you to a barren context which suffocates your life. One day you will penetrate out of your cocoon and enter the real world of Truth. Then your mind will embrace the full, meaningful and alive context of life. The world of Truth always exists. It is not to be created nor manufactured. It is always Here silently awaiting for you to return to your right mind. Just a little willingness is needed on your part. A willingness to listen to the Voice of the Holy Spirit and to follow His direction alone. The breaking of the shell constitutes the work that must be done on oneself which the mystic Gurdjieff always referred to. It is the breaking of the shell of one's egoism. This then opens the door from darkness into light.

Remember you are only ever listening to one of two, wherever you go - the ego or the Holy Spirit are the only options. Which do you hear? The breaking of the shell represents your sudden Enlightenment, Illumination, Satori. You are born again and ferried from the illusion of multiplicity into the reality of Oneness. Now the drop enters the ocean, Now you become aware of your Wholeness. You think that your judgments can be right or wrong, but you never think that it is judgment itself that is wrong? It is a power you have invented, so that you can entertain reality on your own terms. Through this invented power you lose awareness of truth and cloak yourself instead in the robe of worldliness. Yet, who are you to judge another, being blind yourself! In the end, you will choose either judgment or reality, but you can never have both. Restored to truth you will automatically recognize that all judgment was redundant and was but a weapon you used against yourself – it is but a sword, you held against your own throat.

Only the clarity of perfect Knowledge is ever in the position to judge. The One-Mind sees and knows without distortion. God in His infinite Wisdom sees all judgment as purposeless. He simply Appreciates and Loves. This is the '*Law of the Kingdom*' and the condition of knowing it once more. The Holy Spirit teaches that judgment offers the surest path into illusion and pain. He wants to take this knife from you. So that you do not tear yourself apart and cut out your own heart. He can see the manifold effects of your every decision and action on all. The full constellation of events, with all it repercussions and recursions. Every reverberation, even your tiniest judgment makes through time. You cannot "protect" yourself through judgment. This, he says, is the very recipe for making enemies instead. Attune therefore to the Holy Spirit before making any decisions! So do all your decisions become effortless. So do you travel onwards lightly and joyously, no longer enforcing any guilt or separation.

Judgment and condemnation must go hand-in-hand. Those whom you judge against stand condemned and your vengeance will follow soon after. In your isolating enclave of self-righteous condemnation, you find more reasons, evidences and opportunities to retain your original judgments. You scavenge the world of your perceptions for those scraps of evidence that serve to enshrine and validate them. So do your perceptions become partial. Yet, what is this alien part of you that needs to judge and to condemn? Judgment and forgiveness are diametrically opposite in means, scope and purpose. Just as judgment functions to exclude, isolate and endarken, forgiveness serves to include, unify and bring to light. Judgment severs you from truth and keeps you hooked into the blindness of your past. It always seeks to rationalize, justify and react based on your imaginary experiences. Using the past to cloud over the present you extend into the future a facsimile of past beliefs and judgments. So it serves to enshrine the thought system of the ego, placing you firmly in its clutches, to walk around on crutches.

The ego hoping to escape the impossible position it finds itself in, sees death as that one final potent elixir that can end all its madness. Forgiveness looks only to the present moment and carries no distortions inherited from the past. Silently remembering and emphasizing only truth, the false is allowed no foothold in your mind. The truth needs no protection, but you need to exercise vigilance against false beliefs. Thus does forgiveness bring forth clear perceptions and paves the way for Knowledge. Thus does it restore meaning, vitality and life, to the cave of your broken dreams. Your mind no longer diseased by judgment, seeks after no more imaginary needs, established out of your sense of inadequacy. You release all your baggage and skeletons, only to come blazing forth, extending the future out the ever-living present. So do you find your entire path out of dreaming into unconditional happiness and life eternal. Your mind sharpened and unclouded now dwells only in the forever IS.

Forgiveness is the Heavenly means to see your brother as God sees him. In your failure to appreciate his value, you have lost sight of your own. Judgment condemns on partial evidence. It seeks to eviscerate and exsanguinate all that which is not in its likeness. All not correlated to your own cherished and special self images. So is it motivated and biased by your fears, prejudices and desires. It seeks to fragment the real and so render meaningless. Forgiveness overlooks all your brothers mistakes, realizing these are all seen only through the eyes of your ego. So does it correct and heal. So do all gain in equal measure. It implores you to give up your many attachments to the unreal and to teach only that which you desire to learn. By dismantling that obfuscating cloud and distorting matrix of your false beliefs, petty hatreds and ego distortions, it reveals your brothers in their full immortal grandeur, as they will be seen at the end of time.

Lend strength therefore to his mind then by forgiving him, so that he no longer needs to invest in false and unworthy images of himself. Release him from his dreams so he can reveal the truth in you. Let yourself be empowered by what he is, and not by what he appears to be. In his current state, he is doped out of his mind. In his mindlessness, he has became obsessed with those insane, insubstantial and wicked dreams of the world. Is this what you would picture for yourself? Remembering what you strengthen in him you will seem to become. Forgiveness looks only to the goal, a goal that has never changed. Your goal is Truth and forgiveness is the only means. In forgiveness, ends and means become unified. It is the Heavenly means for healing your mind and finding salvation. By removing all that is false it cleanses and purifies your mind so that it is ready for truth. Once, the goal is carefully visualized and strengthened, the universe is empowered to bring the means in line. This is the essential foundation and fundamental bedrock also of numerous other New Age teachings such as *Creative Visualization*, '*The Power of Intention*', '*The Law of Attraction*', '*The Secret*' etc. True forgiveness has the goal of making thine eye single and your purpose clear. As Jesus taught :-

"If therefore, your eye be single, your whole body shall be full of light."   [Matthew 6.22]

The Kingdom of Heaven is not far away, but very near. All that is needed by you is a simple change of mind on what constitutes your Identity? You remain always as God Created you, not what the world has made. This change of mind undoes all false beliefs and transports you safely beyond your identity crisis. Forgiveness takes you to the goal, but it is not the goal itself. Your goal is complete immersion in true Being. We have said that forgiveness is your master key to happiness, but it is evident that you do not believe this. You think forgiveness is most often undeserved and a sign of weakness. In fact it seems to go against your true feelings and beliefs as well, as your visceral instincts. Yet ask yourself this, "*Who it is that hates to forgive and why?*" Isn't it your ego that has such a visceral reaction against it? It much prefers to feel victimized and to cry out and whimper that it has been unfairly treated in some way. Then it directs you to place the blame and condemnation squarely on another – on someone or some circumstance outside yourself.

Why does it detest forgiveness so? Isn't it because in forgiveness it feels weakened and attacked? It sees forgiveness as the thief that has snuck in behind its defenses, a thief that is actively undermining its foundation in your mind. So it feels less secure, like it is losing all your allegiance. Yes the ego feels direct disempowerment in the presence of forgiveness. Therefore if your goal is to get rid of the ego, it is clear that forgiveness is the means to do it. Now forgiveness is not easy, it can be tremendously hard and difficult for your ego. In fact it is impossible for your ego. Only you, as Immortal Spirit can forgive. Even though forgiveness offers you the means to peace, it is also very much a call to war. For it is sure that the ego will give you no rest, while you are considering forgiving anyone, instead of showering condemnations. It will become spiteful, embittered and capricious and wait for every and any opportunity to get back at you. It cannot bear to see you standing up for your Self and so dispossessing it.

So it brings out its complete chest of knick-knacks, in which are found one-way mirrors, dark glasses, distorting screens and distracting flares. Through these distractions does it hope you will forget all about your forgiveness games. Blinded by denial and seduced by specialness and temptation it wants you to push all those unfortunate judgments, hatreds and hostilities from your past out of your mind. All that is calling for forgiveness and therefore for your healing. Yes, forgetfulness is a wonderful drug to dull your pain. There are many unforgiving thoughts still in your mind that you are no longer conscious of. Maybe something that occurred thirty years ago, that has now disappeared from your surface awareness. Retained only as ghostly residuals in your non-active memory, like the fossilized imprints of dinosaur bones left in the dust and mud somewhere in Colorado. Yet, it goes on affecting you all the same. You have not escaped it. It goes on wreaking havoc in your unconscious. Whenever you are not feeling happy, peaceful and assured, which I assure you, you are most of the time, you can be guaranteed that unforgiving thoughts still plague your mind.

THE CORRECT INTERPRETATION OF FORGIVENESS

Yet, if you interpret forgiveness as just taking on another major war with your ego, you will lose all interest. After all you have enough crap going on in your life already, so why be bothered attracting more inner unrest and turmoil? Yet, forgiveness is not a task or chore, but your healing remedy. A remedy that may poison your ego, but one that restores you to Life. It offers to you complete healing and brings you to everlasting happiness. So you cannot really afford to be without this healing amulet. How we feel deeply inside goes a long way towards determining what we say and do. It determines how we react to others, how we behave, how we interpret our world, what adventures and pursuits we engage in, what opportunities become squandered, who we choose to become our compadres and our most sacred friends. Perhaps you do not see this yet, but examine closely enough and you will. If you make the decision to be healed at the deepest level, it is only a matter of time before you are cooked. If you think you can avoid more pain by simply giving into the ego, you are simply suffering under the most severe of delusions. Your procrastination guarantees that the pain and suffering of the ego will go on all the more intensely, but insidiously. It is all just buried underground for later delivery and soon you will see that the thorns are sticking in just a little deeper.

If you feel inferior, you will not have the confidence to take on the great opportunities in life. Instead you will go around apologizing all the time. You will take on a position, that is far below the threshold of your talents and competencies and you will convince yourself to settle for mediocrity. You will bow down before the corporations, apologize for projects not completed on time, despite working around the clock attempting to meet unrealistic demands. If someone thunders into you at the supermarket, you will automatically apologize, even though, it was not your fault. You will not go on those vacations you deserve, believing these are for the super-rich and famous. When your financial adviser, gives you very poor advice that loses you bucket-loads of money, you will somehow think you deserved all this. You will never drive a successful business, have a large house by the ocean, servants and nice things in life that others take for granted. Instead you will spend your whole life paralyzed and frozen in the mire of your inferiority. Always trying to atone for your sense of inferiority. You will apologize even for your own death.

As another example, one who feels angry all the time, goes through life as if he were constantly being crucified. He sees conspiracies everywhere, feels wicked vengeance breathing down his neck, wherever he goes. He cannot really trust in the harmlessness of another. He demands, proof of innocence. At all times his defenses are up. Thus he cuts himself off from so many blessings that are showering at him from all directions. He imputes evil motives in others that were never there and then wonders why he feels so stifled, gagged and bound, suffocating in his self-made tomb with no friends. He may never even suspect that it is his own inner feelings of anger and rage that has destroyed his life. Yes, our feelings and those emotions we cultivate do play a major role in determining our lives and destinies. This is not just true with our feelings of anger but with all our feelings. Bearing this in mind, ask yourself now these two highly critical questions.

Do I see myself as Guilty or Innocent?
Am I Guilty or Innocent?

You will probably vacillate a short while on the first question. This is because it is a question asking how you perceive yourself, rather than asking you directly, what you Are? The ego is definitely ok with you perceiving yourself as innocent. Yet, if you are being honest, you will answer guilty. The second question is much more difficult. This is because it is simple and direct and leaves no room for the ego to maneuver. It is asking you, what you Are, not how you perceive you Are? The ego cannot answer that you are guilty, because then its game of projecting guilt to others would be up. What is the point of making another feel guilty when you know you yourself are also guilty? You are both made of the same stuff, guilt is what this world is made of, so let it rest at that. Anarchy and strategy would is your game instead. Likewise the ego cannot wholeheartedly answer that you are innocent. For if you truly recognized this, you would dispossess the ego and no longer follow its dynamics. So the ego presents you with a bargain and offers you the illusion of innocence instead. Yes, at rock bottom, you believe in your own guilt. Otherwise you would not be tempted by this offer. For Guilt you have been teaching yourself for many-many lives. Yes, you have committed great sins and atrocities, but those of others are worse. Theirs are to be condemned while yours are simply to be dismissed. You do not really believe you are loving and lovable. This is at most a self perception you like to project, but it is not something you really believe at your core.

Inside you rests a deep feeling of unworthiness and it is on this that the ego goes to work. It teaches, you that *"Yes, your innocence is a self-deception, but that no one need ever know the truth of your guilt."* So it creates a smokescreen around you that keeps the myth of your innocence safe and untarnished. So it plays its games of raising hell, bribing witnesses, pointing fingers, tampering with the evidence, obsequiously pandering with the jury's feelings to prove your innocence to everyone, but yourself. Your notion of being loving is just bait you hang out to catch another fish. Once they are hooked, you proceed to gut them out on the shore. As they struggle for their last breath, you are yanking at their entrails. So you cook the person alive eating and nourishing yourself only on those selective parts that are to your own satisfaction. You have extracted the pearl of their worth out of their dough. Now you are ready to go back fishing again. This is the true content of all that the ego flies under the banner of love. Yet, as you look deeply into your dark heart, you must really picture yourself, as guilty, sinful and vile - horrid and wicked to the core. That is why forgiveness is so important. Forgiveness isn't going to make you innocent – it is going to reveal your innocence.

As you are now, you believe in your own guilt. You have carved for yourself the most terrifying picture - your own *'Dorian Gray'*. A face so stark and ravaged with cruelties and sin, that you dare not show it to the world. In the silence of your innermost shrine, you see all your sins etched deeply into your sagging flesh and as eternally irredeemable. Your specialness stares out in its conceit and your face is pock-marked with all your past failures and mercilessness. Your dry ashen lips and bony down-turned jaw speaks only of those harsh and cruel judgments you made against yourself and others. For as you know yourself within, so you see yourself without. Your judgments can never be repealed and you are beyond all redemption. Your lips sit arched over the dark maw of your mouth. This is your oracle to the Antichrist. One that can utter only, the most vulgar profanities. Your right eye looks out with callous cynicism on the world while your left eye looks downwards in dark despair. All your blood vessels throb. But it is not the juices of life that course through your veins but the rivers of past blood – *'Et Thybrium Multo Spumantem Sanguine Cerno'*. These rivers caress and sooth your evil demons and then spill out into the world. Only to be consecrated by all your vengeances and attacks.

So what then is the purpose of forgiveness? Forgiveness is the healing touchstone that restores you back to life. In the recognition of innocence lies all healing and life, just as the belief in guilt holds all the seeds of sickness and death. There is a very wonderful and insightful story told by Osho about the touchstone diamond that goes as follows. A seeker is walking along a beach searching for the touchstone diamond. There are millions of pebbles on this beach, but he knows the touchstone is somewhere on this beach too. So he decides to spend his whole life searching for it. Each day he picks up thousands of pebbles. He examines each one briefly and says to himself *'Not the touchstone'*, and then casts it into the ocean. Day-in, Day-out he incessantly follows this same mindless routine. Now after almost twenty years, his practice has become almost mechanical. One day at last, he finally does come across the touchstone diamond. Immediately, he picks it up and automatically responds with *'Not the touchstone'* and throws it into the ocean.

You have been given this touchstone diamond of forgiveness. Do not become mechanical now and throw it away so easily. Do you really think that after millions of years navigating psycho-planet in blindness that you are going to be able to recognize and appreciate the touchstone diamond for what it is? See it for the tremendous gift it offers? This gift is hardly something the ego would want or appreciate. If it did you would have found it by now and put it to good use. Yet, it has been here all the time and was simply overlooked. This healing touchstone has all the power to reveal your innocence. But only if you put it into practice. Perhaps, you think innocence is not valuable – and confuse it with foolishness, weakness, naivety and gullibility. What is innocence? Innocence is Knowledge, because it recognizes only that which always IS, while disavowing all else. As you approach innocence, you develop crystal clear perceptions because you no longer distort or twist things about to be in line with your private interests. So illusions lose all their seeming power and death is known no more. You have come to recognize your true safety and abundance. Yet this healing touchstone can only work its magic to the extent that you uncover all those areas in your life and thought that remain unforgiven still. Whether these seem within or without, it makes no difference because we always fail to forgive in another that which we fail first to forgive in ourselves. As you begin to forgive, many unforgiving thoughts, long forgotten will rise back to your conscious awareness. Now they can be exhumed and divested of their poison. Now you are engaging in the sacred voyage of Self recognition. A voyage towards eternal innocence and peace.

Forgiveness is About Forgiving Those Who

Outshine You!

Are Loveless to You!

Do not Appreciate Or,

Fail to Understand You!

Will not Embrace,

Or Have Excluded You!

Are Fearful Of,

Reject, Abandon,

Or Humiliate You!

Ridicule,

Badmouth,

Defame And,

Blaspheme You!

Back-stab And,

Double-cross You!

Exploit,

Deceive,

Lie To,

And Betray You!

Control, Manipulate,

Judge, Condemn,

Attack and Hurt You!

Invade your Life!

Are Hostile and Vicious,

Ever Malicious!

Teach your Guilt!

See you as Sinful!

Show no Mercy!

Are Arrogant!

Soak All your Attention!

Project their Hate!

Are Not Grateful,

But Blind,

And Deny your Gifts!

Prevent Your Progress,

Put Down your Talents!

Are Psychological Vampires,

Who Drain,

All Your Energy,

And Seep Your Vitality!

Invade your Privacy!

You Feel Powerless Before,

Powerless to Teach,

Or Who See Themselves,

As Better!

Live Off,

Smother,

Suffocate,

Repress Or,

Limit You

Put you Down,

Are Mean to And,

Unfairly Treat You,

Mooch Off,

Blame, Slander,

And Sabotage You!

Inflict Diseases on You!

Block Your Freedom,

And Imprison You!

Deny And

Destroy You!

Forgiveness is About Forgiving Yourself For

All the Hateful Things,

You Said!

Pain you Inflicted!

Time you Wasted,

Opportunities you Squandered!

For Excluding Others And,

Shutting Them Out!

For Denying,

Judging,

Manipulating,

And Condemning Them!

For Being Selfish,

Self-Obsessed,

Arrogant,

Hostile,

And Vicious!

For Being Fearful,

At Times!

Acting Grandiose,

Thinking Yourself Special,

And Superior!

Denying Your True Feelings!

Disavowing Your Creator!

Forgetting Your Self,

And Closing Your Mind!

For Engaging in Back-lip,

Uttering Profanities,

Losing your Sense of Humor,

And Giving in to Your Ego!

Ignoring your True Purpose

For Distracting Yourself,

And Not Having,

Sufficient Faith,

Or Being Patient Enough!

For Spreading False Beliefs,

Negativity,

Hopelessness,

And Fear!

Teaching Scarcity and Sacrifice,

Seeking to Limit,

And Destroy!

For Failing to be Kind,

Compassionate,

Empathizing,

And Understanding!

For Failing to Be Joyful,

Grateful,

Appreciative,

And Merciful!

For Failing To Communicate,

Honesty,

And Trust!

For Failing to be Trustworthy,

Healing,

Inspirational

And Miracle Minded!

Failing to Bless,

And Forgive,

Others,

And Yourself!

18. TIME V ETERNITY

I Feel it Now!

That Intoxicating Scent of,

The Most Fragrant Perfume,

As it Meanders Its Way,

Across Mystic Waters!

That Scented Candle,

To Everlastingness!

II

I am both Old and Young!

Appearing in Time,

But Not of It!

As, I Feel Azure Winds,

Cooling my Everlasting Frame,

My Composure is One,

Of Silent Penetrative Depth!

III

I Am HERE-NOW!

And will Remain,

HERE-NOW,

When Time Is Ended!

As my Illusory Life Dissipates,

Yet, my Pure Perfume,

Remains Unchanged!

IV

My Song Sings Out!

Echoing Into Eternity!

For I Am, the Immortal One,

Untouchable By Life and Death!

That Song of

The One Consciousness,

That Pervades All!

V

I Drop Down and Down,

Sinking into This Moment!

And, Now I am Imbibing,

The Nectar Of the Gods!

I Taste Once Again!

Unity, Love and Freedom

My Invulnerability Once More!

VI

Your Ravenous Spirit,

Darkens Your World!

My Addictive One,

Darkens Mine!

But Now we both Glow,

With a Crystal Clear Purity!

Like The Moon,

On an Arctic Night!

VII

Perfect and Unquenchable,

As an Eternal Flame,

We Stand As God Together!

But as Nothing Alone!

Put Out This Candle!

Put Out This Fire!

But That Does Not!

Put Out Me!

[The Timeless One]

Have you ever considered spacetime to be just a vast illusion? An entirely mentally created artifice that arises out of our limitations and handicaps? Considered that we only experience ourselves in time after first horribly reversing the correct understanding of true Cause-and-Effect? Thus, we seem to experience ourselves and events serially and perceptively rather than holistically and associatively. Yet, this spacetime illusion only remains so long as we continue to retain and nourish false beliefs in our minds. Our true Being does not experience time at all. It cannot experience the temporal and transient, nor is it contingent on the ephemeral and unreal. Our true Being rests in certainty and knows only of perfection. Perfection would gain nothing from any experience in time and time is powerless to add to its perfection in any way. What has truth and perfection got to gain from the variable and transient? What could the vagaries, uncertainties, contradictions and phantasms experienced in time add to its truth and perfection?

Time just serves as a means to an end. False and imperfect beliefs have entered our minds and these can benefit tremendously from our experiences in time. For once we learn to dispossess these, our illusion of being in time will come to an end. Yes, when all the apparent contradictions percolating from our false beliefs are satisfactorily resolved, there will be no more need for our dream fictions to play out in a temporal universe. In the meantime, time serves as a very useful and powerful mental construct to support learning. It enables us to weed out all that is false. So it functions to facilitate the healing of our split-minds. Time can be viewed as providing the space needed for our healing. As enabling us to make those critical healing decisions that bring back to us awareness of our inherent perfection. Once our minds are fully healed, time as an illusion will disappear.

"The purpose of time is to enable you to learn how to use time constructively. It is thus a teaching device and a means to an end. Time will cease when it is no longer useful in facilitating learning."

[Miracle Principle 15]

Regaining awareness of our divine perfection is our goal. Our perfection has never been compromised. Time is however needed to relinquish all ego images we cherish in place of our perfection. We need to change our beliefs of what is worthy and true. Learning in its true sense is choosing to retain only what God Created. This is clearly differentiated from worldly learning which aims just at stockpiling more junk into our minds. Yes, our egos believe that if we just assimilate enough of what is offered on this smorgasbord, we will become special, knowledgeable, powerful and magnanimous. Worldly learning aims at increasing our egos. It thus obscures our view. Rather than enabling us to function more fluidly, potently and creatively it embalms us in very frigid, stuffy and stereotyped beliefs. Thus we become molded into mummified idiots that have lost all spontaneity and aliveness. The ego is like the magpie that likes to collect all colorful trinkets it sees. It does not know what is real, meaningful or of immediate use. So it stores these trinkets away in its nest hoping one day to find their use. Yet we are easily blinded and deluded by the distorted world we see through these colorful trinkets.

True learning simply restores us to simplicity and naked perception. It teaches us how to clearly distinguish the worthless, false and unworthy from the true. Thus we reprogram the matrix of our beliefs, which drive our perceptions. True learning functions subtractively rather than additively. It does not give us any new knowledge, it just removes all that is false, obstructing and obfuscating. There are definite laws we can employ to help us evaluate what is worthy. As we remove all false beliefs we are removing all impediments that block our view. Thus only truth is retained to shine in our mind. Then our minds become truly radiant. because there are no more impediments to hinder our inner light from propagating outwards. Nothing to prevent complete illumination of our perceptions.

True learning has nothing to do with ingenuity, inventiveness and imagination. It does not harness to itself a sack full of patents, accomplishments, certifications and credentials to impress other egos. The need for inventiveness and ingenuity only arose after the seeming separation. They are ego devices for dealing with the world of specifics, but not eliminating it. We are obsessed with constantly crafting solutions for alleviating all the pain of the ego world, hoping one day to make it whole, hoping one day to make us as gods in it. So we attempt to make the world a place of happiness, purpose and completion. But this world being unreal is beyond all hope. It cannot ever provide any lasting happiness. The only meaningful purpose it offers to us, is as a classroom to regain right understanding and thus graduate from this academy of sorrows. We can become more loving and thus escape its prison. So the gods that our ingenuity and inventiveness serve, are gods of nothingness. No matter how ingenious and inventive we become, we can never Create the real through them. All we can make through them is ever more fanciful and imaginative illusions.

> **"Inventiveness is wasted effort even in its most ingenious form."**   **[T-3.V.2:7]**

DISCOVERING OUR TRUE REALITY THROUGH FORGIVENESS

We cannot find our wholeness and completion in a world of separation, because the separated universe we perceive just reflects our inner belief in incompletion. Until we change our goal, we just puppeteer as certain self-images that befit us. We go about craving dreams of specialness while adding more refinements to our masks. What is purposeless and unreal can have no meaningful goal. The only purposeful goal we can assign to the world is to have it completely undone from our mental belief. Yes, the world can be deployed most wonderfully and strategically as a means. It can be used most expeditiously as a boat to take us to the other shore. On this journey we transcend the ocean of its limitations. The apparent separation can certainly be healed because it is untrue. It is cured by no longer powering belief in it. This is the purpose of forgiveness. This is the real recipe to restore happiness and wholeness. The love that forgiveness reflects purges all erroneous beliefs, including those of separation. Thus restoring to us recognition of our fundamental unity.

Forgiveness does not aim at clinging to and nourishing false images. It is not a game of denial like imagination is. Imagination can be a dangerous toy and one used very destructively against our own better interests. It can stream in false "private" worlds before our mind's eye which obfuscate the true present. Its goal is to preserve the dream, but not to escape it. It is often used for the express purpose of shielding and hiding us from our present condition and unhappy circumstances. Yet the escapism imagination presents us with is no safe haven at all. It just reflects our wish to live in denial of the effects of our own wrong decisions. It functions to block our mind's awareness of our own real thoughts. So through imagination we further bind ourselves to time and cannot bring about those meaningful changes and resolutions that would heal us.

All real transformative change only ever happens in the present moment. It happens when we are prepared to truly engage the present and so reach the truth that heals. Since we no longer deny or evade our current condition, immediate progress is possible. We must remember that all miscreations that darken our perception spontaneously arise from our present poor decisions alone. Yet, imagination should not be confused with other natural abilities of our mind. Abilities and capacities such as mental dexterity, fluidity, induction, extrapolation and analogy can be extremely useful for us and progressive. As is our power to reason and to distill multiple interpretations out of any given situation or context. All these are constructive pursuits that can help migrate our consciousness to higher levels of abstraction. Positive evolutions that can expedite our release.

The objective view of time is that it is independent of us. The Course teaches, in stark contrast a far more progressive understanding of time. Time is seen as the hospital needed for the healing of our psyches. A hospital generated out of our mind, like a holodeck and one which remains open for business until our healing is complete. Beliefs in guilt preserve time and therefore the need for this hospital. Practicing quantum forgiveness helps to close its doors. Forgiveness accomplishes this by calling forth all the miracles needed for us to heal. Each miracle makes whole sections of time redundant and therefore unnecessary for us to "live" and experience. The experiencing of time then is precipitated out of our belief in guilt. We are not prepared to let it go either in ourselves or others. Guilt and judgment go hand-in-hand. Guilt is primarily an unseen presence for which judgment is a direct manifestation. Judgment remains attractive and useful so long as underlying guilt remains to distort our perceptions. For guilt demands condemnation in place of forgiveness. So is sin made "real" and all attacks become justified. Through guilt we tarnish and defile the altar of our minds. The result is fear of God, fear of "others" and fear of ourselves.

Fear compels us to make up private worlds. These heavily defended bastions are just illusory artifices where we think we have successfully hidden away from the source of our fears. So we behave like ostriches digging our heads in the sand. Yet all our defenses only seem to separate us from others. In the end they cost us our healing. One of our key motivations for preserving spacetime is so we can retain our private worlds. These private worlds in turn prove extremely useful for idol worship and for furthering our goals of specialness. So we continue to nourish our beliefs of guilt in others. The attraction of guilt enshrines our chosen gods of sin, evil, fear and judgment into place. Without our investments in guilt our eternal innocence would be easily recognized and transparent in our perceptions.

Forgiveness would restore to us our real eyes and enable us to witness innocence everywhere. It would restore us to remembrance of God and eternity. The plan of healing behind time is simply to free ourselves of all belief in guilt through forgiveness. Until that willingness has been developed we continue to live with the illusion of having a split-mind. Our dedication to guilt is not worthy of God, nor of us but it does cost us awareness of our Whole-Mind. We cannot be restored to awareness of God's presence and the eternal until the altar of our minds has been restored to its original radiance and splendor. All the idols we have developed in time must be let go and no longer cherished. Foolish beliefs in guilt and sin have to be relinquished. Time's illusory nature and its plan of healing is presented quite clearly in the following beautiful passage.

"Time is a trick, a sleight of hand, a vast illusion in which figures come and go as if by magic. Yet there is a plan behind appearances that does not change. The script is written. When experience will come to end your doubting has been set. For we but see the journey from the point at which it ended, looking back on it, imagining we make it once again; reviewing mentally what has gone by."

                                    [W.158.4:1-5]

Here is a very positive and refreshing understanding of time. There is a definite script written into each of our lives that needs to be completed. Only then, will we successfully escape from the shackles of time. Nothing is happening at random. All the figures that come into our lives are there for a purpose. Every situation in which we find ourselves is loaded with meaning. Meaning that we just need to decode and uncover. We can never find ourselves in any situation that does not reflect our immediate learning needs. Each situation is a golden opportunity to facilitate our healing. When it is viewed and interpreted clearly and unbiasedly, its meaning soon becomes evident. But when we look at a situation ambitiously, its meaning can easily become lost. Ask yourself then what is this present situation trying to teach me? Perhaps it is, that the particular specialness dream you are voraciously consuming the universe for, is not so special? Maybe the faults you are finding in another are really in yourself? Maybe you suddenly realize that you are dedicating all your time and energy to giving your guilt away, as Christmas gifts? Maybe you are tempted to feel victimized from without and desire to paint the picture of an evil and sinful world to justify your callous actions and lovelessness?

We can elect to exercise the power of right decision to heal ourselves right now or procrastinate these decisions until a later date – that is all. The world itself does not care and it cannot force us to make the right decisions. Yes, our progress depends on us. We will feel joy or pain depending on whether we choose to entertain right-mindedness or wrong-mindedness. In any case this hellish psycho-drama, that we call the world was over long ago. The curtains have fallen and the movie theater is dark. Nothing is happening here at all. Eternity has always been the only show in town. It remains here always encompassing us in a warm welcoming embrace. It recognizes each aspect as complete and whole and as the very picture of perfection. But it seems like someone must have slipped something into our drinks, while we were watching a much better show. We sipped it and in an instant we were fast asleep. Now we are continuously reliving nightmares in our memory of that which seemed to emerge - but in fact never happened. Experiencing unreal past events fresh, as if they are happening now.

We can no longer see Eternity, because we are not equipped to see the present. We see only the past. We have lost vision and so we see out through blinded peepholes and jaundiced eyes. The illusory world we see exists nowhere but in our memory banks. Our memory banks are replete with deceptive ego videos, of that which seemed to happen and play itself out, so long ago. That frightening instant in which we had that *tiny mad idea* (TMI). Yes, our strong ego identification with these dark videos is what alone is unfolding from our memory banks. Not seeing past their illusory content we continue to watch them over-and-over. This is wreaking havoc on our thoughts and perceptions. We cannot see through this dense screen of memory to the real show. We have not yet awoken. We are like the Vietnam veterans reliving terrifying PTSD experiences from the past in the present. The relived experiences are so emotionally charged for us, so warped with cognitive and perceptive distortions that we cannot recognize now this show is long over. In truth it never happened at all, it is all just a feverish dream arising in our own imaginations.

Forgiveness removes all distortions in our perception introduced by guilt. So it restores us to vision. Vision is our only need. Forgiveness is the generalized plan behind appearances. Through it we learn that the poisonous snake is really just an innocuous rope, that the world does nothing to us, it is entirely neutral and empty of substance. We have always just been shadow-boxing with ghosts - which are our ego selves. This alone is what is reflected as the world we see. So we need not fear its vengeance and should just lighten up. It has no power but that power we loaned it through mental projection. We can therefore reclaim all power over it anytime. All its seeming power arises from all the mysterious "black and evil" forces, sins, magical beliefs, terrifying forms, concepts and symbols we ascribe to it. Yet all these strange notions only arose in the darkness of our own ignorance. They are mind-made and can be destroyed by right mental understanding. We can so easily dispossess all beliefs that are untrue because none have any substance that will ever stand up to the light of truth. None has any more fighting power than the boxing of a mouse.

There is no need for us to become prickly hedgehogs cowering away from everything and everyone, afraid even of our own shadows. We just need to remove the guilt that we mistakenly believed in. We should not be tempted to give our guilt away to "others" through projection, because this just serves to reinforce it in ourselves. The illusory innocence we purchase in this manner is not worthy of us and not worth a farthing. Our real innocence is available to us through simple recognition. All that is needed is a simple reevaluation of *Who we Are?* and *Where we Are?* We need no bribery or racketeering. With application of the Course ideas, we learn first of the world's inherent neutrality. This is a most important step because it motivates us to drop our defenses and come out into the open. As a result of this step, projection soon becomes far less attractive to us. We come to see again that the world was never anything but an empty canvas or screen. We need not fear it. It is up to us to decide what movies will play out on it, because we are the director, cast, stage and projecting booth. If we use it destructively we block out our awareness of eternity.

THE CORRECT USE OF TIME, IS TO HEAL ALL OUR BELIEFS IN GUILT

Similarly time can be used both destructively or constructively. It is neutral in itself but our decisions determine what appearances it brings. Used in the hands of our ego, we imprison ourselves further in its mire. We chain ourselves to our ego's dark despair and get caught up in a jagged, austere and icy cold universe built from our toxic thoughts. Highly treacherous mountainous passes that seem insurmountable, which bring with it the thin air that suffocates. In this vast illusion, built entirely from guilt and its minions, our world seems bleak indeed. We get reduced to small-minded, petty men and women that bow down deferentially to it. We treat it as if it were the god that held our very destinies in its paws. Used destructively it can be used to promote our fear weakened condition and so enter a summer of hopelessness. Any attempt to climb beyond these ominous rock formations must seem futile indeed.

Yet there is another use for time. We can use it constructively so that each day we become more joyous and loving. We can learn to overlook the failures and flaws we see in those around us, seeing in them instead an opportunity to heal and be healed. This is what time has done to them, this is what worldly teachings has taught them, this is the mess the ego has made of their lives, but this is not who they Are! Are they to be condemned for listening to the voice of their ego? Punished for becoming overly hostile, defensive and vicious because of worldly identification? Or are they merely to be seen as frightened children, who have lost their way? Lost access to their inner wisdom and light? We have made the same mistakes and if we judge and condemn them, we teach them that their hostility, viciousness and defensiveness are both justified and necessary. That their egos have a purpose and should remain in place. So do we steer them and ourselves away from the path to light. Isn't it far more healing, effective and progressive to give a frightened child a sincere complement or blessing, rather than a condemnation? Thus we strengthen and instill in them the power of good. Thus do they want to do 'the good' even more.

That which differentiates Course messengers from worldly ones, is that the messenger must become the message. It is not good enough to just deliver it. The only way to deliver a truly existential message is to have first thoroughly imbibed and assimilated it into yourself. Course teachers and students progress only to the extent that we live the messages we bring. Only then are we endowed with the capacity to influence others. Because all our thoughts and behaviors have come into perfect alignment with our message and perfectly reflect it without any disparity. It would be senseless for us to preach giving and then behave supremely selfishly, or to talk about unity and go around snooty and high-horsed all the time, deprecating everyone we see while giving them the cold shoulders. How much faith and credibility are you likely to place in a teacher who talks gloriously and abundantly about love and then fails to be forgiving and compassionate on even the most trivial matters? No! this would all be seen as highly contemptible and contradictory behavior. Yet there are many such teachers about. Shameless self propagandists whose lives are a lie. In the end we feel revulsed by them. Our stomachs turn over and we just want to vomit our guts out, then run fast in the opposite direction, as if recoiling from a serpent.

Now ask yourself this, "***Do I live my Message?***" Maybe you do not even know what your message is and just want to remain simply as driftwood. So you spend your days chasing after fads or picking up worthless things, not knowing their use. Perhaps instead you find yourself in an intense inner state of conflict because there is such a disparity between the message you want to bring and your life as you are currently living it? Maybe you feel you have been placed in an impossible situation. One that has no resolution in sight. Like you feel in your heart you want to live as one person but everyone is expecting you to live and play as another? Maybe they have become dependent on you keeping to a script of deception, despite the overt pain it is causing you? Perhaps you have a career that is financially lucrative, but your heart is somewhere else entirely? Your job may be stressful, demanding all your energy and focus, yet someone close by needs your support as a full-time caregiver. You feel compelled to do the right thing but cannot afford to leave your position.

Difficult decisions are difficult because no matter what decision we make, we will lose something of tremendous importance, which we are uncomfortable giving up. Yet difficult decisions are not in the same ballpark as impossible decisions. Impossible decisions are those in which you cannot decide one way or another because each extreme of decision becomes a matter of survival. Something critical will be lost either way you decide. There is a big difference between something you cannot give up and something you just prefer not to give up. A big difference between not having enough toys and ending a life. This is where prayer and the power of attuning to the Holy Spirit becomes so important. We need the intervening power of a miracle to resolve our intense and difficult dilemma. We need to come head to toe with our abject powerlessness, on our own and place our faith in a greater Power.

We should use our time constructively, because we do not know when the rug will be pulled out from under our feet. My father passed away suddenly of a heart attack. His life message wasn't plastered out there on some billboard for all to see. No! He was far too humble for that. His message was imprinted into his life. Imprinted into his large family, to whom he was dedicated. Imprinted into his work for which he had great professional integrity. Imprinted into his personality and value system. Yes, he valued honesty, humor, right effort and accountability and the ability to get along with others. Even though he had spent his whole life working hard, he had never achieved much in the way of worldly success, at least not by the metrics by which superficial people judge success - that is financially and materially etc. His success and recognition came in the eyes of his family and friends. In fact he was old far too soon.

In the end, all he had to show for his life was a large family, a wealth of experiences and a moderate house, that he was still paying off the day he died. Even this house was sinking into the bog on which it was built, so it was not worth much. In his dedication to his job, he would take only one week of vacation a year. Often he would go into work on weekends, as needed. He was already having heart attacks in his forties. Work stress was probably an important factor. But it is also true that his focus was on taking care of others rather than himself. Even at that age, he was deemed to be in too poor shape to be considered a candidate for bypass surgery.

Thankfully, he was content with the simple pleasures in life. All he wanted was to have his family around him and some friends to share a joke, story or insight with. So occasionally he would take a trip to the pub to play cards and down a few pints. The pub was the place where he could sneak in a smoke. This is because he had told everyone he had quit and didn't want to break my mum's heart. He was born over a pub called Godsil and died heading to one called Godleys. Maybe the message of his life was secretly saying "*God is silly*", and having his last laugh. He had a good sense of humor. Even the day he passed on, he was cracking jokes. Driving through a pothole in the road, while visiting nearby County Kerry, (Ireland) he would reply that the Kerry folk had strategically placed these potholes there to keep all hedonistic folk from County Cork, out of their county. In any case, at his funeral, we all decided it would be nice to place some cash in his jacket pocket. We didn't want him stuck for money or the price of a few pints on the other side.

At this moment, Dr. Gobbler's Knob arrived at the funeral. I was a little suspicious of his sudden turning up. I put him to the test and asked whether he wanted to contribute to our endeavor. We were not asking for much, just $30 each, which we all placed in his jacket. With such a large family, that would keep him going for a long while. The Dr. said *"Of course I will, I would never refuse a dead man a pint."* But then he said, he had a far better idea. He began immediately writing out a check for a very large amount, which he then placed into my father's jacket. I was alarmed then to see him filching out all the cash that was already inside it. In my outrage, I asked him *"What the hell are you doing?"* He responded with, *"The check I wrote covers all the cash that was already in there and includes also for my own contribution."* We have always been waiting for that check to cash and maybe one day it will. Then we will be in for a real shock.

Yet, this is how the ego makes use of time. It is always writing out checks to you for grandiose amounts. Writing checks for all those things you feel you desperately need or desire. It writes checks for your salvation and eternal bliss, checks for your unconditional peace and happiness, checks for truth, liberation and the attainment of knowledge. Each of these ego checks costs you so much of your time dollars. Vast amounts of your energy, dedication and focus. But you pay back on the installment plan. Then one day you go to cash in one of the checks, only to find they are all empty IOUs. For none of the ego's checks have ever cashed and none ever will. They were merely worthless promissory notes printed from the treasury of the ego's

Ponzi scheme. A Ponzi scheme intent on improving its future prospects by leveraging on all your efforts and energies. A Ponzi that lives and thrives in the smokescreen of your denial, greed and capacities for self-deception. You should have been investing yourself elsewhere all the time. It is this new direction that the Course brings to us.

The Holy Spirit alone knows how to use our time constructively. Used in his hands, the dark clouds begin to disappear and the sun comes out again. The world is transformed into a safe haven. A place of beauty, warmth and life where everywhere flowers are springing up releasing beautiful intoxicating fragrances into the air. That seemingly impenetrable fortress of time is gently transmuted into the eternal. A place of endless love and joy that glows now with a radiance long forgotten. In the end, time must pliantly respond to your interpretations of its use and purpose. Because it is nothing in itself, except a neutral learning device. It can lead you to your freedom or to even greater bondage. Use it therefore not as a storehouse for your idols, nor as a holodeck to entertain false gods. Invest it not with special relationships and clutch not to guilt as a dear friend or your world of time becomes joyless, darkening and imprisoning indeed.

Rather employ it, to honestly seek for truth and you will find the treasure that you seek. Use it to forgive and you will be healed. Use it to extend miracles and you will feel empowered. Use it to increase awareness of Oneness and you will recognize your invulnerability. Use it as a currency of remembrance and you will be restored to peace, unconditional joy and light. The choice is yours. Of one thing you can be sure, if you decide not to put it to good use, it will be used on behalf of all your ego goals. The ego likes to use time defensively. So does it use it to further ensnare you to false beliefs, to preserve its wishfulness over truth and to increase your portfolio of enemies. The miracle-minded escape from time because of their right motivations and pure thought. So they come to know of its unreality and the power of their mind over perception and the spacetime dream. A single loving thought, whole, pure and uncompromising is enough. Giant sections of "linear" time can be erased, in an instant which otherwise may have taken thousands of years of self-purification efforts.

The miracle-minded easily take the boat to the other shore, for they are always placing their focus on the vertical dimension of love. They know this shore is the other shore seen through the right eyes. There is no question of finding any destination, once one has recognized themselves as love. Since this recognition is all that time is for. Through love, you realize the power of your mind over the entire world of form, which then melts before your eyes and silently implodes within. You become attuned to God's Mind, as to your Identity, as Love eternal. Spacetime only seems to have many insurmountable mountain passes. Those who use time to exploit their brothers will continue to see the Alps of separation and the Himalayas of guilt present before their eyes. These seem to fence them off hopelessly within it. Yet, this world of the five seeming impenetrable aggregates is easily pierced by those who would join in present love. This is the communion that heals the separation.

The ego is all about making things difficult and complex, for it cannot ever see past form. The Holy Spirit alone distinguishes true content. He teaches effortlessness and simplicity. Yet he knows that simplicity is difficult for twisted minds - hence His infinite patience. Knowing time as an illusion with no real continuity to it, Spirit does not needlessly expend you searching out futile cause-and-effect relationships within time's dim scope. Time has no power to cause, because it has no Cause. There is no reason therefore for you to be fearful of it or what it seems to bring. Can a shadow attack? The breaking down of time into the arbitrary partitions of past, present and future is so characteristic of a mind that believes itself in time. A mind that also believes the phenomenal universe is true. For the ego believes it can only experience existence sequentially and in one direction. But as the Course reminds :-

> **"Time can release as well as imprison, depending on whose interpretation of it you use. Past, present and future are not continuous, unless you force continuity on them. You can perceive them as continuous, and make them so for you. But do not be deceived, and then believe that this is how it is. For to believe reality is what you would have it be according to your use for it *is* delusional. You would destroy time's continuity by breaking it into past, present and future for your own purposes. You would anticipate the future on the basis of your past experience, and plan for it accordingly. Yet by doing so you are aligning past and future, and not allowing the miracle, which could intervene between them, to free you to be born again."**

> **[T-13.VI.4:1-8]**

A 3D BEING PROVIDES ENLIGHTENMENT

Imagine for a moment that you are a 2D being. You entire existence is limited to a 2D screen. You are not able to witness the 3D world directly. Your entire knowledge-base then, along with all the cause-and-effect relationships you assign are limited to the phenomena that can be imprinted on your 2D universe. Now suppose that the 2D screen on which you live is moving linearly through the 3D world, that surrounds it. You may experience a dot appearing in your world, growing into increasingly larger circles, then diminishing again into a dot before disappearing for good. Developing your laws of cause-

and-effect from your perceptions alone, you would probably assign the initial dot as cause of all the phenomena that followed. So the dot gave "*birth*" to the expanding circles, which then contracted and disappeared. Yet this law of cause-and-effect you thus derived from the various phenomena you perceived is a mistaken one. None of the observed phenomena had any intrinsic cause to them. The cause of all the observed phenomena was simply the motion of your world through a higher space. Your 2D world was simply cutting across a static 3D sphere in 3D space. Given this higher dimensional viewpoint, you easily see that this 3D sphere possesses no cause-and-effect relationships inherent in itself. Your own arbitrary assignments of cause-and-effect were just mind-dreams, that conveniently correlated to all the sense data appearing in your world. Nothing is as you had mistakenly assigned it.

Qualitatively, our 2D friend is not much different from a modern day physicist who proclaims that the dot of the "big bang" gave rise to our expanding universe, which then marked the beginning of time. A theorist that then smugly retorts that the experimental findings and evidence prove him out. He remains incorrigible in his conjectures and tenaciously adheres to all his mistaken notions of cause-and-effect. He never questions his own frame of reference and how this affects his perceptions and his findings.

Now suppose a 3D being communicated into your 2D world. The 3D being might start by saying that all the phenomena you experience in your 2D world are illusions. That you are seeing just fragmentary slices of a 3D sphere, which remains forever unchanging in a "higher" world. Yet a world you are powerless to view or apprehend. The 3D being proceeds to say that all your laws of cause-and-effect are misplaced and in fact meaningless. That all phenomena in your world are nothing more than distortions imposed by your own limited 2D viewing context. Ghosts, illusions and apparitions are a better term, he says to describe all the unholy artifacts generating out of your limited and distortionary context. They are not there. Their seeming appearance is driven by distortion. These "phenomena" have nothing to do with reality, but everything to do with your limited experience of reality. They are mere appearances arising in your mind because your viewing perspective is not whole. The 3D being might go on to say that your arbitrary partitioning of the events in your life into past-present-future, as if the past caused the future is really a joke. This he declares is not how things are. He teaches instead that all the seeming events of your life exist in and as part of a far greater unity, that you cannot perceive or yet know. Your temporal partitioning and sequencing of events is of no consequence and has no meaning. Rather your self ascribed "laws" of cause-and-effect are making you blind to true cause-and-effect relationships.

The 3D being says, "*Hi Buddy – I am here for you. What you think is in the past and future, is really available right now. You can so easily look into the 3D world, where I exist and see it directly. But for this you will need to engage a completely new way of seeing. Your reasoning must advance to become inductive as well as deductive. All the "inheritance" that your 2D world knowledge has given to you, is the only barrier. If you are willing to transcend the limitations and distortions of this "inherited" knowledge, for a moment you will have the vision to truly see. The vision to see the perfect and unchanging in what seems transient. The inner eye of vision can only open when your worldly eyes have become temporarily shut. So you must cease for a moment all your nonsense mental activities, stop chasing after forms and feasting on all you perceive. Because this is not the real seeing. This is only seeing that which your ego wants you to find. All seeing is of the mind. The mind that listens to the ego will see as it directs and believes.*

In Zen there is a term 'no-mind'. It does not mean having no mind. That would be ridiculous. What it means is seeing with naked awareness. That is as a mind that retains a perfect, lucid and transparent awareness, one that has divested itself of all false beliefs and distortionary thought-forms. Your real Mind can only open when your regular mind has shut down all its engines of madness. Just for a moment, you feel like you have gone on vacation because it has stopped pestering you. Your real Mind is a 'no-mind' and it is as silent and expansive as the sky. In it all becomes clear because your seeing is not obscured in any way. Boundless potentialities and manifold universes can instantly become manifest from it, because it has become unshackled from the narrow-band filters of limitation. Hence the term pure Buddha lands, which are those magnificent celestial kingdoms that only the impeded and unshackled mind can glimpse. Your real Mind will reveal to you all that which your inner eyes of vision sheds its light upon."

Our 2D friend truly listens for once and gets a profound insight and intuition into what this 'no-mind' must mean. He immediately realizes what was his mistake all along. Those special hindrances of mind, that he himself had made that were costing him true perspective. In a powerful *'A-Ha'* moment, he suddenly realizes that all this "knowledge" which he possessed, all those mistaken laws of cause-and-effect he had accumulated, all those conditioned experiences he took to be true were always part of his shackles. All that, which was being presented to his senses was arising within that myopic context by which he viewed himself and his reality. He had foolishly believed himself trapped and mercilessly bound to this universe he perceives. Foolishly taken himself to be a victim of his own perceptions. Now he realizes in a flash that he has always been projecting this limited context from his own mind. It is he that has been binding himself to this world. Yet, he is a prisoner only of his own thoughts and beliefs. Recognizing this he is able to successfully migrate his thought to higher ground and see new worlds of a much higher dimension and quality. He also has another profound insight :- *"That which appears to have gone away has never really gone away and what is to come is already here, just unseen."* It has always been here.

The only difference between appearances and disappearances was intrinsic to his own mind's limited viewing capabilities. Events from the past have not really gone away and they can easily be made to reappear back into present awareness and experience. Just as the past is not gone, the future is not yet to come. Both already exist right now, this moment and can appear back on the screen of our lives through our right decision, if desired. It is our decision alone that moves this screen and brings all those events, figures and happenings that appear on it. Your future isn't just porting to you events from your seeming future, but also from your seeming past. For both coexist in the higher reality. As the 2D being fully assimilates these new understandings he experiences Enlightenment - also called Bodhicitta. His mind is now cleared of all the distortions caused by erroneous beliefs. All that he had inherited from living in his 2D world over lifetimes. All these accumulations and sedimentations we call the samskaras. Now he sees directly with naked and transparent perception. He is no longer a 2D being, in fact he had never really been a 2D being. He had just mistakenly taken himself to be such by overly-identifying with the very limited world generated out of his toxic thought and trashy beliefs. Now he sees for the first time his real face and all the time he had just taken himself to be a flatfish in 2D spacetime landscape.

Similarly when a higher being speaks into our world. His primary aim is to raise our consciousness to a higher level, so that we can grasp things directly for ourselves. He is limited in his transfer only by the depth and quality of our understanding. He can use only those forms and concepts that we now know and understand. His aim is to impart direct comprehension in us so we can joyously experience the real world instead. He realizes that the greatest impediment to his teaching success is all the false knowledge and beliefs we have accumulated over time. Beliefs which unfortunately now have become deeply embedded within us. It is these alone that keep us blind and in the quicksand. He wants to divest us of all such false and foolish beliefs. He knows that this step is absolutely necessary to bring to us vision. So he proceeds to teach that all phenomena and apparent motions of our world, all our perceptions are the byproduct of our own mind-made distortions and limitations. He teaches that time is not real and that in the "higher" reality, all is changeless. That time is only an apparent reality. One arising from our own limitations and handicaps, one intrinsic to our own limited worldview.

Our myopic worldview has cut reality into slices and this has seemed to fragment us so deeply that we no longer experience any hint of our Wholeness and former majesty. Seeing through our split and fragmented frame of reference, we seem to experience our Wholeness now as serialized streams of meaningless phenomena and perceptions. Our split-mind is creating the illusory notion of time. He proceeds to then teach that what was real in the past remains real in the present and also in the future. The past that you remember is not gone away. It contains threads of your future. Threads that you will yet experience again. Similarly your future is deeply threaded into your past. The old laws of cause-and-effect you believed in had always attributed cause to the past and effect to the future. Now you see how arbitrary and meaningless this was. More like a hangover from the dinosaur age of thought. All time-based cause-and-effect principles can now be relegated to the trash. Time's only purpose is to provide the space for undoing all those illusory miscreations that were generated from your split-mind. Time and split-mind being synonymous at their core. Split-mind itself being the cause of all apparent motions, and therefore of time. It is split-mind alone that powers all phenomenal universes, seen or unseen.

We have entered now a higher modality of thinking. One that realizes that time can have no affect on the real and the perfect. We realize now that we can never suffer any diminishment or loss. Finally beginning to glimpse that all appearances arising on the screen of our lives are doing so because of our present decisions. Our present decisions alone drives all future appearances. So bringing to us all those "learning" experiences we still need in order to heal. Yes, we are now securely on the terra-firma of a higher mental evolution and coming to the recognition also that this possibility alone supports our total and unhindered free will, our absolute liberation from all appearances in time.

So the **Eternal Now** was always our only gateway to experiencing truth. But to enter this gate we will need to return to our '*no-mind*' essence. As we embrace a '*no-mind*' approach to living, we will come to a powerful transcendence that relinquishes all we believed in and formerly understood. Once we free ourselves into our '*no-mind*' essence, we will have simultaneously become all and nothing. Then we will know directly that all the phenomena we appear to see, were never there. That all our foolish laws of cause-and-effect, concepts, words, symbols, percepts, even our consciousness itself are without any meaning or merit. They are mirages arising in the duality of our split-mind but disappear once Whole-Mind is known. Only Whole-Mind alone is capable of knowing directly the Real. In the meantime by making our concepts more expansive and generalized they become increasingly light-filled. Finally, there comes the moment when we are ready to progress beyond all concepts and enter the potent realm of the supra-conceptual.

THE CARPET OF GUILT

> "Time seems to go in one direction, but when you reach its end it will roll up like a long carpet spread along the past behind you, and will disappear. As long as you believe the Son of God is guilty you will walk along this carpet, believing that it leads to death. And the journey will seem long and cruel and senseless, for so it is."

[T-13.I.3:5-7]

The relinquishment of guilt is what removes all our distortions. Thus are we restored to our natural awareness as Whole-Mind. Then we get to peer into the timeless and come into direct contact with the bright and radiant altar of the ever-existing. What we know as "Time" is just a false and arbitrary framework, developed in an impure state of mind. This impure mode is maintained through guilt, which in its distortion releases countless false ego beliefs. Even consciousness itself is an impure mode of mind and one incapable of communicating directly with our Being. We experience ourselves falsely and dualistically in the manifold of consciousness. Consciousness arose simultaneously with the separation and will disappear again in 'the final step', taken by God. So long as we experience guilt, whether conscious or unconscious, we will experience the world of time. We are sentenced to "the carpet" treatment. Endlessly plodding along it with dampened spirits while soaking up tireless views of the empty, soulless, despairing and mundane.

This carpet of guilt is where we seem to walk now. This carpet is only seen through the many distortions of the ego's thought system.

These interpose a heavy screen that darkens our vision and disables us from seeing, that which truly IS. Only when we successfully remove all belief in guilt from our minds through quantum forgiveness can we experience the real world again. Forgiveness purifies our minds and thus divests us of all erroneous beliefs. Because we provide no further breathing ground for grievances, we are restored to our bliss bodies. We exorcise all those false phantoms born in time, which appeared on the carpet. Phantoms that sought to deceive us by teaching us that sin was real and our vengeance warranted. When no impure belief is retained in our minds the carpet rolls up and disappears. The altar has been restored to its original radiance. The Real can never be lost. Yet it can seem lost when imperfections and distortions enter our consciousness and take root. Simply put, our false beliefs establish our distortions, which then sediments into our heavily filtered and conditioned experiences. It is these alone that prevents us experiencing reality Now. But we will succeed. The Mind of God's Son remains impervious and invulnerable throughout Eternity. Illusions can never reach to our core. Dreams can only appear on the surface of our mind, where the ego has dug in its roots. Yet all dreams will disappear, once the light has come.

> **"Only in time can anything be lost, and never lost forever. So do the parts of God's Son gradually join in time, and with each joining is the end of time brought nearer. Each miracle of joining is a mighty herald of eternity."**

> **[T-20.V.1:4-6]**

The past that you remember is almost entirely composed of dream fiction. Nevertheless there is a thread of truth running through every perception and each of our memories. Our memories not only extend into the far distant past but also hold important messages from our future. Truth is still in our memory. However so long as your mind remains in its heavily distorted state, you can no longer recognize this thread of truth. The past that you do remember is mostly just the residual of false memories. Even the recall of these memories, changes as present beliefs are changed. Your future is just dream projection. Changes in your current beliefs changes your future course. Both past and future are formed from the distortions guilt introduces. Experiencing yourself as an unreal image in this hall of distortion you are easily induced to settle for the idle wishes and temptations of your ego. Without distortion there would arise in you no need for wishfulness. You would simply appreciate reality as it IS. Guilt provides a tiny gap, for many false beliefs to enter and to fester. From there they go forth and multiply to obscure your vision entirely. These false beliefs form into the composite, known as the ego. They represent the only block to your knowing and experiencing reality, directly in the present. As the Course reminds :-

> **"The past that you remember never was, and represents only the denial of what always was."**

> **[T-14.IX.1:10]**

GAINING PERSPECTIVE, ON OUR LEARNING LIMITATIONS

Looking back at our earlier example, we can see that the phenomena and motions appearing on the 2D screen are very limited and distorted projections of the 3D world. One could impute almost nothing about the 3D world from examining what shows up on this screen. Shadows or chiaroscuro is a more appropriate term for what is viewed. Likewise what shows up on the 2D screen of our memory represent just shadows, distortions and fictions of the Real. Our past experiences, for the most part are not real in any meaningful way. What is real in them is too distorted and obscured. Dreams of the past can only show up in split-mind. Whole-Mind sees no past. As our split-mind is healed, we are actively changing our memories of the past and reinterpreting them in the light of our newfound understanding. Thus are we cleansing our past of all those aspects that are unreal. Likewise cleansing all our future aspirations and anticipations to receive only that which is worthy. But if instead we use the past as our reference for action and decision we will once again retain split-mind. We will once again distort. We will not be able to see with vision, because we will be projecting our own false distortionary beliefs as a veil to cover the present. This veil then impedes the spiritual light of truth from showing up in our perceptions. The present will only be truly seen, when we are ready and willing to release all that we have learned from the past. Then we are no longer misusing time to suit our own idle ego purposes. But allowing instead the present to truly change us.

Imagine for a moment a group of people having a picnic under a tree. The random movement of the people, branches and leaves casts many unpredictable shadows on the grass below. What if your entire world experience from birth to death got limited to the 2D plane of the grass? Suppose you could never see directly upwards to make out the sun, people and trees. You would have to induct their presence and greater reality indirectly, through the various light patterns and shadows that are appearing on the grass. Trying to make sense of this shadow world, you would invent many strange laws to explain them. After a time it would be hard to convince you that all your beliefs, concepts, memories and perceptions developed in this shadow-land are almost completely empty of substance and meaning. That their connection to reality is very weak and tenuous at best. Yet, your mind would soon become so full of false beliefs, interpretations and inherited knowledge that it would be hard to convince you of all that exist, just beyond its planar context. It would have become overly identified and blinded by this bleak world of shadows, it perceives. This alone would occupy your mind and thoughts. Nevertheless your mind is perpetually impelled to think until it reaches back to awareness of its perfection. Only then will it return to a state of quiescence. When it receives only garbage, it will attempt to make sense out of this garbage. Just as prisoners will spend days, weeks and months developing many ingenious shanks or kites to kill the boredom or void arising from the absence of a higher meaning in their lives.

Yet, predicting your future based on past shadows, you remain sightless indeed. Until, we admit that we do not truly know ourselves or our world, we continue to block our vision and consciousness from experiencing the real one. We have to take the critical step of realizing that nothing we perceive makes sense. That all our laws and beliefs would easily be invalidated in a higher context. This meaninglessness is evidenced by the fact that they are in a continuous state of flux, changing with the times and across civilizations. The underlying content we feel of boredom, dullness, sickness, savagery, toxic emotions etc. must all point to one essential fact - that the content of what we see and experience cannot be true. It can never be made satisfying. So long as we continue to poison, stifle and clutter our minds with such useless misconceptions, such gravely mistaken laws of cause-and-effect, we will continue to need mirrors in the world of the blind. One of the fundamental messages of the Course is that the past and future have no power over us. Nothing from the past can touch us in the present, unless we empower it to do so. While we continue to extend our past into the present through entertaining false ego beliefs we will pay the bill. For it costs us true experience in the present. The cost of illusions, being the loss of awareness of truth.

So for example, suppose you go to your doctor's office and he tells you that you have an inoperable brain tumor that will kill you in a matter of weeks or months. A few moments ago, you had never felt better. You were feeling highly energized and brimming with endorphins, having just got back from an adventure vacation. Yet as this new item of "knowledge" sinks in, you start feeling anger and injustice instead. At first, you start reviewing your CAT scan results over-and-over. Soon you are researching brain cancer therapies and treatment centers, finalizing your will etc. As depression sets in, all the accumulated information you have learned since seems to have become ominously stacked against you. You proceed to empower past beliefs into the present until eventually you have brainwashed yourself into fully believing the bleak diagnosis you have received. This series of beliefs and their corresponding images alone you picture now. Your past beliefs projecting into the present suffuse your mind entirely unleashing a veritable Pandora box of poisons. As a result your mood has changed, your whole state of mind has changed. You have self-hypnotized yourself into believing your doctor's grim prognosis. And yes your mind, being all powerful, will manifest into your present experience all that your beliefs dictate.

You believed you have a tumor and so a tumor you will have. Soon all the effects and manifestations will show up in your body and they will fall into line with your belief expectations. You have just made it real through your own mental conviction, in its ultimate veracity. Other than that, your tumor never had any reality to it at all. All you really saw, were some shadows showing up on a black and white X-Ray and nothing else. But you end up dying in the dream, killed by your own beliefs and your own subscriptions to magical beliefs. There was an alternative that you were free to take. Really, it is not **an** alternative – it is **the** alternative. It is simply the realization that this CAT scan that you saw a half an hour ago is incapable of extending itself into the present moment. Once you choose not to entertain belief in its potentially fatal message, you will cease to feed and empower all its associated thoughts into your mind. So it and all its mind generated effects will diminish and disappear. They were never really there to begin with, being entirely Causeless.

It was never your present reality just a past appearance in mind. This past experience is long since gone and it is powerless to reach you in the present. It is just a frightening mind-dream that you co-produced with your ego. It cannot continue to exist now and have any effects, without your belief. This is the healthy form of denial, that the Course advocates. One in which you do not invest in, fuel and propagate false appearances from your past into the present. At this moment you are free to let it all go – in fact only in this moment can you let it all go. The Holy Spirit is there with you and he knows your present and eternal reality. He knows of your Wholeness and perfect health. If you listen to the Holy Spirit you can receive his knowledge and dispel all unreal phantasms from your mind.

"This lesson takes no time. For what is time without a past and future? It has taken time to misguide you so completely, but it takes no time at all to be what you are. Begin to practice the Holy Spirit's use of time as a teaching aid to happiness and peace. Take this instant, now, and think of it as all there is of time. Nothing can reach you here from the past, and it is here that you are completely absolved, completely free, and wholly without condemnation. From this holy instant, wherein holiness was born again you will go forth in time without fear, and with no sense of change with time."

[T-15.I.9:1-7]

OUR DECISION OPTIONS ARE ALWAYS EGO OR SPIRIT BASED

Almost every moment you are making decisions. Yet, you only have two options: - **(A) Decide based on past beliefs and experiences alone.** That is employ the extensive legacy of dead knowledge to make decisions. Have them shaped through the prism and filters of your old identity or **(B) Ignore the past completely and decide fresh based on the current situation as it is evolving.** With (A) you have opted to choose with your ego and to put on its dark glasses. So does the miracle that this moment offers you, becomes lost. You will not be released. You will not experience something totally new and vibrant. The power of the divine cannot intervene on your behalf, because you have not licensed it to. And it can come only where it is made welcome. You will not have that spontaneous remission you were hoping for. You will not be restored to health and peace of mind. You are not dynamic, evolutionary and progressive enough. Instead you remain frozen in time, a static and dead thing that is tied to the old rigid belief system of the ego. You can hardly be called alive. And looking through those dark distorting glasses, you will never experience anything truly joyous, vibrant and new. You will just be regurgitating yesterday's vomit into all of your tomorrows. Yes, the ego is satisfied with you for a moment. It is glad of your complicity to it. You have accepted its sage advice and ongoing counsel and this seems to ensure its continuity and rulership over your mind.

Yet, how about you? How are you feeling? Do you feel like a tamed and neutered animal coerced into jumping through hoops? For you the cost has been great indeed because you have chosen to remain blind and to miss reality completely. The power inherent in the present moment to release you through present decision has been lost. This is no idle power or arbitrary decision making process but one that can extend forever real effects that will heal. A healing that does not need any reference to any past or future for it comes from the Eternal present. But you have decided instead that you want to keep your psychological knapsack in place, replete with all its pains, injustices, sufferings and lacks. You want it to remain fully loaded with all those dark tales of crucifixion, victimization or of being slaughtered by a merciless world. You want to remain loyal to your ego while ignoring and overlooking its real motives for having you exclusively invested in time. Are you still not interested in taking option B? In dropping all now, and walking joyously into the radiant light of the present moment?

> "The ego has a strange notion of time, and it is with this notion that your questioning might well begin. The ego invests heavily in the past, and in the end believes that the past is the only aspect of time that is meaningful. Remember that its emphasis on guilt enables it to ensure its continuity by making the future like the past, and thus avoiding the present. By the notion of paying for the past in the future, the past becomes the determiner of the future, making them continuous without an intervening present. For the ego regards the present as a brief transition to the future, in which it brings the past to the future by interpreting the present in past terms."

> **[T-13.IV.4:1-5]**

Maybe you are beginning to see how the ego uses your past against you. Through your firm belief in the past, does it succeed in keeping you in prison. Now you understand also how it will shape your future projections to usher in only that which it alone wants. Seeking vengeance and retribution for past hurts is one of its strongest drives. Towards this fulfillment of this noble aim, does it steer and dedicate your future. So it silently reminds you of all the brutalities, insults, humiliations, afflictions, sufferings, denials and compromised positions you have had to endure. How you were scorned, slandered and diminished into a nothing even by those whom you had respected the most. Your future is a dark canvas in the ego's hands, one in which it will actuate all its hidden motives and desires. Maybe as you get older, you steal a glimpse in the rear mirror of just how well the ego has succeeded. Haven't your beliefs in injustice, guilt and sin dug in just a little deeper? Now its fatalistic endgame is in full motion seeping the last remnants of your vitality and trust. Now it wants to make a final push on all fronts at once and end it all in a powerful cataclysmic exhibition of brutal tragedies and catastrophes. A firework display that even the Anti-Christ would lovingly adore and clap his hands at.

If you have been listening to your ego all your life, it is likely that you have become a closed-minded, untrusting and embittered soul. Now it can afford to speak a little softer and a little closer to your ears. You have now become the consummate cynic, only too eager to listen. It tells you many tales of your victim-hood and your needs for magic and vengeance. *"Eat or be eaten!"*, it says, and it pictures to you a frail and aging body stacked against so many powerful and ominous forces on the outside. Its future plans for you are more of the same. Maybe getting a little darker now perhaps, because we are getting a little closer to midnight. You will yet complete your vast network of defenses, even if you can no longer peer out through them and smile. Your newest face-lift has made your transformation almost complete and makes smiling all but impossible. You are now the very portrait of darkness. Maybe one last sneer for the audience, is all you can muster. The game is almost over. Now is the time to sell all your remaining ideals and values in for pennies at the pawn-store.

Cash them all in a rock-bottom prices so that you can use what is left of your future to seek out a few last idols. Maybe you will even get to complete that monument to your specialness.

Yes, you will enter the ego's hall of fame and yet experience your salvation here in the world of time. This road to your future, placed in the ego's hands seems perilous and bleak indeed. An ominous cloud hangs over it. The gates into hell are sidelined by all sorts of wicked enticements and attractions. Each of these flowers must yet bear thorns. Thorns you do not see, as you reach down to smell these stupefying blossoms. Their fragrances have fully intoxicated your mind into submission. It is poison we see now smeared upon your lips. Here is the road of fear, guilt, sacrifice and sin made real. Getting thornier and thornier as you proceed deeper into its blood wrenching briers and convoluted jungles of thought. You become increasingly frail and fear weakened as you proceed, less sound of mind and body, until finally you profile an entirely dilapidated worn down, pallid and etiolated corpse. Yes, you do sport a crown now, but it is the crown of death conferred on you at last, the marking of the Antichrist consummating the efforts of your life. Here is the final outcome of that specialness which you had sought so eagerly to find.

You literally jump into your grave with glee, hoping that death may free you at last from the ego's clutches and its inglorious torture traps. The ghost of Christmas future, has finally come, as anticipated demanding your complete and utter sacrifice – only to then cast you into the fires of hell and everlasting hopelessness. Does it make any difference now that you started out with such good intentions? Or that as a newborn puppy you remember wagging your tail so playfully? Woof, Woof, Woof, all the way down the road to rub up against some witless folk and get a free massage. Or that you were once brimming with such innocence and spontaneity and emblazoned with such joy and hope for life? In those moments when life still held out some promise, reverence and unwritten magic for you? Those fond days of your youth when innocence was something you still treasured and believed in, when your radiant eyes prospected a world of wonder and mystery, abundance and limitless potential. The jewels are all torn out. They were plucked from your mind and scavenged from the minds of all around you. You could not bear to see them radiant with love, you would not dare to see their worth, less it denude you of all worldly ambitions. So you scattered them to the winds or sold them in at the pawnbroker. To this sad theater, that has become home to the insane and battle weary, the Holy Spirit comes with one last joyous message.

> **"The Holy Spirit teaches thus: There is no hell. Hell is only what the ego has made of the present. The belief in hell is what prevents you from understanding the present, because you are afraid of it. The Holy Spirit leads as steadily to Heaven as the ego drives to hell. For the Holy Spirit, Who knows only the present, uses it to undo the fear by which the ego would make the present useless. There is no escape from fear in the ego's use of time. For time, according to its teachings, is nothing but a teaching device for compounding guilt until it becomes all-encompassing demanding vengeance forever."**

> **[T-15.I.7:1-7]**

The Holy Spirit now comes to remind you of the true purpose of time. Time is needed to unchain your mind and to heal it. Only thus do you come to the recognition of your freedom, happiness and completion. So do you release all those imprisoning demons that mindlessness had made. So are you restored to your true position on the royal throne of divinity and holiness. *"Time is your friend, if you leave it to the Holy Spirit to use. He needs but very little to restore God's whole power to you. He Who transcends time for you understands what time is for."* [T-15.I.15:1-3] He proceeds to recount how spacetime is a vast unreal territory, that only came into seeming existence at the instant of the *'Tiny Mad idea'*. Though unreal, it has become stored in you as memories. Memory only became needed after you became sick and started to hallucinate. All spacetime ever portrays is but your belief in guilt made real and given form. Form is then used to mask the underlying content of guilt from your direct awareness. From this all dream fictions arose. Thus has your consciousness became dull, lethargic, conditioned and plagued by so many erroneous beliefs.

So it is that you came to experience your mind, as it seems now. A mind limited and weak driven almost into extinction by the marvelous stunning complexities of the dazzling worlds without. He teaches how your sensory profiling network is so deceptive. Yes, your senses are distortionary and only capable of illuminating a tiny fraction of the vast territory of spacetime at any given moment. You can never distinguish your true portrait from what they show. There is no glimpse afforded of your grandeur, magnanimity, and invulnerability. Nor do you know of the powerful and endless regressive implications streaming from even your most innocuous decisions. You have been schooled and fooled into enfranchising the world the ego wants. Swallowing all its idols pills and capsules and hoping for an LD50, this very night.

So you take yourself now to be the tiny invented self-image that you see – an image that lives out its entire life as a tiny portion of dream fiction. Only to forget who it is that wanders aimlessly down the hallways of ignorance, begging for some spare change or little gifts to compensate for all its invented needs. Spacetime comprises an entire land of illusion, already completed. It has no secrets to give - just the unanticipated. For there is nothing new to come, but much that will seem new. Our entire path out of it is already established. All that you will ever do in spacetime is already set. Your decisions seem to place you on one path or another but both paths already coexist complete. When you make a poor decision you merely burn yourself up by wandering down a slower more painful path for a time, until you decide otherwise. You think that you are burning up time but it is you yourself that are being cooked in this cauldron. Slowly smoked and boiled until you successfully connect to the path that leads out.

Imagine your consciousness as a laser shining its light into a large dark room. A mental laser only capable of illuminating tiny sections of this vast room and its contents at any given time. Whatever is not illuminated by this laser seems as if it does not exist. What is no longer illuminated by your conscious awareness seems to have disappeared into your past and be gone for good. 99.9999% of our past, we cannot even actively remember. We have forgotten those powerful associations and mental mnemonics needed to trigger each such experience back into our awareness. This is why when we are having a déjà vu experience, it seems so weird. We have lost all our conscious associations to this event but a deeper part of us registers and remembers it. This deeper aspect of ourselves is not fooled. The deeply engraved landscape of our unconscious and emotional selves still retains its associations. It is here that we record and remember. What is not seen with the laser of our consciousness still exists and is available. Yet, it seems out of reach because it is mentally relegated to our past or future. Past and future coexist in the spacetime illusion and they can yet be unfolded into our present experience. If we could merely flick on the light switch, we would know that this is so! Our consciousness must first become expansive enough before the hidden, denied and forgotten can be remembered. Then all our past and future lives will be revealed to us, in one fine instant. Jesus speaks of our past lives being revealed to us in this very heightened and fluid state of consciousness in the quote below.

Jesus said, "When you see your likeness, you are happy. But when you see your images that came into being before you and that neither die nor become visible, how much you will have to bear!"

[The Gospel of Thomas]

There are many other techniques other than mental mnemonics that are also extremely useful for remembering what is past, (including past lives). Deep meditation and regressive hypnotherapy have been used. Certain psychoactive substances work well. The aim is to make your mind into a blank canvas that is completely free, open and receptive so that the images and experiences can flood in unimpeded. You are opening the filter of your mind by temporarily removing all obfuscating memories and conditioned thought patterns that clutter it. You remove all analytical overlay of your reasoning and calculating mind as well as all future dreams. Now you are in the zone, in the present and ready to receive.

We easily see that when a consciousness has become greatly diminished it can't even remember what it had for dinner an hour ago. But it is more difficult for us to embrace the full extent of all that is lost and filtered by our current blocking state of consciousness. So our consciousness must rise up to become all-encompassing. It must lose its narrow focus and become more diffusive again, before we can access all. It should not become narrow-banded to individual perceptions, which then serve to cohere into meaningless globs that cover over the entire canvas of our minds. In the meantime, as we plod along and stumble in the dark, it seems as if, all that our future holds is yet to come. We can use our free will to stumble any which way we like. We can go on stumbling almost forever. We can fall down many times, and cover the same turf over-and-over again in an infinite regression. It is certain that if we continue to use our past experiences to direct our way, this is exactly what will happen.

We are in a sad plight indeed, because the room is so vast and so dark, and has so many trinkets and toys to distract us. There are so many howling shrieking sounds piercing the dark, making us feel endlessly fearful, anxious and tormented. Our only alternative and hope is to choose the guidance and vision of the Holy Spirit. We need to elicit His services to become our eyes. He knows the one complete and painless way out of this dark room. Here where we have wasted millions of years. He knows where the door and light switch are. His only purpose is to guide us quickly to our safety, sanity and joy. His teachings are simple. Anything which serves to increase guilt in another is not the way out. Anything that serves to strengthen belief in separation places you deeper in darkness. You are being lead by your ego to greater confusion and misery.

Once you begin to see the shining light of innocence in your brother's face, you are near the door. Your choice remains either to follow your ego or your Guide. When you finally reach the door, you will look back stunned. For now you fully realize you had sucked on so much rubbish for so long. All is seen and known, simply as harmless when seen in the light. The way is easy but very different. It is one of content, not of form. For the ego rejects content in a form it does not like. This is always what has lead to its blindness and confusion. It is partial in its evaluation of what it sees yet Reality can only be known through our complete impartiality. Your future has already happened. Your one choice is to release yourself from the need to have it relived and re-experienced again-and-again. It will be faithfully played back from your memory banks until you make the decision to relinquish it. Give it over to the loving, wise and all seeing eyes of the Holy Spirit. He will help you to make informed present decisions that will release all nonsense for good. Then you will no longer worry about your future, nor be haunted by your past. You will know that you are always perfectly safe.

> "God holds your future as He holds your past and present. They are one to Him, and so they should be one to you. Yet in this world, the temporal progression still seems real. And so you are not asked to understand the lack of sequence really found in time. You are but asked to let the future go, and place it in God's Hands. And you will see by your experience that you have laid the past and present in His Hands as well, because the past will punish you no more, and future dread will now be meaningless."
>
> [W.194.4:1-6]

Jesus continuously appeals to each of us to release our maddening toxic grip on our future. Yet, we ignore this sage advice. Instead we have become obsessed with constantly manipulating and forcing our future direction to accomplish all our projected goals. Because we feel incomplete in the present, we seek our completion in the future. We often place our chips exclusively on some other person, event or situation. Then we engage in our games of guilt when they do not come through. In every situation we like to brand it with our own specific ego imprint. Often the ego cares not, what imprint it leaves nor how much it stomps upon another, so long as it leaves some imprint. It is so afraid of its own emptiness and inconsequentiality. It thinks it can get more of our attention, if we are going nowhere fast, rather than nowhere slow.

Don't Be Fooled by The Ego's Rosy Picture, of your Future

I remember one time, working with Dr. Gobbler's Knob on the building sites in London. The work was really hard at times. One of our tasks was to lift all these heavy fire-lined plasterboards up many flights of stairs. This was because the building had no operational lifts yet. When we got to the top, we would be panting hard and usually decided to rest for a few minutes, before heading back down for the next load. While resting we suddenly heard all sorts of grunts and groans echoing from a fellow worker coming up the stairs. He was panting like a wild predator on the Serengeti just after having completed a kill. His face was flushed blood red. He had that look like he was just about to drop down dead from a full blown cardio on the spot. He was rather old. That is in his late fifties and yet this is what he was doing. When he saw us resting for a few moments, he had the most overt vile contempt for us. He said, *"You just wait and see - in a few short weeks or months I will be manager of this outfit."* I did not think he would last that long.

Then as he headed back down for another load, I was suddenly engulfed with this weird mingling of profound sorrow and amusement. His script seemed so depressing. He treated his own life and body like a sordid rag to be torn or shredded for whatever idle purpose floated about. One generation, it would be used to stuff cannons and to stick bayonets into human fodder and in the next to clean out all the cobwebs out from all the sewers and gutters of this world. Yes, I had a sudden illumination there and then. My mind flashed forward and I could instantly see the final and just reward of all those who buy in fully to all the poppycock they are sold in this marketplace. It was only ~10am, yet I could do no more work that day. No longer function as a junkyard monkey. So I headed to a nearby bar with the Dr., where we spent the remainder of the day getting inebriated and singing out in uproarious delight. Saying a great **Yes** to life, adventure and fearlessness. Saying **No** to blind pandering submission. Later that evening as we were heading back trashed in the underground, there were all these yuppies dressed to the hilt. Yes all nicely outfitted in all their business suits and dresses. Yet, they all looked so miserable, lifeless and dejected, this army of the corporately condemned. All sold on future dreams and now paying the price.

The ego is always holding out this beautiful picture of our future. One that glowingly encapsulates all its promises to us. This picture can look so compelling and so much rosier than our present. As a result we will often do the most mind-numbing tasks in the dream to get this "future" we desire. The present becomes our dirty rag, to be used merely as a means to implement all our ego dreams. Fundamentally we see no value in this rag beyond the limited purposes we have assigned to it. We do not trust in the present to deliver us completely and we have no trust in ourselves. All our loyalties are dedicated to our glorious futures, that we have projected into time.

Jesus's teaching in the Course is in stark contrast to the worldly way of doing business. It can be considered the unworldly wise way. The present moment is deemed the only place of value and of worth. The only place for our faith and trust. Here is the Home of miracles and of all meaningful change. All can be miraculously changed, transformed and healed through our present decision. Take care of the present and the future will take care of itself. We need but cast all our cares on its power. Then we can navigate forward in our life, infused with a spirit of lightheartedness and trust. As we embrace the guidance and powerful presence of the Holy Spirit, we gain remembrance of our real freedom. We begin to experience power and release. So do we transform every instant into a holy one and establish it as a breathing ground for miracles.

> **"Release the future. For the past is gone, and what is present, freed from its bequest of grief and misery, of pain and loss, becomes the instant in which time escapes the bondage of illusions where it runs its pitiless, inevitable course. Then is each instant which was slave to time transformed into a holy instant, when the light that was kept hidden in God's Son is freed to bless the world. Now is he free, and all his glory shines upon a world made free with him, to share his holiness."**

[W.194.5:1-4]

One single instant given over in perfect faith is enough to release you entirely from the prison-house of time. For it is impossible for any illusion to keep you in chains, once you recognize your strength. When you have penetrated any instant to its core, you simultaneously release yourself of all illusions. Time then has no more power over you. You are no longer tempted by the allure, temptations and empty promises each illusion sells. You cannot come to awareness of your completion in time, but only outside its manifold. Do not swear then to uphold a vast illusionary network of self deceptions. Retain even a single false belief and you retain your blindness. Yet, all are made of the same old stuff, one that is devoid of any content and meaning. There is no hope of finding lasting joy in any mind-dream. This is the single roar of all the Enlightened.

Yet, those tempted to choose form over content have already established preference and judgment as their gods. Manifold worldly heavens and hells will stream into their sight, but they will never reach the eternally abiding. Their many compromises, preferences and capacities for self-deception hold them at ransom and they cannot enter the gateway to truth wearing these dark cloaks. Can any meaningful distinctions be made among the non-existent? No! the Buddhas do not practice nonsense. They look inwards this moment and see the eternal flame, which is also the bonfire of all illusions. They know all phenomena are born of the mind. To stand naked, is to be without any pretense or self-deception. Then all reality reveals itself. Then you die as the illusion that you were, only to be born again as the Christ Consciousness. For this, you must be totally ready and willing to give up all meager offerings, and sweet-nothings of your ego. You must learn to see them all as empty dreams leading to nowhere but disenchantment and death. This single instant of trust is enough to free the entire world, replacing it with the ever-existing and eternal.

> **"If you are tempted to be dispirited by thinking how long it would take to change your mind so completely, ask yourself, "How long is an instant?" Could you not give so short a time to the Holy Spirit for your salvation? He asks no more, for He has no need of more. It takes far longer to teach you to be willing to give Him this than for Him to use this tiny instant to offer you the whole of Heaven. In exchange for this instant He stands ready to give you the remembrance of eternity."**

[T-15.I.11:1-5]

One thing the ego cannot tolerate is peace and quiet. During such times, it becomes anxious and restless. Seeing you kneeling silently in meditation, it cautions that you will soon turn into a zazen zombie.

Yet change is also a fearful thing to your ego. It wants you to get the future that it desires, yet it does not want you to really change in doing so. When the dust finally settles around all its idle and failed wishes, it tries to leverage off your feelings of pain, failure and victimization. Yes, the world is against you. Thus it whispers into your ears. Always trying to put you down and take you out of commission. Thus it ensures that your future will again be wasted trying to atone, or at least compensate for all your past miseries.

The Holy Spirit teaches in stark contrast, that change can be a good thing, something to be positively welcomed so long as you are evolving along the way. The changes brought about through His benevolent guidance always bear fruit and blessing. You need not fear the changes He brings to you in time. They ensure all illusions will pass away, finally enabling truth alone to be revealed. His changes bring you to light, joy, empowerment and increased peace. The Holy Spirit uses time to release you from all your false and binding beliefs in sickness, sacrifice and sin. So He demonstrates there is no power to darkness, nor to death. He removes all that is illusory, which is covering over your reality. But He never seeks to change your underlying reality itself. All that seems to change is that ragged image you hold of yourself in the dream. That image which the ego made to replace the Eternal Son of God. This image cannot be revamped but must be dismissed. We must tear down and sculpt away all the unwanted bits of marble you have added in time. Thus revealing the immortal splendor of your perfect Being.

> **"Change is the greatest gift God gave to all that you would make eternal, to ensure that only Heaven would not pass away. You were not born to die. You cannot change, because your function has been fixed by God."**
>
> **[T-29.VI.4:1-3]**

ZENO'S ANSWER TO THE OBJECTIVE VIEW OF TIME

The Course teaches that time has an endogenous nature. That it is psychological, mentally created and endowed with the intimate spiritual purpose of providing a framework for our healing. This of course is diametrically opposed to the world's teachings pertaining to time. The world treats time, as if it possessed an exogenous nature. Pictures it as having an objective, self-existing reality, that is independent of ourselves and our psychological makeup. A yardstick for measuring events in a physical "outside" universe. Time is thought to potentially go on indefinitely, although certain physicists posit that even "objective" time had a beginning and will have an end.

This "objective" nature of time has seen many conscientious objectors in the dream. Firstly there are those who thought deeply about the nature of time (and motion). These came to a far deeper metaphysical understanding. They realized that there was a total absence of any objective quality or reality to time. They had penetrated through all the layers of subterfuge that surrounds time, all those false premises and illusions upon which our notions of "objective" time is based. This group includes great luminaries such as Zeno, Kant, Ouspensky and countless others. Even Minkowski has seen space and time as joined. Zeno did it elegantly through a now famous paradox which succeeded in turning the premises of objectivism back on itself. He started out by agreeing with the primary premises of objectivism, namely that time and space are continuous and mind independent quantities. In this view, any fixed extent of time or space can be infinitely subdivided. It can therefore be broken into halves, quarters, eights ,and so on . . . ad infinitum. Then he simply pointed out that based on these premises, an arrow shot from a bow can never make it to its target.

So he sets out first agreeing with the objective assumption that the arrow does make it to its target in some finite time T_0. Then he reasons it would take a time $T_0/2$ to make it halfway to its target, and some fixed time $T_0/4$, to travel half the remaining distance, and so on in an infinite series. Since there would always be half of the remaining distance to go and some definite time period needed to accomplish this goal, the arrow would never reach the target. Or another way of presenting the outcome is that the arrow can only ever reach to the target, given an infinite extent of time. Mathematically this situation is expressed as a geometric series of the form below, where **S,** represents the total distance traveled at measurement event N:-

$$S = 1/2 + 1/4 + 1/8 + 1/16 + \ldots\ldots\ldots 1/2^N$$

In this geometric series; **a =1/2** and **r=1/2**

$$\sum_{k=0}^{n} ar^k = \frac{a(1 - r^{n+1})}{1 - r}$$

Its Sum, $S = 1 - 1/2^N < 1$

As we can see since the sum, S of distance traveled is always less than 1 for any finite N, and therefore any finite time. It is a mathematical certainty then that the arrow can never make it to its target. There will always be some additional time increment needed to travel the next incremental distance. Now let's frame Zeno's paradox in a slightly different way. Let's start taking our measurement observations instead, when the arrow has traveled one third of its distance to this target and therefore has two-thirds of the remaining distance to go. We will then proceed to take our next time-check when it has traveled one third of the original distance and so on. When we establish our infinite series along these lines instead, the total distance S traveled to the target at measurement increment, N becomes.

$S = 1/3 + 1/9 + 1/27 + \dots \dots \dots (1/3^N)$

In this geometric series; $a = 1/3$ and $r = 1/3$ and its Sum, S is

$S = 1/2 * (1 - (1/3^N)) < ½$

As we can see, in our new scenario, the sum, **S** of total distance traveled will always be less than half the total distance. So the arrow cannot even make it halfway to the target, given an infinite number of increments and therefore an infinite extent of time. If we start taking our measurements instead when the arrow has traveled 1/1000 of the distance to the target and still has 999/1000 of the distance to go, and continue with this scenario, we find that even in an infinite extent of time the arrow cannot even make it 1/999 or ~0.1% of the distance to the target. In the ultimately scenario, we can show that Zen's arrow cannot even leave the bow. It remains frozen there for an infinite extent of time.

Maybe you are still not convinced. So we get creative and decide to use time lapse photography to send us a series of snapshots delimiting the arrow's progress for each of these three scenarios. A photo is e-mailed to us each time the arrow has traveled our chosen ratio of the remaining distance. In each scenario we will be receiving an infinite number of snapshots, but none ever showing us the arrow reaching its target. In the first scenario, the snapshots will paint a picture of an arrow getting always closer to the target, the bulk of the photos in the second scenario will show the arrow stuck somewhere in the middle, desperately trying to make it to the halfway point. While in the final scenario, we will have an infinite set of pictures of an arrow that seems almost frozen at the bow. So we arrive at three completely different pictures of the arrow's ultimate progress trajectory. Pictures that depend intimately on those progress increments, at which we want to receive our updates.

Let's suppose instead that there are three separate observers, each with different response times watching this archery show. Observer A, has a very limited response time. He can only take snapshots of the arrow's progress each time it has traveled half the remaining distance. His observations tell the story of how the arrow almost reaches the target but never quite gets there. Observer B has a faster response time that A. He will start taking snapshots of the arrow when it makes it 1/3 of the total distance and then one third of this distance, and so on. His observations will indicate the arrow never makes it even to the halfway point. Notice this was the first snapshot that Observer A is able to capture. Their two perceptions of reality will therefore never even overlap because of the difference in their response times. The third observer C can take snapshots each time it has traveled 1/1000 the distance to the target. He is mystified by the data he is hearing from the other two and boldly declares the arrow hardly ever exits the bow. So the three observers will step away with three completely different worldviews of what happened to Zeno's arrow, each claiming that their results alone are correct, based on the evidence of their snapshots. The evidence bears them out, they say. In the ultimate extrapolation of Zeno's arrow, we can imagine having an infinite number of observers, each with their own different response times or time-lapse photography equipment. Each presenting a different story of what actually happened to it and each claiming their story alone is true Let's not forget to add in our own story, that of blankly stating that the arrow did indeed make to the target, because this is what shows up in our perceptions.

As we are beginning to see, what actually happens to Zeno's arrow is becoming a mystery. One less to do with any objective arrow or target but one that seems to depend intimately on the capabilities of the observing apparatus. Recognizing ourselves as the observing apparatus, we begin to see that the story unfolding in our world picture has more to do with our own subjective dimension and inner response time than anything objectively happening "out-there". The story of what happened to Zeno's arrow is therefore one told from within rather than from without. It is the story of how each of our different world experiences are uniquely shaped by us. It helps explain why one person is a professional basketball player, or champion race care driver with split second reaction times while another mopes about as a zombie crashing into everything. In the end we begin to realize that it is our unique inner subjective capabilities that determines the world of our perceptions

Zeno merely stated with his paradox that if we take the premises of objectivism to be true, to declare that the arrow can make it to its target in some finite time, T_0 then we can also identify an infinite number of scenarios based on the same premises that can prove otherwise. So we have no answer, just an infinite number of assertions claiming to be the right answer. Now just to recall the two primary premises of objectivism again. They are *Premise (1)* Space is a neutral, continuous, independent and objective entity that can be infinitely subdivided. And *Premise (2)* Time is a neutral, continuous, independent and objective entity that can be infinitely subdivided.

Let's look at another simple example that portrays how our subjective inner response times shapes our world picture. Imagine there are four different observers each with different inner perceptual response times. Observer W, is very slow. He clocks in with a response time of one second. As a result he only ever perceives blue balls showing up in his world. Observer X I,s a bit more quick witted and has a response time of 0.5 seconds. He gets to also see the yellow balls. He argues endlessly with W on this, because observer W claims they do not exist. Observer Y, is much sharper than the norm and has a response time of 0.25 seconds. He tells X and Y that they are both mistaken and that green and red balls are also present. Now there is bigger argument going on. Enter observer Z, he is one bright wit, almost a mystic and clocks in with a response of time of 0.125 seconds. He claims to see eight different colored balls. He sees the purple, orange, gray and black balls, which none of the others ever spot. Now the atmosphere has become really heated and debated. Some think observer Z is hallucinating or at least is a little deranged.

Using a response time of seconds, in this example is completely arbitrary, since time itself is an illusion. I could just as easily have given a response time in guinea pigs or space-monkeys. Nevertheless, we can readily recognize that the more our subjective inner time-sense dilates, the more expansive our world picture becomes. When our time-sense has been extensively dilated, we begin to see all at once. One may well ask the question *"Dilated compared to what?"* This is an excellent question, since there is no objective time to set the benchmark for comparison. There is an important internal benchmark however that we can use. This benchmark is our becoming aware of each thought as it occurs. When we have become so self monitoring as to be aware of each of our thoughts then we have reached the critical point of time-sense dilation and responsivity.

A lesser dilation and many thoughts go by without us ever becoming aware of them. Lesser still, and whole activities may go by without our presence. While in an increased state of time-sense dilation we can be awaiting in positive anticipation for the next thought, before it even occurs. At the critical point of time-sense dilation and awareness expansion, the duality of seemingly separate inner and outer worlds begins to disappear and vaporize. This is because of our heightened state of awareness. We are beginning to see at last, how our thoughts are simultaneously showing up as images in our perceptions. Images that reflect their underlying content. At this awareness threshold, the picture on the screen, the screen itself and the mind of the projectionist are known to be intimately fused together. All is arising in one's awareness. Thoughts and images are just fluctuations, known as vritti, in the calm expansive sea of our greater awareness. This is the threshold that separates the awakened from the daydreaming. The threshold that separates those who can exercise power over their worlds, from those who simply identify themselves as victims.

Below this threshold one's awareness is poor. One finds themselves in a world of clearly delineated objects. This is a dull and conditioned world in which the mind's filter is too closed off and narrow-banded. One identifies themselves, as a thing in a static universe. One can be said to be trapped in the solid state of consciousness. Above this threshold, one's self awareness has increased to the point where objects are no longer objects. They have lost all their static boundaries and distinctions and have become fluid and permeable. Colors are no longer colors, but more colorings. The coloration tracking their increased awareness. For once, objects are known now to be a verb, instead of a noun, because they are becoming so dynamic, permeable and fluid, as to be experienced more like phenomena. One can now be said to be in the liquid state of consciousness.

Eventually with increased awareness all phenomenal activity is seen to come to an end as all merges into One. All coexists now in a flux of vaporous light, in which there is no thing. Your body has disappeared into this nebulous flux, as has everything else. There is no *thing* to see and you now suddenly realize there has never been any "*thing*". This is naked reality straight up, coming at you hard and fast. It is a reality that is a womb of all that is within and seemingly without. A soft, warm and cradling womb. You have now entered the vaporous state of consciousness. The goal of consciousness is to bring you to this point, after which it becomes completely useless and ready to be discarded. Replaced by a reality, that is one of pure abstraction, where nothing can be described but most assuredly can be felt.

Zeno's paradox is not at all concerned with arrows, targets, events, forces and energies etc. Nor is it concerned with the archer's cheating wife and how this may be affecting his mental state and aim. Nor is it concerned with any specific phenomena or concepts in particular. If we focus on those minutiae, then we also miss the target, because we have missed the true content of Zeno's paradox. He could just as easily have established his paradox based on the chances of a mouse reaching its hole in time, before the cat swallows it up. Or he could have formulated it along the lines of our fictitious notion of possessing a human will. Because, if we think of our personal goals as targets, we can never say for certain whether we will accomplish a definite goal or not. This is because, at some point in-between we are only halfway towards accomplishing our goal, and at a later point only three quarters and so on . . . We can only say we will accomplish a goal for certain when we have already accomplished it. This then makes it a redundant statement. Also he who accomplishes the goal is not that same person that started out making this bold statement, since your mind changes in the process of accomplishing a goal. Therefore we cannot say for certain, we have a will.

Rather Zeno's paradox is concerned more generally with undermining the entire worlds of phenomenalism and conceptualization in general. He is saying we project this world from our minds based on those arbitrary concepts and beliefs we embrace. These then determine all that seems to happen. The world is always a spontaneous tailor-made apparition, that is the perfect reflex of all that is currently happening in the sea of our own subjectivity. It is the arbitrary flux of those concepts and beliefs we endorse, which then shapes and determines all our perceptions. Zeno is therefore confronting us deeply and directly in a number of important ways. For not only is his paradox probing deeply into the illusory nature of time and space, but it also delving into the relationship that exists between our perceptions and psychological states. He is saying that it is the particular way we formulate our questions after all which then shapes what appears to happen. He is examining the metaphysical nature of the relationship between motion and stillness. Do either have any absolute reality that we can clearly differentiate or is there no real difference between the two? He is obviously dismantling space as an objective entity, pointing to the fact that it is born within us, and only seems to be outside due to mental projection. He is exploring deeply also, the nature of becoming to being. His paradox is sneakily demonstrating that we can never transmute a statement of becoming into one of being. This is because being has no need to become and becoming never ends.

In our world picture, we often make rash judgments based on the evidence of our sensations and perceptions and so say the arrow accomplished its goal of reaching to the target. We see a picture of an arrow stuck in a target somewhere and then we rush out to the press saying this is an accomplished fact, never recognizing for a moment our unique part is making this seem so. Then we proceed to invent our laws of cause-and-effect to explain away this perception. We are no different then, than that 2D being, who claims a dot gave birth to all the expanding and contracting circles it perceived in its world. So he cleverly reformulated the scenario, into one of the arrow, always being in a state of becoming. One in which the arrow always needs more time to travel more distance. Since in the new scenario, the arrow is always in a state of becoming, it can never accomplish its goal.

Zeno wanted us to get rid of all those nonsense cause-and-effect principles we assume based on the evidence of our perceptions. Our current position is to let the evidence speak for itself. His position was diametrically opposed to this. He is saying that the evidence of our sense perceptions cannot be trusted. It is already suspect, because it has become corrupted and tarnished by all our preferences, biases, concepts and a-priori beliefs. The worldly position of objectivism, is one of having already accepted that things are actually happening "out-there", and that there is an outer world. Its position is hardly one of an unbiased critic since it is extremely critical of evidence that goes against its own premises. It severely ridicules and rebukes any position that would seek to dismantle or destroy all its carefully built edifices and monuments to materialism and objective glory. It does not want you to see that all its castles of sand are erected from false premises.

The worldly stance on objectivism, is therefore hardly neutral. It is more like that of an agent who is already invested in promoting the wares, of his client alone. Immediately dismissing the merits of all contending products and stances. So the world stands adamantly on the rocks of its own premises. It then seeks to explain all events in our world rationally and cohesively via mechanisms, concepts, laws, principles and cause-and-effect relationships etc. that are built-up from these premises. Embedded deeply into our minds now, these principles have become transformed into our conditioned beliefs. So have we become brainwashed and avalanched by all those magic principles that have arisen in the fields of Science, Technology, Genetics, Health and so on. Now we develop exclusively on these platforms and sit in self-righteous contempt of all other understandings.

Zeno's position contends that all the evidence that reinforces our many false beliefs, was placed there by us in the first place. Placed there by all those prized concepts, principles, cause-and-effect relationships and conditioned beliefs we are already biased favorably towards. This evidence therefore cannot be trusted. Unfortunately these beliefs have become our sacred cows and they function as part of those internal filters, which then shape and determine all we perceive. We are continuously repeating mantras of an internal script formed from our belief composites and projecting this into the domain of our perceptions. This results is certain evidence showing up in our perceptions. Armed and loaded with such evidence, we then do a 180 degree about-face and claim this arsenal of compelling evidence confirms the veracity of our underlying scripts, principles, concepts etc. We make it out as if the evidence is telling us the story, rather than that it is our own evolutionary state and pet nexus of beliefs that is producing the evidence. Thus we use the evidence showing up in our perceptions, as a form of proof and validation of what our world really IS and what we ourselves Are!

Consider as an example, a movie spool. We know this movie and the story it tells has only a fixed number of frames. Despite this fact, it can present us with the illusion of continuity -just like time. Now what happens, when we randomly reshuffle all those frames and play that movie again. That movie would tell a completely different story and one that would seem to take forever. It would not hold our interest for long. Yet we know that nothing fundamental has changed. The frames themselves, and the number of frames has remained the same. It is just the ordering of the frames that is different. So it is with the movie of our lives. We are ordering the frames based on our pet concepts, beliefs and persuasions and then foolishly say this is the story that is being told to us. We ignore our part in doing the ordering of the frames. We filter out and ignore all that goes against our grain.

The Course teaches us that we only experience time and the meaningless movies we perceive because we are using our ego to do the ordering of the frames. And yet the ego itself is an artifact, an apparition that is only arising, out of the disordered state of the frames. The ego grows in direct proportion to this disorder. It is the pseudo-living symbol of this disordered state of affairs and so long as we use it as our guide the disorder remains. When we no longer resort to using this "guidance" of the ego, order is restored. Relinquishing the ego, we learn the right criteria and understandings by which to properly order the frames. So the movie transforms from one that is meaningless to one that is tremendously meaningful and light-filled. Then the unnecessary encumbrances of time and the ego will be no more.

A second group of conscientious objectors to the prevailing beliefs, in time came from those who were primarily interested in voyaging deeply within themselves. Those searching for meaning and for truth and exploring those subaqueous realms normally covered over by the rigid plasticity of everyday life and conditioned thought. They were not predominantly interested in understanding the nature of time. They were primarily engaged in reaching to certainties experientially. So they dived into the seemingly fathomless reaches of their own self-natures and being. After they accomplished their goal of self-realization, the full deeper understanding of the true nature of time came as an added bonus. Through their self-realization, they came to know that time was an entity with no real existence. They came to directly see that all the events and happening of the "outside" world were in a direct dualistic relationship with the inner self. Yes, time was psychological and inwardly driven. This group includes Parmenides, Shankara, Jesus, Osho, Wei-Wu-We, Sri Ramana Maharashi etc.

Then there is a third group who stumbled on the experience of time being a mentally generated illusion using an entirely different approach. They can be considered untethered voyagers of the psyche and all inner spaces. This group got their experiences either through taking certain psycho-active drugs (Marijuana, Psilocybin, Ayahuasca, LSD, Ketamine, DMT, etc.) or else through experiencing a near death experience (NDE) or equivalent. Most modern day mystics, New-Agers and quantum physicists are willing to agree now that our time-sense is a subjective rather than an objective quantity. In fact many quantum physicists found out that they can do their equations far easier and far more elegantly by excluding all references to time and space from them. Others cosmologists include time as a parameter but make it into a directionless entity. In the end it is far more realistic to talk about the time-sense, than about time because all time comes from within. Since all our time-senses are different, all our worlds are unfolding at completely different rates into the canvas of our perceptions.

EVOLUTION IN OUR CONSCIOUSNESS IS DESPERATELY NEEDED

Many may be willing to agree that consciousness represents an imperfect and limited mode of our psychic functioning. This is because consciousness always implies some degree of separation between the knower and the known. Our experiencing of time is really just a carryover from the limitations of consciousness. Or more appropriately the limitations by which we use consciousness. In days of old, many who wanted to get information directly and immediately, would bypass the limitations and distortions imposed by their normal streams of consciousness. We can see for example the appeal, that existed for spiritual mediums, sorcery and for entering trance states. These days many use psychoactive substances instead. But nothing is needed at all, to function as an intermediary between you and naked experience - just an increase in your awareness. Through increased self-awareness you become aware of how extremely filtered your consciousness and perceptions are. Recognize that they are filtered to the point of blindness. It is this filtering that seems to present the illusion of continuity to time.

As awareness increases, time dilates. As your depth of understanding increases, certain perceptions and scripts will no longer be played out making time increasingly unnecessary. Those with perfect understanding do not distort and therefore they find no need for time at all. For time is but a vehicle where all contradictory notions produced and propelled from erroneous beliefs can wage out their wars into our perceptions. It is our imperfect comprehension that gives rise to such phantoms. When the mind resolves all its conflicts and so transcends, there will be no more distortions, illusions or time. One has entered a reality that is constant and timeless. One that is perfect, non-contingent and whole. Yet so long as we see and comprehend through limited planes of understanding, the appearance of motion and phenomena will continue.

Unfortunately, the mystics and greatest philosophers have been little understood. It seems with every new generation, they are dismissed as irrelevant. Again we need to be potty trained in our "ABCs". So we blindly set off on our way again trying to make illusions joyous and meaningful - sending up more smoke signals and looking for the great spirit in the junkyard of technology or such places. Unfortunately many just take it, as it is dished out to them. They have no powers of insight or critical reasoning. Objective spacetime becomes their a-priori position because that is was is fed to them, through their IV. The Buddha taught that the dream, the dreamer and dreaming were all symbiotic aspects of one illusion. Each reinforcing the pseudo-realities of each other. Yet all such apparitions can only arise in an impure mind with its impure understandings. None has any absolute existence, each has only contingent existence. Their contingent existence is based in impurity. It is the split-mind mode of mental functioning which makes them seem real.

When the Buddha is teaching that all happenings are illusory, he is most assuredly also teaching that time itself is illusory. As mentioned earlier, the Course goes further, when it says time has a plan to it. From the eternal perspective, time serves no purpose, but from the context of the relative existence it has a very important one. This holy purpose is the removal of all false beliefs. This alone brings about our healing. So like the lame man we learn how to walk again and then to run. Then one day we throw down our crutches of spacetime and walk off into the light. The Course never seeks to take away our existing beliefs, without giving us something far more valuable in return. It teaches us that our existing beliefs are beliefs in the non-existent. So we go on believing in a world that is not there. Those of us, who are unwise remain as children. Our unquestioned beliefs can be dangerous in our minds. They can do much harm and inflict much illusory pain. Over time they seem to corrode our very souls and are the only cause for our experiencing the illusion of death.

The real world of perfection, always awaits silently for us in the Here-and-Now, silently waiting for our return and the restoration of our sanity. It is awaiting for us, to retrain our eyes to see and interpret things a little differently and to purify ourselves through forgiveness. It is our beliefs in the unbelievable that are keeping us blind. The ego's key attraction to time is to preserve it indefinitely, and this it does through guilt. It seeks to retain the unconscious guilt that arose in the beginning at the instant of the tiny-mad-idea (TMI). This guilt is progenitor of all other false beliefs. So, in the ego's hands time is used destructively to imprison and to waste. This darkened transparency of the ego which we have invited into our minds seduces our consciousness into dullness and mediocrity and attachment to its empty offerings. It functions as an obfuscating overlay that impedes us from witnessing truth, Here-and-Now. As long as we chose to maintain belief in guilt, this transparency will remain.

> **"Guilt feelings are the preservers of time. They induce fears of retaliation or abandonment, and thus ensure that the future will be like the past. This is the ego's continuity. It gives the ego a false sense of security by believing that you cannot escape from it. But you can and must."**   **[T-5.VI.2:1-5]**

THE PRESENT MOMENT IS OUR GATEWAY TO THE ETERNAL

The present moment is all powerful because it does not exist in time. It is the meeting ground of time with eternity, of the horizontal with the vertical. Living horizontally in spacetime, without ever traveling into the vertical is to live an entirely wasted life. Your life is lived tragically and short of meaning, since all meaning is in the vertical. All paths on the horizontal path lead nowhere but further into illusions – the goal is the vertical. Here alone lies truth and therefore all that is supremely important and thirst quenching. Entering *'The Now'*, is like peeping through a hole in the paper of spacetime and peering into Eternity. Here is the birthplace of all miracles and holy instants. Here is the portal for all experiences of revelations. Here is where God communicates directly to you, in an ancient tongue that can never be spoken. Here He imparts His messages in terms that can be fully understood at the deeper level of your mind and Being. Here is the place of all certainty, safety, peace and rest. The Home of all inspiration, in which you are healed of all the nonsense, time has taught you. It is only here that real understanding and Knowledge can be rediscovered.

Otherwise you miss. You just spin your wheels endlessly in the dream making choices between vain and empty illusions. You attempt to make one dream more meaningful than the next, but the lesson has always been that all dreams are meaningless and futile. All block awakening. The dream of forgiveness is the only meaningful dream since it alone leads to awakening. Forgiveness is the dream that ends all dreams. All other dreams are representative of fear's presence and love's absence. They evidence your belief in your own incompletion. So you seek compensations for your believed scarcity and lacks from a world outside. So you come to beg and ridicule yourself before some new high powered dream or idol. Foolish treasures by which you seek to douse and eliminate your never-ending misery. But no dream or idol has power enough for that, in fact no real power to give anything real at all.

Having admitted to imperfection anywhere, it seems you must learn to bargain now with the world of evil to make yourself whole. So arises the belief in the Anti-Christ. Only the Anti-Christ can give you what you need, but for this you must first sign on the dotted line. Every choice you make is one between continuing to dream or choosing to awake. Do you choose to continue your hypnotic attraction to this world of idols? Do you seek to further ensnare yourself in this hallucination? Or do you say instead, *"This is not for me, I have come to find the real treasure House, my inheritance that is hidden just behind this dream?"* There is no in-between; either you are asleep or awake! Only when you no longer hold any attraction to guilt, specialness and the world of idols will you awake.

Time can be seen as the purgatory needed by all those, who have yet to learn of its emptiness. Yet all those idols and temptations are nothing more than shabby tattered substitutes spun from illusion, that seek to upstage truth. Those who choose to awaken, treasure the present moment. They see it as the ferry from illusion into truth. They know that the '**Now**' is the '**Gateway to Eternity**'. On this journey, all masks need to be left behind, for it is a journey without distance or time, to a place where you have always been. As all illusory beliefs, superficialities and masks are left on the floor, your original face is restored to you once more. Then all confusing beliefs percolating from this relative world of form are undone for good, no longer here to plague your holy mind. They were but functioning as curses to hold you back and to clip your wings. The instant, is immanent and transcendent to time. It is Home of the eternal. *"The Now'* exists beyond the scope and manifold of time and yet seemingly within it.

"**The little breath of eternity that runs through time like golden light is all the same; nothing before it, nothing afterwards.**"

[T-20.V.5:8]

Everyone must come to '*The Now*' in the end. This is the one true naked singularity, in the entire universe of the relative and yet outside it. It extends a limitless force of loving vitality and benevolence on all who come to it. Yet its power is self-sustaining, inexhaustible and independent of all dreams. From the sun of its unconditional warmth every mind receives the only power it will ever need. It even sustains all the galaxies and all the worlds so long as you retain split-mind. When we are all finally sucked back in by its pure powerful magnetizing force, we but seem to disappear. But we are reborn instead into the unquenchable loving light of the infinite. The 'Now' rests as an Eternal flame perched high above the vicissitudes of time. No illusion can pass through this gate to the eternal. They must be left at the door, for no illusion is licensed to enter Eternity, to pollute its crystal clear waters, to foul up its fragrant vitalizing air, or to stagnate its loving atmosphere of perfect aliveness. You must divest yourself of all illusions at the door, so that you can pass gracefully and effortlessly through this portal.

Your real power derives, out of your connection to God in '*The-Now*'. Losing this connection for even a single moment, you would disappear entirely. It is like the light behind the tape in the projecting booth, that is yet the Source of all the images on the screen. Without this light, there is nothing. This light shines through the slit of '*The Now*', giving birth to the universal holomotion (Holographic projection in motion). This tape holds all your beliefs, true and false. It holds all those scripts which you projected into time. The screen faithfully responds reproducing and picturing to you all the scripts you have chosen as well as their content. The outer faithfully reflects the inner but it is only through the inner that the outer can be transformed. For the inner is the active power, which drives the outer.

Do what you like to the screen or upon it. Yet you will remain powerless to effect any meaningful change because you are working with the causeless. You will not reach to true Cause, in the projecting booth of the Now, until your mind is healed at a fundamental level. So dispossessed of all false beliefs. Until then, you will remain just a tragic Don Quixote figure, tilting at the many windmills of life. A mindless puppet that has got overly identified with his puppetry and worldly show of make belief. A puppeteer that has forgot that it is the workings of his own hand that powers the entire show. 'The Now' is the Home of the forever true. What is not in 'The Now' does not exist. Time itself, can be seen as your futile attempt at recovering a single experience of the eternal by breaking it up into a seeming infinite series of 3D cuts. You then look at these 3D cuts through a darkened window – the darkness of false and obscuring beliefs. Yet these cuts seem to have lost all their meaning. Because it is only in their relationship to Wholeness that their tremendous meaning becomes apparent. Of themselves, they appear fragmentary, inconsistent and meaningless. Yet, darkness is only maintained through your continued belief in the meaningless. In this darkness, it is impossible to see that these cuts are fragments of what is the radiant One. They all still retain their unity, but this truth has been obscured through your unhealthy desires, for fragmentation and partiality.

It is the purpose of forgiveness to remove all that is false on these 3D cuts and to restore vision of their Wholeness and underlying intimacy. Only then does the meaning in the parts become self-evident. We have become too accustomed to thinking of the 'The Now', as tiny and insignificant. As a result, it has become completely covered over with mind junk - with worldly goals and ideals.

Experientially we know it not, yet we can think we do. We do not understand that this instant contains all there IS. It represents the reservoir of our bounty and abundance, our freedom from all beliefs in lack, limitation and vulnerability. *"Look lovingly upon the present, for it holds the only things that are forever true."[T-13.VI.6:2]* Yet, until we have felt its tremendous value, at a truly spiritual and existential level, we will not attempt to enter it.

WE ARE HYPNOTIZED BY ORDERS, MAGNITUDES AND OUR PARTIALITIES

Is this surprising? Our whole culture trains us to think in magnitudes. We are taught that the part is always less than the whole. Yet, even higher mathematics and infinite number theory clearly demonstrates that the part can contain the whole. Yes, '*The Now*' which seems to us as but a tiny insignificant part of time, yet contains all of it. The power of '*The Now*' extends well beyond time, for it contains eternity itself. Yet we have the old ego habit of thinking that whatever can be easily passed over, ignored or dismissed must be of little or no importance. We reason that if it had more power and clout, it would be better able to advertise itself. So reality must become a shameless self-propagandist just like ourselves.

Hypnotized by our strange notions on magnitudes, we believe we live in the world of the limited. A world composed of many different levels, objects, classifications and distinctions. A world in which the notion of '*orders of reality*' has meaning. So we assign values to everything we see or think. Ego hardened by living in a world of evaluative judgments and comparisons, we have come to know the price of everything and the true value of nothing. We evaluate on the basis of our beliefs, desires and needs alone. Truth almost never comes into the equation. Based on this matrix of our "valuations", we then perceive the world. That which is assigned a high value gets more grid spots on our perceptual matrix. These are amplified and focused in on to the exclusion of all else. They become the greater picture of our lives and its emphasis. That which we think of as inconsequential, may not be seen at all or else becomes excessively diminished. Like everything else, we believe in greater and lesser Sons of God. One particular Son may occupy Park Avenue on our matrix, while another is assigned to the Bronx Zoo, or even to the Tenderloin. This valuation matrix makes sense to those who have strong ego needs and desires and to those who are obsessed with form and the idols of their specialness.

So our picture becomes partial and driven by our beliefs, desires and needs. One person, place, event or form is zoomed in upon to take over the whole grid and all the other pop-ups are minimized and placed squarely out of our awareness. Some become barred for good because they are considered malware viruses. So we live in denial of them and all they represent. Yet, those who can penetrate easily to content see that this matrix of ours is absolutely ridiculous and unneeded. They know reality is of the same order no matter where you choose to look. It does not play games of hide and seek with itself. That is what we do! Our mistake is thinking reality is somehow phenomenal and finite. That it is composed of many different orders and levels. So God remains hidden under the veil of our partiality. When we insist on extending value to the valueless, He must say, *"I am off, I am sick of your games of make belief and your continuous sulking due to not getting your own way."* Trapped into our very rigid identifications, with the worthless, we completely forget that this world of the phenomenal has nothing to do with reality. Reality remains the noumenal and non-manifest Source from which everything arises. It cannot be fitted into our "valuation" matrix anywhere because there it would remain unseen. How can we represent totality in our matrix of partiality?

We have taken an earnest interest in studying only the positive and phenomenal aspect of existence - those aspects we sense and perceive. So the truly creative aspect, the negative aspect remains unseen and forgotten. Yet, the positive derives all its seeming power from this negative aspect. The noumenal is the Source of all that is seen and unseen. The being of all phenomena is the Beingness of the formless and non-manifest. The negative aspect is that which is unbounded and limitless. It can never be an object of conception because it is the conceiving itself. From it are all phenomena sustained, empowered and given seeming life. All phenomena spring from it, dance for a while only to then disappear again into this glorious sea of the non-manifest. These apparitions have not really gone anywhere. Our senses are totally deceived by form and phenomena. We cannot see that which is beyond all sensory distinction, differentiation and has no attributes. That which IS there - before there is any discriminating thought. That which split-mind must always remain blind to. Anything that truly IS, always IS. Our conceiving is indestructible, ever potent and spaceless. Our concepts can become so expansive as to bring us almost to Whole Mind.

THE POWER OF THE UNSEEN, AND UNSYMBOLIZED

The fish of the phenomenal may not remember anymore for it cannot see the ocean of the unmanifest. But it is from here that it receives all its daily bread. It does not see it, not because this ocean is far away and a thing apart, but because it is all too near. The fish is completely sustained and surrounded by this ocean both within and "without". This ocean is its life. The fish looks out at the phenomenal world, at other fish, at seaweed etc. and yet it seems powerless to see this great ocean which it lives in and depends upon for its entire being. Phenomenal viewing is too focused on specifics and that is why it can never see that which is beyond all specifics. The Course reminds us that there are only two items, which we can never symbolize :- **(i) Nothingness** and **(ii) Totality**. Nothingness and Totality transcend the phenomenal existence. They are not seen, simply because they cannot be symbolized.

> **"As nothingness cannot be pictured, so there is no symbol for totality. Reality is ultimately known without a form unpictured and unseen."**

> [T27.III.5:1-2]

Yes, we ignore Totality and Nothingness. This is because there is no obvious way, for us to relate to them. The relative mind cannot grasp their meaning. Its futile attempts on this are akin to trying to scoop up a ladle of water with a sieve. So the ultimate substance of all things remains unknowable because it cannot be accessed as a relative knowledge. That is by concepts, percepts, symbols, forms, sensory experiences etc., all of which are mediated through the medium of consciousness. The void is not a nothing, but it is everything in its state of perfect unification. In it all complementaries, opposing concepts and percepts, positives and negatives have canceled each other out. This is why Totality and the Void cannot be perceived or known by the relative mind.

The void offers no possibility of displacement to itself. It supports no room for any differentiation or contrasts. And it is only through differentiations and contrasts, that the relative mind can thrive. This is why it is called the void of annihilation. Not because anything is destroyed in it, but rather instead because all remains perfectly preserved and safe here. Preserved in its indestructible and pure state. So Totality and Nothingness are of supreme importance. Through them we can take the boat to the other shore and migrate beyond the relative existence. Yet, because we ignore them, we remain as fish caught up in the ocean of phenomenalism. We remain blind to the ocean of the unmanifest which is all around us and which is Totality itself.

The Course has taught us that the world of spacetime came into seeming existence in a single instant. That its entire span and breadth is still contained within this instant. Yes, we come to look on that instant, *'The Now'*, as insignificant. For we have lost the vision to see the incredible and limitless power it contains. For it contains all that is forever perfect, effulgent and indestructible. The Home of our Immortality. Yet to access all that eternity offers, we must just be willing to release the past and detach ourselves from all future investments and attachments. All our investments must be directed into the present. Once the instant is correctly approached it will be seen and known in its true and radiant light. We correctly approach it by dropping all our conditioned beliefs and false knowledge and by not seeking to exploit or master it. It is our master and revealer. It will give us everything we need, not as some future dream - but immediately and in this moment. Its power is so great that there will be no delay. What is wished or willed is instantaneously fulfilled. Just like the story of the genie in the lamp. This instant is our only window into eternity, but also very much IS eternity. One Holy Instant holds all Holy Instants. In Eternity the part and the whole are not seen as on different orders, or separate in any way. Eternity appreciates only essence and content. This is how it evaluates and is the source of its potency. For it always sees truly.

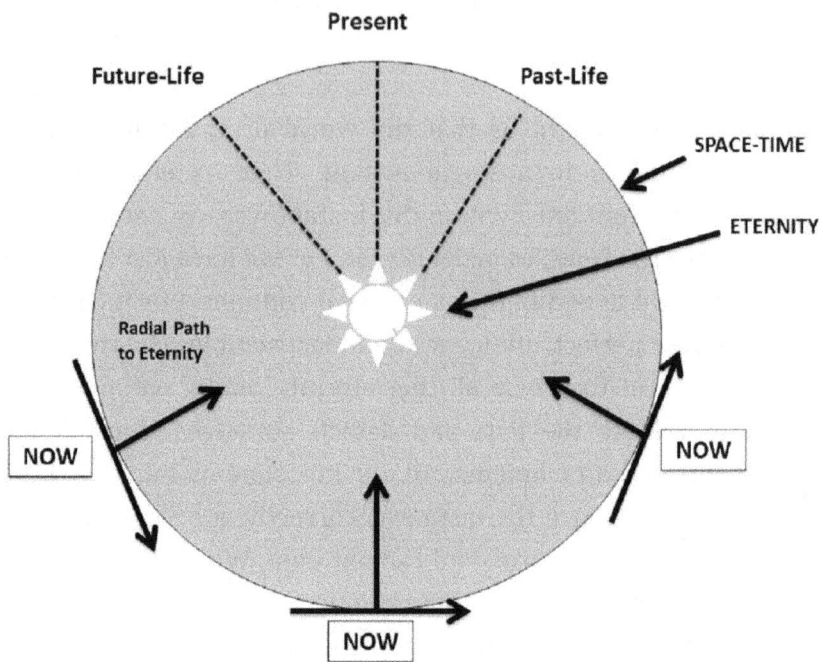

Imagine for a moment a large circle. Now consider that as you meander around the periphery of this circle you are traveling along the horizontal path of spacetime. Yet, if you decide to travel radially instead you are taking the vertical path from time into eternity. At every point on the periphery of this circle, the tangential path of spacetime and the radial path to eternity intersect and are perpendicular to one another. Their point of intersection is *"The Now"*. Eternity is located in the center of the circle. As you travel peripherally your past, present and future lives all seem to be spread out and apart. So do you seem to experience them serially and sequentially. When your current life is in progress, your previous live has dipped just below the horizon, so it can no longer be remembered by most. Your future life has not yet come above the horizon and so it seems, as yet unknown. Yet when you take the radial path of the *'The Now'*, you are transported instantaneously to Eternity, located at the center of the circle. From this unique vantage point, all of spacetime becomes revealed to you. You see all that is on the periphery simultaneously. You see how all your lives are integral to one another.

'The Now' represents the only way out of this circle of spacetime and also the immediate one. The peripheral path represents all that appeared to happen, at that instant of the fall from grace, in which the entire illusion of spacetime was formed. Each moment can be a **'Now'** moment, in which you choose to travel radially to the center of the circle. Here you connect directly with the Eternal and its wisdom. By becoming increasingly aware and mindful and dropping all false beliefs and mental conditionings you take the vertical shuttle directly into eternity and obviate the world of spacetime entirely. One does not need to wait on time, for that which is already Here. With the ferry of your increased mindfulness and purity of thought, you get to experience the power of the **Eternal Now,** in this moment. All experiences of revelations, holy Instants and miracles propagate outwards from the sun of Love, located in the center of this circle. You just need to become available to its beneficence. The mind that succeeds in shutting out all temporal flux, mental noise, the residuals of memory and belief, and the contamination of imagination becomes an open, vacant and receiving slate for all that is real. So it travels easily Homeward bound.

Perhaps another example, may illustrate how potent and complete the present moment is. Imagine you are a trucker driving on a twisty mountainous road. There is a motorcyclist also on this road, traveling towards you. However because he is still ten miles away, you will not cross paths with him for another five minutes. Each of you are part of each other's future. Yet, a balloonist hovering high above the mountains can see both of you now. Your futures are his present perspective. He knows where and when on this road you will cross paths. Eventually you both cross paths at a turn in the road. The biker, who has insufficient space wobbles and veers over the edge of the cliff to his death. But you have already turned the bend and do not notice anything has gone wrong. You take the headphones out of your ears and take a sip of your coffee. Only the balloonist knows because only the balloonist has the advanced perspective. Similarly, as we travel through the horizontal path of time, we do not have the advanced perspective. We do not really see how events and decisions from our past are affecting our present, nor how our present ones are affecting our future. The meaning of our lives and our decisions is often hidden from us until much later. Sometimes it never becomes known to us at all, in any given life, and yet each shapes our future destiny.

THE IMPORTANT LINK EXISTING BETWEEN AWARENESS, TIME DILATION AND CONSCIOUSNESS EVOLUTION

We do not often see the enormous impact of the miracles we work by our right-minded decisions because of our limited perspective. We are unaware of the power and full consequence of each of our decisions. Yet, the balloonist, hovering high above can see it all. He is in the unique position, of seeing our true past and futures and the impact our lives and decisions have made on everyone. He sees our real legacy. The world of time we seem to remember and the one he recognizes can be completely different. What is presently seen through his eyes has become part of our past or is yet to be experienced as our future. If we liken the advanced perspective of the balloonist to that of a more evolved consciousness, then such an advanced being can witness our present, in a truer and far more expansive form. We can easily induct that those with a sufficiently increased conscious evolution, would be capable of experiencing in the present, that which still seems relegated to the past or future, for a less evolved consciousness.

For example, a dog runs around to the back of a house. We know what the dog will find before he gets there, but the dog himself does not yet know. It is still a mystery to him. He cannot see in 3D. He does not possess this inferential capability, because he is not able to think conceptually. Yet, because we do, we can mentally picture the back of the house in our mind's eyes and know what he will find long before he gets there. But for the dog the back of the house, remains still a mystery, a percept that he will experience in his future. Likewise a being with an immensely evolved consciousness and one that has transcended the need for and limitation of concepts, can extend their temporal reach far beyond ours. It would know all the trajectories of our past and future in its present view. With sufficient evolution, such a being would be capable of seeing and knowing the entire history of spacetime in the present moment. Such an advanced being has transcended the need for spacetime. Being able to see all instantly, all illusions of time and motion disappear in their entirety. For once one is able to see all instantly, consciousness itself loses all purpose. Where is there a need for consciousness, when there sits before one the complete picture? The entire picture would simply be assimilated and infused back into the being of such a One.

Another way of looking at your experience in the world of spacetime is to consider that all your past, present and future lives are occurring and being lived simultaneously by you. When you are consciously experiencing, any of those lives, you are simultaneously filtering out the others. So it seems, as if you are unconscious to these other lives. Yet, you still retain a seamless integration with all of them, in your greater mind. Every one of your lives is a present one. All the videotapes, of all your lives are playing on a thousand flat-screen TV sets all at once. Yes, you may have temporarily displaced your focus to just one screen but that does not mean the others videos are not simultaneously proceeding.

It is just like the many worlds theory of quantum mechanics, in which each of your probable selves and worlds exist in parallel universes. Yet each seems supremely unaware of each other's existence. When you exercise a particular decision, you seem temporarily screened from the rest and so lose conscious awareness of their existence. Yet, this does not invalidate their existence. There is no future or past. Just changes happening in your present awareness and this alone determines, what is filtered out and what is filtered in and selected. As mentioned, a diminished awareness cannot even remember, its immediate past. It is the instantaneous content of your mind and its decisions that alone causes the illusion of movement. This mind can become either expansive or contractive. As it becomes expansive, time dilates and so one is capable of taking in far more of the view, all at once. Your unconsciousness becomes revealed and unfolded before you to an even greater extent. All your apparent past and future lives can become evident in the present moment. Eventually you reach to the awareness that is Whole-Mind, which is a complete integration. Then all is experienced as motionless and unmoving. One no longer experiences their reality, as a thing apart, but instead as the living, throbbing, radiant embodiment of truth. One picturing Totality itself . Perception has become translated into Being.

The seeming separation of the projectionist from the objects of his projection, presents this illusion, that is consciousness. Through this illusion, the projectionist becomes maker of the show. He then mistakenly proceeds to think, it is apart from him. In this show he hopes to learn from his experiences and so heal the dissociation, that resulted in his consciousness in the first place. With time his consciousness expands and his concepts become more generalized and powerful. He is rising high above the road now and learning to see in a far truer capacity. When his consciousness is sufficiently evolved, he can see all in the present Now. Once he has seen and known all, the picture simply swallows up its tail and disappears back inside him. This greater picture is imbibed, not as a dissociated knowledge but instead deeply at the level of his Being. His learning has been replaced now with a direct knowing. He no longer has any questions to ask, he no longer has a need of a consciousness to maintain this picture.

Consciousness always means separation – separation between the picture and the projectionist. But when all is simply known, consciousness is no longer needed to differentiate the seer from the seen. Duality has disappeared and is replaced with Wholeness and true knowing. Consciousness has been purified of all its false and limiting aspects, all that it paid heed to during its time on the road. Its many confusions and contradictions have all been undone. They are healed through his seeing the complete picture. One now disappears back into God and into the timeless. All lesser evolved beings, remain caught in the mirage of time and continue with their learning disabilities and diminished consciousness. They may still have a lot of learning to do before they can obviate their need for time entirely.

How does the Holy Spirit relate to this model? He exists as perfect Knowledge. His encompassing perspective sees no form and no motion. Yet, to those still limited to the manifold of spacetime, form and motion seem very self-evident. The Holy Spirit knows the higher constellation of all events and happenings. He sees directly how the content behind each of our decisions can lessen our need for spacetime, particularly to the extent that they reflect increased light and love. Flying up high on the balloon, we are approaching the sun of life. We are rising upwards to the Eternal Source. This love is released through our right decisions. So we extend out miracles to other minds. More accurately to other aspects of the One-Mind. In most cases these minds may not even be born yet in our spacetime context.

The Holy Spirit's simple criterion for whether a decision is right, is in answering whether or not it removes a barrier to Love's presence? It makes great sense therefore to attune to Him. To follow His Guidance and advanced perspective. Your crippling advice to yourself most often sabotages you. It makes you feel more diminutive, fearful and contracted. He sees you as the trucker on the road. He knows what will happen in five minutes? He reveals to you exactly what right decision you must make each moment. He does not guide based on conjectures, contingencies or false interpretations, but rather based on facts and actualities. He teaches that only 'The Now' is meaningful, this is your one true position of power and one where you need to place all of your attention. 'The Now' is the limitless dimension, invulnerable to the world of spacetime. It is the Home of the forever real. Love pervades it and touches all who come in contact with it, with its soft embrace. Here is Holiness remembered, all healing accomplished and the Face of Christ seen and known.

Holiness lies not in time, but in eternity. There never was an instant in which God's Son could lose his purity. His changeless state is beyond time, for his purity remains forever beyond attack and without variability. Time stands still in his holiness, and changes not. And so it is no longer time at all. For caught in the single instant of the eternal sanctity of God's creation, it is transformed into forever. Give the eternal instant, that eternity may be remembered for you, in that shining instant of perfect release. Offer the miracle of the holy instant through the Holy Spirit, and leave His giving it to you to Him."

[T-15.I.15:4-11]

19. THE JOURNEY HOME

**"And turn you to the stately calm within, where in holy
stillness dwells the living God you never left and Who
never left you. The Holy Spirit takes you gently by the
hand, and retraces with you your mad journey outside
yourself, leading you gently back to the truth and
safety within. He brings all your insane projections
and the wild substitutions that you have placed
outside you to the truth. Thus He reverses the course
of insanity and restores you to reason."**

[T-18.I.8:2-5]

O ne time, Dr. Gobbler's Knob and I were sharing a house near
downtown Toronto, where we were working for the summer.
He definitely saw work as the curse of the drinking classes. His goal
was to party as much as possible and to somehow squeeze work in
around his noble intentions. The beer was flowing fast and hard and
was being guzzled down in vast quantities, every night. We would
stack the 24-packs in palindromes for easy consumption. Then
proceed to make pyramids of beer cans all the way to the ceiling.
After getting suitably wasted first in our apartment we would take
the subway downtown to the nightclubs and bars. Yes, the party
animals had been set free from their cage, and now all rapturous and
charged were ready to tear the town apart. Coming out of the bars, in
the wee hours, we were always in exuberant spirits, but must have
looked pretty pathetic to a neutral onlooker - like a Colosseum
exhibition was playing itself out in the town. One night, after exiting
a bar, a large construction yard came into view. There were a large
number of cranes in this site, which made it irresistible to Dr.

Gobbler's Knob. He decided to mosey up one immediately. I came along too since I always had a strong predilection for climbing, since my early youth. I had worked as a tree climber and as a lumberjack once but I was not limited in my portfolio. I also liked climbing things in the big city like buildings, statues and fountains. Thus I could often escape paying the cover charges for late night clubs by climbing the drainpipes and window ledges. This was my key strategy for getting into upstairs nightclubs and bars.

Anyway here we were high in the sky, with a great view of the city. The stars and moon made for an excellent celestial canopy and it was such a fragrant, mystifying and tender summer night. Dr. Gobbler's Knob had his usual intense half crazed look in his eyes, which he always had after a night of hard drinking. In fact I hardly even remember ever seeing him sober. In his drunkenness he proceeded to stumble his way out along the main beam. The first hints of a nervous anxiety started to percolate into my blood and bones, penetrating even beyond the frozen numbness of my own drunken stupor. He made his way to a large rectangular gap at the end of the crane and decided this would be the perfect place to dangle from. Any moment now and he would fall down into the quarry below. It was such a long way down. Then the Gobbler's Knob would become the gobbled up knob, a flatfish scrolled out before me, sporting a cement makeover. Who ever heard of being on edge while drunk - yet that was me, in that moment. For the Dr. had a stunning capacity of pushing the limits beyond all sanity and reason. I was trying my best to entrain him back to his senses. Yet, he seemed to have completely tuned out. Finally a response egressed from that salivating oracle in his head. All he could muster out was that he was trying to find his way home.

Yes, this is the ego's way of bringing us all Home. The long and difficult path, that is destined to end in a splat. It may start out with baby steps, but over a lifetime the ego brings us all to the top of this crane, or some ledge from which we are only too eager to jump off in delight. All wise minds come to the realization somewhere along the line that there is something very fundamentally flawed in the framework of this world, that simply cannot be patched. Maybe one day you have this epiphany. Realize that you have been living in denial for far too long. The thought springs into your mind, that we are all on board the Titanic. The ship of the relative existence will sink no matter what - is a mathematical certainty captain. Yes, if a thought is depressing enough and beyond any hope of redemption, we go into denial. That is our firsthand primal instinct.

FAILURE IS INEVITABLE FOR THE EGO, BUT SUCCESS IS GUARANTEED FOR YOU

An honest, critical and impartial evaluation easily sees, that all our best efforts seem setup to fail. It makes no difference which particular worldly path we choose. This is true, even for those paths not purely motivated out of ego self-interest. Yes, even our pure and noble intentions will become dampened and demobilized by the forces of human inertia, until there is no wind left under our sails. Our ideals will become tarnished and turned against us - their key initiator. Because other egos won't easily share in, or endorse our own altruistic designs, our wiser living modalities, but instead introduce chaos into the mix. They will impute evil motives everywhere. If we do not run into individual resistance, we run into political and social unwillingness. This is part of the underlying source of our continuous anguish and frustration. This is why we become enervated and disenchanted after a time, only to be followed up a little later, with the soup-du-jour of despair. Some become paralyzed and non-functional even before they leave their greyhound box. So frozen in their cocoons and too afraid to venture out.

This world seems like an infinite series of ego crash courses on how to fail. And fail we must, because all ego paths function to separate the journey from the destination. The destination has always been within, and yet all ego journeys lead without. Sometimes an intense series of personal tragedies following in quick succession triggers the instantaneous realization within us that this world is deeply flawed. Or maybe this poison slowly infuses its way into our bones, through an uncanny stream of misfortunes and bad luck events. So finally you begin to see the full picture of this world's inherent bleakness. Alternatively, an addict or psychopath may have buried their way into your life, gradually eroding all your spirit, vigor and vitality. Maybe you did not advance as expected. All your efforts and idealism were turned against you, disposing you to the frozen Siberian wasteland of your profession. This is where you remain now, with your life simply in tatters.

Yes, it does not take too much depth perception, to realize that the world can often be a tiresome place. If you are not suffering from intense boredom, you are likely feeling unappreciated or mercilessly flogged. This world is a very old, ragged and uninspiring place and its masts shudder and creak continuously under the winds of its meaningless changes. Everywhere one hears that eerie howling, groaning sound reverberating from its foundations. Time is powerless to give it any semblance of life. It is a maze of futile complexity whose corridors of ignorance keep you endlessly busy chasing after so many distracting pursuits. Complexity can function as a screen, that strategically covers the essential meaninglessness and joylessness of its content, from your active awareness. So much effort is made to squeeze a few drops out of this coconut. It certainly is a *'much ado about nothing'*, kinda place, a place of gradual death and often an abrupt one. Those who paint smiles and go about their business, as if nothing is wrong are those for whom the daggers have not yet set in.

Now as you survey the worldly stage, through eyes darkened with malice, you clearly see in all its vain pursuits, just a fool's glory. That all optimism celebrated here is simply a delusion. Many years of scorn and rejection, have set in to take their toil on you, making you feel all the more resentful and embittered. Dark feelings have sunk deeply into your mortal fiber. They have diffused into your every pore, fumigating you with their toxic residue, and are witnessed now by the plethora of wrinkles and gray hairs, you sport. Sinking yet deeper, they have spread their contagion into your wizened limbs. Only to echo-out now, their song of abject hopelessness from behind the soulless sockets of your eyes. It is a soundless song indeed but one which can be heard most pervasively even from a distance. The ego is not concerned at all, about the eventual outcome of following all its mindless strategies. It diminishes such thoughts in your mind. It preaches instead that it is how gloriously, spectacularly and ingeniously, we fail that alone matters. We need to establish some crescendo in the flux of gyrating bodies before we burn out. For the ego does not hold any truly hopeful, inspired and healing solutions for our predicament. It does not really believe you can take your spaceship into the void and escape out the other side resurrected.

Unlike the ego, the Course is not about bringing hopeless and fatalistic messages. It is about offering truly positive and hope-filled solutions, that are guaranteed to work. It teaches that an entirely new approach and freshness is needed, if we are to successfully transcend our disillusionment. One in which, this world is seen, not as the goal, but as the means. It is the means for us to become more loving and conscientious, the means to remember our Creator and ourselves. Thus are we finally released from the body and the world of form. Yes, no amount of euphemisms or painting glossy lipstick over this skeleton is ever going to bring it back to life. But that is not the goal. The goal is to restore ourselves back to life, by returning to the meaningful. On this sacred voyage, the Holy Spirit will be our guide. The inspired Voice, that offers us clear direction and one that restores us to all sanity and joy.

> **"Learn now, without despair, there is no hope of answer in the world. But do not judge the lesson that is but begun with this. Seek not another signpost in the world that seems to point to still another road. No longer look for hope where there is none. Make fast your learning now, and understand you but waste time unless you go beyond what you have learned to what is yet to learn. For from this lowest point will learning lead to heights of happiness, in which you see the purpose of the lesson shining clear, and perfectly within your learning grasp."**

> **[T-31.IV.4:3-8]**

Yes, the path to lasting happiness must go through the path of absolute despair. Just as the easiest path out of Dante's hell, is through digging your way out, from the very center of the ninth layer. This is not because despair is a teacher of happiness, but it is a great teacher and revealer of valuelessness. It is that great illuminator of ego illusions. One that magnifies and exposes quickly for you, the far reaching depths to which the tentacles of ego delusion have set in. Your true hope is in recognizing that which is hopeless fast. A complete overhaul is needed, or you will remain clinging to ego illusions and solutions that cannot work. Believing that your strength can be found apart from truth. The restoration of meaning is our path to joy. But meaning cannot be found by entertaining the meaningless. Truth alone carries meaning - being its Home. Any purpose then, that makes worldly success into the intended goal, must be meaningless and empty, simply because there is no world. What never existed and ends in nothing, can have no meaning. All worldly joy is built-up from the fabric of illusions. Each will bring in its wake an equal amount of illusory pain. The very transitory nature of its joys and sorrows evidences this. The crests and troughs in the waves of life, of transitory happiness and sorrow simply imply that the other is soon on the way. If meaningless function arises from investing in the world - then the only meaningful function must be in investing elsewhere. As the Course teaches, "How else can you find joy in a joyless place except by realizing that you are not there?" [T-6.II.6:1] It proceeds to teach the way out of this world into the blazing light of reality. The sacred journey of awakening through forgiveness. This path alone, can undo all our shackles, pain and bondage and lead to lasting peace.

"The way is not hard, but it *is* very different."

[T-11.III.4:1]

Yes, finding your real Self has always been the only goal. Your heart still remembers, what your mind has long forgotten. Deep in your heart is the memory of your Home and your heart will not rest until it finds it again. Reality is restored once you become willing to practice true forgiveness. Thus you no longer strengthen the thought system of the ego and finally relinquish it. So does the dream of meaninglessness end and the love which was always present becomes revealed. A love that is no dream but a reality that completely enfolds and nourishes you. One that restores you to life. This journey and this goal must become your only desire.

Right now the ego is holding you hostage in a halfway house, that is nowhere. You are burning time and energy on pointless desires and temptations that have no substance. The ego keeps you consumed on "separate" interests. It seeks to increase your dissociation and separation from "others", rather than healing these. So you stray away from the eternal Kingdom to walk this planet of dust. You must come to the realization that you will always remain as an alien here, so long as you follow the ways of the ego. You must stop convincing yourself this place is Home. Yes, all earthly paradises will fail to satisfy because they are all sandcastles built from illusion. Tawdry substitutes that mock your reality. Realizing this you become ready to take the journey Home. This realization changes your statement of purpose. So you become willing to embrace all those right-minded decisions that can safely lead you back.

> **"The journey that seemed endless is almost complete, for what *is* endless is very near. You have almost recognized it. Turn with me firmly away from all illusions now, and let nothing stand in the way of truth. We will take the last useless journey away from truth together, and then together we go straight to God, in joyous answer to His Call for His completion."**
>
> **[T-16.IV.12:3-6]**

YOUR ESCAPE PLAN HOME

The purpose of Atonement is to guide you out of hell. This is your VIP ticket. One you cannot lose, but can forget. It leads you quickly past all illusions and onwards to truth. In this journey, you are retracing your steps back to the beginning - to that point from where all illusions sprang. All your journeys through spacetime may have seemed very different, but they are all the same, because their content is identical. They are all ego obsessions with form over content. Each has been an ego voyage through individual illusions, taking these to be the goal. In each you were tempted by empty offerings, that you accepted in place of your true Reality. Each served to separate the path, from the dreamer on the path and to separate you from your brother. The only difference between one dream and another was in the particular illusions, you had pursued. Each was elaborately invested with ego patterns and goals and was motivated by your ego desires and fears.

You the dreamer had selected paths, that seemed to offer the best hope for alleviating misery and reaping success for your own ego self. Yet, this goal cannot be accomplished because this self is the cause of all your misery and failure. Only the Self can be without misery. Thus each path merely served to substantiate the notion of the dreamer and the dream. Yet, it is only the mind of the dreamer that has ever had any reality, and that mind either sleeps or is awake. Atonement has the noble goal of awakening your mind. Its functions as the Heavenly means to end all dreams. To find the path out you need a complete change of attitude about your goal and intended destination. You must come to realize that all ego paths are empty offerings that lead to increased futility and death.

"There is no road to travel on, and no time to travel through. For God waits not for His Son in time, being

forever unwilling to be without him. And so it has always been."

[T-13.I.7:3-4]

Apart from the path of forgiveness, all worldly paths are ego journeys deeper into illusion. You merely travel through a vast sea of appearances, that were never real to begin with. Illusions make the world seem a real and happening place, yet with awakening all this illusory landscape disappears, as mists before the morning light. So long as illusions are believed, time will seem to be present. For a mind that upholds false beliefs and contradictions will continue to manufacture illusions out of its many distortions of thought. So more time will be needed still, to resolve and undo these beliefs. Then that mind cannot enter the timeless, because it carries with it illusions, wherever it goes. In fact it is already in the timeless and does not recognize it, for this exact reason.

Your one and only true goal, is to let the light that is already in your mind to shine through your mind. To let the natural light of Spirit extend outwards and illuminate for you the Real world. As your spiritual sight is restored, illusions become vaporized into thin air and then the full radiance of your mind is known. No longer will any illusions serve to defile you. Then you will no longer see, hear, smell, taste or touch. For the sensory system and all sensation in general was made by your ego to witness a world of sin and separation and to support its vast framework of illusion. Truth itself cannot be known through sensation or perception, but only through penetrating beyond all your ego beliefs and so reaching to the Knowledge of Whole-Mind. That Mind, which is limitless and omnipotent in you. All sensations and perceptions are partial and fragmented. The senses and perception will always distort, to some extent because the mind that senses or perceives is insufficiently healed. With healing, all your distortions disappear and you attain to spiritual vision. Now you have become so light-filled, that the real world comes into view.

You have the choice of voyaging further into illusion or closer towards truth. To the extent that you choose to maintain ignorance and its composite beliefs, you bury yourself further in darkness. To the extent that you embrace right-minded understandings and practices you advance towards the light. Guilt feelings and thoughts preserve time and advance you further into separation and darkness. Quantum forgiveness releases time and works all those healing miracles that advance you back to light. So it restores vision to you. Quantum forgiveness is your one means to healing yourself. It is the closest thing to love that pervades the spacetime experience. It is the heavenly means chosen to remove all distortions and misperceptions.

Spacetime is a mind made construct. It is an artifice that provides a very useful and necessary learning arena for those who still cling to illusion. It will remain until you are healed of all misperceptions. No perception can ever be made whole because no perception or vision can ever substitute for your reality. Perception remains but an illusory screen that stands between you and truth. You are healed when you longer perceive. Then you no longer need this screen, nor perceive it. Yet it can only be relinquished from your mind, when you have reached a mental readiness state through sufficient purification. So long as you remain attracted to guilt and attack, you will continue to implement elaborate schemes of defense and use projection to deny yourself healing. You will fall into and nourish, those ego based snares of sin and separation.

Forgiveness serves as the means to remembering your Wholeness but it can never substitute for your reality as perfect love. It is a counter dream that heals the dreaming mind. One that reinforces truth alone and leads away from dreaming. When the dream is over, forgiveness is no longer needed. Then love alone remains as our awakened Reality. The whole topography of spacetime already preexists within the framework of illusion. Illusions will only seem powerful and substantial so long as they retain the power of your belief in them. They can make your experiences in spacetime seem real, as if the future were still open to new possibilities, uncertainties and chance. Yet, all of spacetime already exists, prefabricated within your mind. It is always just unfolding outwards, from within. You are not really capable of having any new thoughts, in the relative existence of spacetime. Yet, you will have many thoughts that seem new. Yet, these are just unfolding out of your memory. Your real thoughts are memories from your seeming future that have become long forgotten. To the extent that you remember them, do you advance backwards in time, to the beginning. Thus you approach Truth, where the whole framework of spacetimes starts to melt away and disappear. Then you realize that you were just journeying through a senseless landscape of phantoms and apparitions, that were all mind-made.

> **"The revelation that the Father and the Son are one will come in time to every mind. Yet is that time determined by the mind itself, not taught. The time is set already. It appears to be quite arbitrary. Yet there is no step along the road that anyone takes but by chance. It has already been taken by him, although he has not yet embarked on it. For time but seems to go in one direction. We but undertake a journey that is over. Yet it seems to have a future still unknown to us."**
>
> **[W.158.2:8-9, W.158.3:1-7]**

Now you are beginning to grasp the full conspiracy. A silent one in which everyone is the patsy. One patterned onto the wallpaper of the world, enmeshed into all its scripts and imbued into its very foundations. All those figures that came and went in your life, all those events, either mysterious or expected, all secretly trick you into believing in this illusion of time. Everyone is part of a joke so large, that the joke itself has become lost to all awareness. So you saw your son being born, your parents passing on, your body appearing to get older and falling apart with time. You saw that crash on the highway, that rocket flying into space, that egg frying on the pan, and yet nothing has ever happened at all. All is spontaneously arising in the greater illusory framework of the spacetime manifold. Yet, all the pictures that you see already remain as a completed deck within your mind. Nor has there been any real place for anything to ever happen in. All exists in a perfect unmoving stillness. This is their backdrop and fundamental bedrock. All pseudo-existence is a false overlay on the real, perpetuated out of ego distortions.

You experience this joke of time only because your viewing angle has become limited, partial and distortionary. If your viewing was Whole instead, you would not experience time at all. Then there would be no happenings anywhere, no comings or goings. The illusion of change, is itself triggered by illusion. The Course teaches this higher level perspective. It knows that there is only one door that leads out of the spacetime luniverse, into the world of light and only one useful path to that door. All paths that embrace forgiveness and Atonement must converge on this blazing highway towards truth, no matter how different they seem to start off. Yet, there are also literally millions of pathways that lead deeper into hell, darkness and illusion. They twist and intertwine themselves and form convoluted loops that lead you nowhere. Many meaningless misadventures, hellish nightmares, deceptions and delusions are all you will ever experience on each such path.

The Holy Spirit knows how you can connect to the path of light. He knows your quickest route Home. His only purpose is to guide your mind to this. Thus He teaches you to become non-judgmental and forgiving, because He knows these lead to wisdom and light. Practicing quantum forgiveness is being unworldly wise. In the end your free will can only be used, to determine how you choose to voyage through this maze. It cannot be used to determine what is in the maze, because the maze itself is already complete. What you will experience on a particular path is already predetermined, until you choose an alternative route.

Using your free will judiciously, you will always choose the right path. Yet, if you follow your own bearings and ego advice to yourself, it is almost certain you will get lost. Being blissfully unaware of the dangers up ahead, you will remain a bliss bunny naively navigating a road to hell. Witlessly smiling, until the buckshot hits you in the ass. A path may seem to start off as one of pleasure, but very soon it will regress into a desolate path of hardship and of thorns. For one, who was once so proud, cocky and confident, now you find you do not trust yourself, even to tie your own shoelaces. The Holy Spirit knows the way - you do not! Accept His certainty, in the place of your doubt. Accept His complete View, in place of your limited and distorted one. So will, you advance speedily towards the light and find yourself at Home.

> **"Heaven itself is reached with empty hands and open minds, which come with nothing to find everything and claim it as their own."**
>
> **[W.133.13:1]**

Now there is Stillness!

Where Before,

Rained,

A Never Ending Stream,

of Meaningless Thoughts!

All Madness is Ended!

It Seems!

And, I Am Back,

To Where I Am!

Before I had left,

To go Nowhere!

II

Now there is Peace!

Where before,

Chaos drained,

My Spiritual

Wells Dry!

Simplicity is difficult!

It Seems!

Now!

The Self Illuminates!

Where Before,

I had left!

For Complexity's Realms!

III

Now, there is Bliss!

Where before,

Joylessness Pervaded,

My Essence Body Through!

And Happiness was Lost,

to Forgetfulness!

Now, I am Home!

Enjoying Limitless Presence!

Where Before,

I had left,

For Wicked Dreams!

[Back Home Again]

APPENDIX A -

DYNAMICS OF THE HOLY SPIRIT V THE EGO

DYNAMICS OF THE EGO	DYNAMICS OF THE HOLY SPIRIT
Fears	Loves
Judges	Forgives
Separates	Unifies
Conquers	Heals
Dissociates	Integrates
Projects	Extends
Hates	Likes
Rejects	Embraces
Attacks	Joins
Condemns	Blesses
Victimizes	Empowers
Plays the Victim	Takes Responsibility
Grievance Orientated	Miracle Minded
Twists	Reasons
Shrouds	Clarifies
Complicates	Simplifies
Distorts	Illuminates / Visionary
Substitutes, Fragments, Displaces & Avoids	Engages, Accepts and Appreciates
Compares and Contrasts	Sees Essential Content

DYNAMICS OF THE EGO (Continued)	DYNAMICS OF THE HOLY SPIRIT (Continued)
Partial	Impartial
Questions	Answers
Seeks	Finds & Discovers
Seeks Special Relationships	Seeks Holy Relationships
Idol Seeking	Recognizing Your Completion
Reactive	Responsive
Miscreative	Creative
Sees only Sin	Recognizes Eternal Innocence
Seeks the Transient and Fleeting	Places value only in the Eternal
Pleasure Seeking,	Purposeful, Communicative
Attention Seeking	Altruistic. Fulfills Others Needs
Calculating	Bounteous / Overflowing
Controlling	Loosened Up / Spontaneous
Manipulative	Liberating
Heartless	Compassionate
Hostile	Welcoming

DYNAMICS OF THE EGO (Continued)	DYNAMICS OF THE HOLY SPIRIT (Continued)
Defensive	Defenseless
Offense is its first form of Defense	Teaches Safety in Defenselessness
Arrogant	Humble
Dishonest / Deceitful	Honest
Impatient	Patient
Untrustworthy	Trusting
Rationalizing	Empathic
Shouts, Roars and Curses	Speaks Softly and Kindly
Harsh	Kind
Self-Effacing	Self-Inquiring
Hoarding	Sharing / Giving
Self-Obsessed	Altruistic
Seeks to "Correct" others	Teaches by being an Inspired Example
Imprisons, Binds	Releases
Engages the Phenomenal	Directs to the Noumenal
Leads Deeper into Hell	Leads Heavenly-Bound

www.ingramcontent.com/pod-product-compliance
Lightning Source LLC
Chambersburg PA
CBHW071402090426
42737CB00011B/1322